TARGÓWEK

STN. for
RADZYMIN

KAWĘCZYN

R A G A

ka STN. for WILNO

Targowa

EASTERN STN.

To Lublin & Lwów

GROCHÓW

River
Port

Grochowska

Paderewski
Park

Zieloniecka

Waszyngtona

ew Railway
Bridge

Poniatowski
Bridge

SASKA
KĘPA

GOCŁAW

U

ks

Czerniakowska

U.S.A St.

OW

L

A

LAS

nki
k

SIEKIERKI

ów

SIELCE

Chełmska

karnia

CZERNIAKÓW
Miasto Ogród

Sobieskiego

Powsińska

The Wars

3 6

also by George Bruce

THE STRANGLERS
RETREAT FROM KABUL
SIX BATTLES FOR INDIA
DICTIONARY OF BATTLES (revised and updated)

George Bruce

The Warsaw Uprising

I August – 2 October 1944

Rupert Hart-Davis   London

Granada Publishing Limited
First published 1972 by Rupert Hart-Davis Ltd
3 Upper James Street
London W1R 4BP

ISBN 0 246 10526 7

Printed in Great Britain by
Richard Clay (The Chaucer Press) Ltd, Bungay, Suffolk

Contents

List of Illustrations and Maps

7

German troops of Ukrainian origin sheltering behind the colonnade of the Opera House in Theatre Place.

A German tank advances through the burning City Centre.

The Germans advance, September 1944. A Wehrmacht officer shouts orders to his men.

German troops advancing through the ruined housesof the old town.

The last days of the Uprising. The wounded Poles were without food, water or medical aid.

The final capitulation. General von dem Bach witnesses the signing of the document of surrender by Colonel Iranek-Osmecki and Colonel Dobrowolski.

After the surrender, the citizens of Warsaw are forced to leave their city before its final destruction.

Maps

Warsaw (endpapers)

The Russian Advance, 15 July to 1 August 1944 (page 90)

Foreword

The purpose of this book is to present the story of the Warsaw Uprising of 1 August 1944, and also to give some idea of the policies and of the people responsible for the events which made a heap of rubble out of one of Europe's finest cities, and killed some 250,000 people. In Britain, the Uprising has become little more than a memory. This is to be regretted. The Warsaw Uprising not only presents a drama of unexampled heroism, ending in appalling tragedy, but also provides us with the first example of full-scale urban guerrilla warfare.

I have tried to be impartial, yet I have to admit that this is a book of some bias. Deeds of savage cruelty culminating in a massacre of some 40,000 civilians were committed by the Nazis. It is impossible to be impartial about such things, though one can be objective.

In order to reveal how the Uprising was launched it has been necessary to cover in some detail the growth, training and development of the Secret Army as well as the motives which inspired it. And for this I have turned to the official documents of the war-time Polish Government-in-exile.

I also acknowledge the help Jan Ciechanowski's London University PhD thesis *The Political and Ideological Background of the Warsaw Uprising* afforded me, as well as books about the Uprising in Polish by Colonel Adam Borkiewicz, Mr Jerzy Kirchmayer, Mr Zenon Kliszko and Mr Alexander Skarzincki.

I am indebted to a number of people who have helped me in various ways; more especially to Mr Adam Zamoyski for translations; to Mrs Czarnocka, archivist of the Polish Underground Study Trust, and to Mrs Oppmann, archivist of the Polish Institute and Sikorski Museum, for help and guidance; to Colonel Iranek-Osmecki in London, Colonel Stanislaw Komornicki, Captain Tomaszewski, Mr Alexander Skarzinski and Mr Wladislaw Bartelski in Warsaw for interviews and personal statements; to Mr Andrzej Broniarek and Mrs Anna Broniarek of the Polish Interpress Agency, for facilitating my researches in Warsaw; and to Mr Pawel Cieslar, Mr Josef Garlinski and Mr Jerzy Kedzierski.

I and my publishers also wish to thank the Polish Institute and Sikorski Museum for permission to use extracts from *History of the*

9

Polish Armed Forces and *Documents on Polish Soviet Relations*, Vols I and II; and Interpress Photographic Agency, Warsaw, Prasa Agency, Warsaw, the Radio Times Hulton Picture Library and the London Polish Library for the photographs used. Finally, I wish to thank the staff of the Polish Library for kindness and help, as well as the staffs of the London Library and the Ministry of Defence (Central and Army) Library.

1/   September disaster, 1939

Thursday, 31 August 1939, was still another day of brilliant sunshine and blue cloudless skies in Warsaw's hot dry summer. The Vistula river, winding like a ribbon of bronze round the eastern suburbs, had fallen to barely five hundred instead of the normal six hundred yards wide. A pattern of white sails tacked back and forth in the fitful breeze over the rippling surface. The Poniatowski Bridge and its neighbour to the left, the Kierbedz Bridge, were clogged with traffic. The harvest was in, and horses and carts from the country jostled for place with heavy army lorries from which the red faces of young peasant troops peered wistfully.

Over the parched grass of the Royal Park a few soldiers still on leave walked arm-in-arm with girls, or watched the fat carp in the fish-ponds stir sluggishly beneath white and rose-coloured drifts of fallen petals. To the south of the city, in the Lazienki Park, mothers and children promenaded sedately around the lake and through the woodland to the Botanical Gardens.

At a first glance everything seemed normal, a typical, lazy day in a season rich with summer's pleasure, except for the absence of Warsaw's usual gaiety, the lack of young men among the holiday strollers, so that it looked for the moment a city of middle-aged and old men and women. And the bells, deep and low, or thin and high, of Warsaw's innumerable churches pealed a little urgently, a chorus of anxiety or warning.

Poland was near the abyss. Radios in the crowded cafés blared out the news that the Polish delegation had arrived in Berlin for final talks with Hitler, but only the simplest people believed that he intended to negotiate. From the officers of the General Staff in the austere and historic War Ministry building in Saxon Square to the correspondents of the international press in the Hotel Bristol bar, all knew by now that Hitler had massed his new tank armies along Poland's borders. The really well-informed hoped that Britain and France would honour quickly their pledges to aid Poland if Germany attacked.

A smoky red sunset ended the last day of the old era in Polish history.

Hitler invaded at dawn on 1 September 1939 with fifty-eight divisions, fourteen of them armoured or motorised, supported by 1,400 fighters, dive-bombers and bombers. Poland, in contrast, put into the field barely thirty divisions, mostly cavalry and infantry, with just one motorised brigade. The Government had delayed full mobilisation at the request of Neville Chamberlain's Government in London, which up to the last moment had tried to appease Hitler.

Poland now became the first nation to experience the new type of swift mechanised attack called blitzkrieg, or lightning war, in which an entire country could become a battlefield. All the tactics which Germany would use in 1940 to break through in the west she now rehearsed. Nazi parachutists in Polish uniform blew up bridges, railways and telegraph lines to prevent unified command from the outset. Fifth-columnists, the so-called *Volkdeutsche*, or Germans with Polish nationality, spread panic among civilians so as to choke the roads with refugees. Low-flying aircraft strafed them there and in the villages. Hitler waged war against the entire Polish people.

During the first two days the Luftwaffe destroyed almost the whole Polish air force of nine hundred aircraft, large numbers of them on the tarmac, where they were grounded for lack of petrol. Against great numerical and mechanised superiority many of the Polish divisions, everywhere fighting with great courage and determination, retreated eastwards to a line formed by the rivers Vistula and Narew. The country to the west was quickly overrun, with large masses of troops encircled and destroyed.

German mechanised strength was certainly decisive. But still another factor in defeat were the unrealistic strategic ideas of Poland's General Staff, stemming from a foreign policy which had seen Soviet Russia as the real enemy and Germany as a possible ally. Clearly, the Polish General Staff had not, until it was too late, planned for a war in which the country fought alone against an enemy three or four times stronger. And this unrealistic thinking led straight to catastrophe. Polish strategy stemmed from the belief that she would be fighting alongside an ally powerful enough to give her decisive superiority over the enemy. And the anti-Sovietism of her pre-war military dictatorship showed that the ally was certainly not Russia. General Romer, the Polish Chief of Staff, summarised his views of Poland's strategy thus:

> Our general strategic situation at the beginning of the war will be favourable, and therefore from the very beginning of hostilities we must prosecute the war as actively and rapidly as possible in order to bring it to a victorious conclusion as quickly as possible. At the beginning of the war we and our enemies will be operating in enormous areas with poor transport facilities (*i.e., in the USSR*). Our principles must be taken from the lessons of the Napoleonic Wars, from the first battles of the World War (particularly on the

Eastern Front), and from the last Russo-Polish War. Our salvation lies in a war of movement.

And upon these impracticable ideas Poland's military strategy, tactics and training were founded. These were for an offensive based on manoeuvre by infantry and cavalry but without modern weapons and weak in fire power. When the enemy proved to be Nazi Germany, this unrealistic strategy was hurriedly replaced by defensive tactics, with almost no defences prepared, aimed at holding back the Nazis until Britain and France could mount an effective attack in the west.

But the Nazi tactics of blitzkrieg and total war quickly overwhelmed Poland. The President of the Polish Republic, Ignace Moscicki, the members of the Government and the Commander-in-Chief fled the capital on 5 September for a small town in the south-east near the Rumanian frontier. Warsaw, the departing Government proclaimed, should be declared an open city and be surrendered without a shot.

Thousands of lives and irreplaceable works of art might well have been saved had this policy been followed. It was perhaps the prudent and sensible decision, but such an ignoble acceptance of alien domination was foreign to the Polish character, hardened as it had been by 150 years' struggle for national survival against predatory neighbours. Besides, British and French armies, people still hoped, would soon launch a decisive attack in the west, overrun Germany and save Poland at the eleventh hour. So the citizens of Warsaw, led by the para-military organisation of the Polish Socialist Party, decided to resist.

Two days later, on 3 September, armoured spearheads of General von Reichenau's German 10th Army, having advanced 140 miles in a week, crashed into Warsaw's southern suburbs. While they pounded the city with heavy artillery and while the Luftwaffe smashed it from the air, leading politicians of the three main pre-war Opposition parties[1] banded together with civic leaders to set up a Defence of Warsaw Committee. In the absence of the Government it was headed by the Lord Mayor, Stefan Starzynski. It included Mathew Rataj, of the Peasant Party, M. Niedzialkowski, of the Socialist Party and General Michal Tokarzewski, military representative.

The Socialist Party, and the Jewish socialist organisation, the Bund, then issued manifestoes calling on their members who belonged to the military reserve to rally in defence of the city. The Socialists took the lead, mainly because they were strong in the capital. For four days, while the Nazis hammered it with bombs and shells, recruiting went on. Thousands volunteered but the military commission accepted only trained men, either from the reserve, or from their own para-military organisations. The rest, whose lives they had no wish to throw away, were put to work digging trenches, tank traps, erecting barricades, laying anti-tank mines.

The citizen soldiers were mostly factory and transport workers, students, shop assistants, reinforced by a few hundred regular soldiers who had escaped to the city after the dispersal or surrender of their units. By 11 September the Germans had surrounded the city and were attacking with tanks and infantry as well as artillery. They penetrated the western suburbs, but the volunteer battalions repulsed them, mainly by the deft use of petrol bombs. 'I was one of 460 men, fully equipped,' recalled a member of one of these battalions.

Half an hour after the heaviest raid on Warsaw, in which Smocza, Elektoralna and other neighbouring streets were completely destroyed, I took the oath of allegiance – an oath of loyalty and fidelity to Poland, but with no mention of the President or the Government. After the ceremony the battalion set out for Praga and took over the defence of the sector Zacisze-Elsnerowo. We remained in this sector until the capitulation. The battalion fought well, and even occupied the enemy's positions for a brief while. Fighting started every evening about 6 p.m. with our attack, and lasted till dawn. During daylight German planes bombed our positions three or four times a day and destroyed trenches and munitions stores. Many of our number fell, many more were wounded. Those who were only slightly injured returned to their posts as soon as they had received first aid.[2]

But the defence was foredoomed, for courage and devotion could not outweigh the lack of aircraft, anti-tank guns, water, food and medical supplies. Day and night the city was swept by artillery fire and smashed by bombs from aircraft which dived to a mere two or three hundred feet above the roofs. Warsaw finally surrendered on 1 October, when it was almost without food or water and thousands lay dead or dying. Volunteers' legion documents were burnt to keep them out of Nazi hands.

Meantime, three historic events had sealed the country's fate. The remnants of the Polish army, encircled by the Germans, surrendered by the end of September. Thousands were taken prisoner, but thousands more escaped to France. Secondly, on 17 September, Soviet Russia, with troops and political commissars, had invaded the large areas of undefended eastern Poland assigned to it under the Nazi–Soviet Pact. Thirdly, believing there was no hope now that these two military giants had between them torn the country apart, President Moscicki, the Government and the Commander-in-Chief crossed the frontier into Rumania, Poland's ally, at the end of September. There, further disaster awaited them. Contrary to the treaty between the two countries they were interned, because of Rumania's fear of Nazi or Soviet intervention.

The Polish people had fought for the cause of freedom and had resisted tyranny. They were now prostrate.

The Nazi terror regime began. Through the battle-scarred city German soldiers in fine uniforms goose-stepped in long grey columns.

Cobbled streets trembled beneath the steel tracks of hundreds of tanks, Luftwaffe squadrons roared overhead. The hereditary enemies of the Germans, the Poles, were utterly defenceless, watching fearfully, or praying in those of their churches that had not been blown to pieces. They soon learned the fate of their country. It was to be erased from the map of Europe, just as completely as it had been in the third and last partition by Russia, Austria and Prussia in 1795. Having occupied western and central Poland up to the line of the Bug river, Hitler incorporated the northern industrial province of Silesia and the northwestern half of Poland into the German Reich. And of the remainder he created a German colony, called the General-Government, its capital being Cracow, although it included Warsaw. Nazi Germany then had a total of 21,200,000 Polish citizens in its iron grip.

The nation which gave birth to Copernicus and to Chopin was now to become a community of slave-labourers for Adolf Hitler. The regions incorporated into the Reich were to be totally Germanised by wholesale seizure of farms, houses, factories and the mass deportation of residents. Hundreds of thousands of peasant families were uprooted from their homes, their work, their land and bundled off to unknown places miles away in the General-Government.

Soon after dawn, convoys of lorries and armed SS men drove into the villages. All the exits and entrances, including the smallest field paths were guarded, with machine-guns trained on the village. SS detachments ran from homestead to homestead, shouting '*Heraus!*', beating on doors with rifle-butts, driving the inhabitants into the roads while their houses were looted down to the smallest trinket.

The SS men then drove the peasants — men, women and children — with kicks, fists and rifle-butts into lorries. Those who resisted were shot dead. In the villages of Sola and Jelesnia a number of women were shot when they tried to run away among farm buildings. Eventually the lorries carried their human cargo off to assembly points where, usually in the open fields, in rain, frost or snow, they were kept for as long as three or four days until a train load was ready. The journey, in unheated cattle trucks, lasted from three to fourteen days in the bitter cold of the Polish winter.

The survivors, once thriving peasant farmers, arrived at their unknown destination with nothing more than a small bundle. German farm workers were moved into their homes without delay. Mass expulsion emptied the cities of western Poland also. Poznan, the capital, with 270,000 inhabitants and a history of flourishing cultural, commercial and political life, was stripped of its inhabitants street by street. The citizens were first ordered to clean their homes from top to bottom and leave a supply of necessities, together with all kitchen utensils, bed linen and furniture for the incoming Germans. Marched or driven off to rendezvous points, they were kept there until they could be removed either to labour camps or somewhere in the central General-Government.

For this region, Hitler had decreed, was to become a reservoir of cheap labour and of Nazi military requirements. Its parliamentary institutions were suppressed, its political parties dissolved. Its universities were closed and their contents looted or destroyed. Museums, libraries and art collections were removed to Germany. All schools except a small number of elementary ones were shut down. A Nazi administration was clamped on the people and the Polish legal system gave way to the German Criminal Code, with death penalties for trivial offences against Nazidom. A starvation diet and a policy of genocide was to be the fate of Poland's citizens.

Warsaw especially was to suffer Nazi savagery. The first great European city to make a determined stand against Hitler's armies, it had paid heavily for this in terms of loss of life and destruction of beautiful paintings, sculptures and buildings. The Nazis saw Warsaw as a focus of resistance. 'We have in this country one point from which all evil derives: namely Warsaw,' exclaimed the Governor-General of Poland, Hans Frank[3] in a speech to Luftwaffe officers on 14 December 1943. 'Were there no Warsaw in the General-Government, we would be spared four-fifths of all the trouble we have to contend with. Warsaw is and will remain the focal point of disturbance from which restlessness is being spread all over the country.'

This 'evil' sprang from the historical role of Warsaw in the nation's 150-year fight for independence, which began with the Kosciuszko Insurrection of 1794. Polish soldier, democrat and reformer, Kosciuszko had sailed to America in 1776 to join the American revolt against British rule. He became a colonel of engineers, and finally chief engineer of General Green's Southern Army. For his part in victory, Congress promoted him to brigadier-general and awarded him a large grant of land. But he felt compelled to return to Poland in 1784 to fight under Prince Poniatowski against the Russians and to lead the uprising of 1794 against them. The Warsaw Uprising of 1794 did not actually launch the Kosciuszko Insurrection of that year but it was of vital importance for its alliance between the lower strata of Warsaw artisans, led by the shoemaker Jan Killinski, and the Jacobin military intelligentsia of the day.

A similar alliance was the November 1830 insurrection against Tsar Nicholas I's rule and occupation, launched by the Warsaw School of Infantry cadets. Again, the Warsaw revolutionaries played an important part in the nationwide rising of 1863. Later, the Polish Socialist Party led the Warsaw proletariat in the anti-Russian uprising of 1904–7. In trying to defend the city against the Nazis in 1939 the citizens of Warsaw had followed this vital tradition; and inevitably Hans Frank's efforts to crush every growth of Polish resistance were in the first place directed against Warsaw and its citizens.

Warsaw was also Poland's cultural centre, with an influence in national life far greater than its 4 per cent of national population, or one million, three hundred thousand people, suggested. It held about nine hundred schools and forty colleges and scientific institutes. Its professors and students amounted to 40 per cent of the country's scholars, and 50 per cent in the field of technology. More than half of the total of Polish periodicals were published in Warsaw, while its libraries and archives held 56 per cent of the nation's valuable books, documents and papers.[4] Industrially, the capital was a potential powerhouse for the Nazis, with ninety thousand factory workers and twenty-three thousand independent artisan workshops, amounting to 12 per cent of the national total. In order to gear this to their war machine the Nazis needed to crush armed resistance there.

Everyone capable of leadership in the capital was listed by the German Security Police, specifically its Department IV, the Gestapo.* The list included Poles and Jews, scholars and artists, army officers, civil servants, students, schoolteachers, artisans and politically conscious labourers. Arrests of civilians began immediately after the surrender of the capital, when the Gestapo raided many houses and seized the first batch of those who were to disappear for ever. Among them was the Lord Mayor, Stefan Starzynski, who had done so much to organise resistance in September.

Manhunts, street round-ups, street executions and mass executions in the forests soon followed. They were part of a campaign of genocide laid down in Hitler's decree on 'the strengthening of Germandom' of 7 October 1939, which demanded 'the elimination of the harmful influence of nationally alien population groups constituting a danger to the Reich...'[5]

The Nazis took over two Warsaw prisons to carry out Hitler's plans. These were the Pawiak prison and the women's section known as the Serbia, kept solely for political prisoners in the hands of the Security Police. But men and women suspected of links with the underground were taken first to the Gestapo Headquarters in Szuch Avenue, renamed *Strasse der Polizei*. Here, in the former Polish Ministry of Religion and Education, they were kept for days or for weeks, and tortured, whatever their age, to obtain information.

Fear and anguish gripped the city. Green-uniformed security police and Nazi Death's Head battalions started to comb the streets at night with the names and addresses of outstanding men and women obtained from official Polish files. Nobody felt safe. In a desperate migration to try to escape the executioners thousands of people criss-crossed the city shortly before the curfew hour to an alternative sleeping-place usually in the house of a friend. At night, recalled Stefan Korbonski, one of the leaders of the Peasant Party who had escaped captivity in the Russian zone to return to Warsaw, the deserted streets echoed to the Nazi patrols' heavy footsteps. Behind blacked-out windows the

* *Geheime Staatspolizei* = Secret State Police

17

city kept vigil. No one knew where the searches and arrests were to take place. Restlessness and anxiety made sleep impossible.

Hungry, often without work or homes in this stricken city that lacked gas or electricity and where horses and carts did duty for the once noisy and familiar red trams, the people of Warsaw seemed without hope in the autumn of 1939. But already resistance was stirring. First steps towards the formation of the Secret State and Army had been taken.

2/   Birth of the Secret Army

On 27 September 1939, while Nazi phosphorus bombs spread streams of fire over the roofs of old Warsaw and heavy artillery shells crashed indiscriminately into workers' homes and eighteenth-century palaces, Lieutenant-General Rommel, Polish C-in-C of the Warsaw region, sent urgently for Major-General Tokarzewski. This dynamic officer with piercing blue eyes had returned to take part in the defence of the capital after German Panzers had routed his infantry division in the west earlier in the campaign. The two men met in a map-lined room of the War Department building in Pilsudski Square shortly before it was blown to pieces; and General Rommel, on behalf of the Polish Government about to seek refuge in Rumania, authorised Tokarzewski to set up and command the military underground.

The Secret Army was born there in Warsaw, within sight of the eternal flame to Poland's unknown soldier, which was still burning brightly, though most of the Doric columns on each side of it were shattered.

Tokarzewski promised solemnly that he would 'assume full responsibility for the organisation of armed resistance against the occupying powers, and the preparation of the country's moral and physical readiness to begin open warfare when conditions were favourable'.[1]

Tokarzewski's hard and dangerous task was made more difficult by Poland's political leaders during the last two decades, who had alienated the majority of those people to whom he would now have to turn for popular support. After the First World War, a stormy period of weak, short-lived governments was ended when Marshal Pilsudski seized power with a military *coup d'état* in May 1926. Forming a 'non-party' centre bloc, Pilsudski had then steered an uneasy course between dictatorship and democracy. Aided by a group of 'colonels' who governed as he decreed, he became the nation's 'moral dictator'. Believing the USSR to be Poland's number one enemy, he nevertheless opposed German pressure to join a campaign against her. He imposed a strongly authoritarian constitution on Poland in 1935 and died a month later.

His group of near-fascist colonels then passed legislation reducing the

19

people's electoral power and moving nearer to a totalitarian system. As a result, the Socialist and Peasant parties boycotted the 1935 elections; only about 46 per cent of the electorate voted. The Government won, but lacked real popular support.

In 1936 General Smigly-Rydz was promoted to Marshal and thrust forward as Pilsudski's successor. He fostered the growth of the Camp of National Unity, a Catholic, nationalist and anti-semitic organisation, which the Left parties saw as fascist and opposed in every way. The great ten-day strike of August 1937 during which the Peasant Party, supported by Socialist strikes in the towns, stopped the movement of all food supplies, was the climax of this opposition. Street fighting followed between the army, the police and the strikers, with a heavy death toll.

Marshal Smigly-Rydz eventually gave in to the opposition to fascism and the so-called Camp of National Unity was checked. A year later, in September 1938, President Moscicki dissolved Parliament, but he refused to allow measures of electoral reform already passed to take effect in the forthcoming elections.

The outcome was that in this crucial period, with war already looming on the horizon, the Opposition parties boycotted the elections. As a result they presented the Government with an easy victory. However, in the municipal elections which followed, the Opposition parties reversed this false achievement by winning 639 seats against the Government's 383, a clear index of national feeling. But Marshal Smigly-Rydz held on to power throughout the ominous spring and summer of 1939.

Poland therefore entered the war with a totally unrepresentative Government, backed by the Army but opposed by the nation. Swift defeat followed and despite its heroic resistance a flood of bitter feeling against the Army swept the nation—a mixture of despair, cynicism and disbelief. Amid this revulsion of feeling, Tokarzewski had now to begin creating a new underground military force. It was no easy assignment, working under the noses of the triumphant Nazis.

He enrolled some two hundred officers willing to stay on and help. In disguise, hiding from the ever-watchful enemy, carrying false identity papers when in the streets, they worked hard, and by December 1939 had created the framework of a secret military underground throughout both the German and the Russian zones of Poland, with headquarters in Warsaw.

But a skeleton command of officers was not enough. Tokarzewski wanted popular support and to get this he had to obtain the backing of the three main pre-war Opposition political parties and their paramilitary organisations. These organisations could supply the Secret Army, which he had named Service For Polish Victory, with large numbers of loyal young soldiers. So early in October he turned to the political leaders still in Warsaw.

One or two of them had ventured cautiously to meet again, despite the Nazi threat of death by torture or a firing squad for political activities. Stefan Korbonski,[2] a leader of the Peasant Party, had escaped from captivity in the Russian zone to this new and quite unfamiliar Warsaw — dangerous, war-scarred, with the empty, blackened window-frames of crippled houses gaping on to streets where Germans in grey-green uniforms barked angry commands.

One morning in October Korbonski made his way to the modest four-roomed apartment of Mathew Rataj, former Speaker of the Polish Parliament and a leader of the Peasant Party, who had already become a focus of secret political activity. Rataj, a man in his late sixties whose fine-drawn features had grown gaunt and his hair white since the Polish defeat, welcomed Korbonski cordially, but made him promise secrecy. He then revealed that with Niedzialkowski, the Socialist Party leader, he was organising an underground civil authority throughout the country in defiance of the German administration. It would be composed of the main parties of the pre-war political Opposition and exclude altogether the bankrupt right-wing parties of the former Government.

Inspired by the prospect of armed struggle, Korbonski met Rataj frequently after this to help plan the structure of the secret civil authority. He warned the old man of the danger of Gestapo arrest which as a known political leader with many visitors he obviously risked. Rataj shrugged. 'What can I do?' he exclaimed. 'I cannot keep the doors locked all day long. I might move to another place, but I won't do it. This is my home.'[3]

Two Gestapo officers arrived at his home a few days later and bundled him off in such a hurry that he had barely time to dress. Shocked by the arrest and aware of the urgent need to discover the reason for it in case the underground had already been discovered, Korbonski boldly walked into the former Ministry of Education building in Szuch Avenue, then the Gestapo Headquarters, and pretending to deliver a parcel for Rataj politely asked why he had been taken in. Korbonski was lucky to escape with his skin; he learned nothing, but came away convinced that the arrest was a routine matter not linked with suspicion that the underground movement had begun.

Korbonski met Niedzialkowski some days later by appointment at 8 a.m. in a café. The Socialist leader was a burly man with a mop of dark hair, double chin and frameless spectacles, who kissed the hands of the two pretty waitresses and cracked jokes with them before conferring with Korbonski. In a stage whisper he then invited him to deputise for the unfortunate Rataj. Korbonski agreed, and learned from him that the political leaders were trying to form a political committee which could be linked with the burgeoning military underground.

Tokarzewski, who saw Poland as an independent social democracy after liberation, had lost no time in making contact with Niedzialkowski. Some agreement was achieved, but the politicians complained that the military wanted to control everything, which ran counter to their wish to keep the underground civil–political authority free of military influence. Niedzialkowski, zealous and active, played the key part in these negotiations.

But on 23 December the Gestapo called at his apartment and took him off to Szuch Avenue at midday for a preliminary interrogation. They then let him go and ordered him to report again the following day. Niedzialkowski inexplicably missed this chance to go into hiding. Some vestiges of trust in the Germans still remained, for Niedzialkowski actually went back. He was imprisoned, and some time later shot in a mass execution in Palmyra Forest.

To lose both him and the no less able Mathew Rataj in a few weeks was a setback, but the men of the infant underground accepted their perilous situation and meeting as and when they could, always in different houses, achieved some accord. By the end of the year the secret underground state had taken first form in the Political Liaison Committee, made up of representatives of the three main parties. General Tokarzewski was also a member and together they drew up the *Statute of the Service for Polish Victory*,[4] which was an agreement on general aims between the political and military underground.

It charged that the organisation should 'undertake a decisive and unrelenting struggle against the invader in every field of his activity... until the day of liberation of Poland within her pre-war boundaries.' Secondly, it should reorganise the Polish Army; and thirdly, create the nucleus of a temporary national authority in Poland. These aims were amplified in an Ideological Declaration which proclaimed:

> The struggle for the independence of Poland against the Germans and the Russians continues. It will continue until our final victory is achieved. Every Pole has the duty and the honourable right to take part in this struggle. One of the conditions of its success and of the effective use of all our forces is the uniformity of its leadership over the entire territory of Poland. Subordination to the leadership and loyal co-operation with it are the least we expect today from every citizen.

Significantly, the declaration added that 'our enemies are all totalitarian ideologies, and, today, in the first place, Hitlerism and Bolshevism'. Finally, it promised that the structural foundation of the Polish state and its social and economic system 'will be decided by Parliament, assembled on a wide democratic basis after the restoration of independence'.

Thus the Declaration demanded uncompromising hostility both to Nazi Germany and to Soviet Russia, with no hint of willingness to compromise for the sake of national survival. This was called the 'two enemies' doctrine. And the leaders of the Secret Army would cling to it to the very end.

22

But meantime a new Polish Government had been set up in Paris and was planning a rival underground in Poland. When the former Government was interned in Rumania and therefore unable to govern, the President had resigned in favour of the Speaker of the Senate, Ladislas Raczkiewicz, who had already gone to Paris. The new President had appointed as Prime Minister General Sikorski, a distinguished soldier but no friend of the military dictatorship which had led the country to defeat. Sikorski formed a government composed mainly of politicians of the pre-war Opposition parties who had escaped to France. It set up a 'parliament' of nineteen members and raised again the banner of the Polish Armed Forces, drawing on thousands of soldiers from the country's defeated armies who had sought freedom abroad. These troops formed the nucleus of the Polish divisions who fought in Norway, North Africa, Italy, France and Germany.

In October General Sikorski, C-in-C of the Polish Armed Forces as well as Prime Minister, now formed the second secret armed force in Poland, the *Union for Armed Struggle*. He nominated the right-wing General Sosnkowski as chairman of a committee of ministers responsible for Home Affairs, and Commander-in-Chief of the UFAS, though subject to his own orders. The Statute of the UFAS declared that its task was to 'co-operate in the reconstruction of the Polish State through the means of war'.[5] It was to be the only secret armed force in Poland, all other underground groups were to place themselves under its command; it was to embrace the whole nation, be above party politics and base itself on 'strictly understood principles of hierarchy, obedience and discipline'.

General Sosnkowski, whom he had chosen to command the Union for Armed Struggle, was not welcomed by the left-wing political parties upon whom the movement depended. A tall, burly soldier with bushy eyebrows, a sharp manner and an inborn distaste for politicians, he had been Minister for Military Affairs under Marshal Pilsudski during Poland's rout of the Bolsheviks in 1920, had been anti-Soviet ever since and was rigidly against any kind of collaboration with Soviet Russia.

Two military underground organisations now existed in Poland: Tokarzewski's Service for Polish Victory and the Union for Armed Struggle, formed by Sikorski's Government-in-exile. 'Already, today, if the need arose, it would be possible actively to take the field and by so doing inspire the masses,' Tokarzewski reported to Sikorski in optimistic tone on 14 December 1939.[6] But Sikorski at first jealously refused to recognise his organisation and finally did so only with reluctance, on condition that it was wholly subordinated to his own Union for Armed Struggle. At a meeting on 26 February 1940 Tokarzewski and the political leaders in Warsaw accordingly all swore to support the work and plans of the UFAS as the sole secret military organisation called into being by the Government of the Republic.

23

For better or worse, the fortunes of the Polish underground were now permanently linked with General Sikorski's Government-in-exile, whose varying fortunes depended upon its fluctuating relationships with Britain, the USA and Soviet Russia. But having subordinated Tokarzewski's organisation Sikorski decided that this General would best serve the underground elsewhere.

He divided the entire underground into two regions, German-occupied and Soviet-occupied. Colonel Stefan Rowecki was given command of the German zone in Warsaw. Tokarzewski was ordered to proceed to the Russian zone, with headquarters in Lwow. The order caused anger among the politicians in Warsaw, because they had grown to like working with Tokarzewski; and since he had commanded the Lwow military district some years before, they believed he would quickly be recognised by the Communists, denounced to the Russians and seized.

They persuaded him to postpone his departure while they argued with the Government in Paris by coded radio. But Sikorski decreed that underground work was equally dangerous in both zones and that Tokarzewski's knowledge of the Lwow region would be useful. So towards the end of March 1940 he departed. A Russian patrol seized him while he was crossing the frontier between the two zones. He was thrown into prison.

Responsibility for the Secret Army in the Russian zone fell on Colonel Rowecki's shoulders in Warsaw. A coldly professional soldier and a veteran of the 1920 Polish–Russian War, Rowecki was guided in the initial organisation of the Union for Armed Struggle by Sosnkowski's Organisational Order Number 1 of 1940[7] which directed that the UFAS should be a small, élite group, foundation of a larger force that could be used to launch an uprising. Upon these principles Rowecki planned its organisation.

It was to be composed of provincial, regional, area, sector and outpost commands, with staffs, special diversionary-action platoons, and combat platoons situated in operational strongpoints. Outpost commanders could lead locally raised platoons. A platoon, about 50 men, was to be the basic organisational and tactical unit. The reserve included all undisbanded military organisations whose members comprehended military tactics and operational procedures. The UFAS was to draw upon this to replenish its ranks and would be used fully on the outbreak of a national insurrection. The mass of the community should be ready to take up arms in a general volunteer movement.

Rowecki and his regional commanders began a campaign to unite all the many secret military groups in the country. Few of the smaller non-political ones resisted for long the pressure to merge with the

UFAS. For military purposes officers and men were subordinated to the UFAS Command, but in their own separate units up to battalion strength, and with permission to keep their own social or professional traditions. They were free, so long as they were not hostile, to work on the underground political front for the kind of post-war Poland they visualised, and so long as this was non-communist.

Three political parties held out against Rowecki's efforts. First, the right-wing anti-communist, anti-semitic National Armed Forces movement of the National Youth Organisation. Fascist in outlook, its members even regarded the Union for Armed Struggle as pro-communist. They were to develop a programme of military action against Soviet partisans and the Communists based on the belief that German defeat being certain, its occupation of Poland was temporary and that Russia was the worst danger.

Second, the Communists, who although they had not re-formed the political party that Stalin destroyed in 1938, began to organise themselves in underground cells immediately after the defeat, Warsaw being their main centre. Communist groups included the Worker-Peasant Militant Organisation, the Friends of the Soviet Union and the Liberation Struggle Union,[8] whose membership included metal workers, railwaymen, tram drivers and public utility workers. It formed an underground military group under the command of Marian Spychalski. The Communist groups, in Warsaw and elsewhere in Poland, combined plans for liberation from the Nazis with plans for a Marxist social system brought about with the aid of the Red Army as it advanced against a defeated Germany. Thus, from the earliest days, the Communists were on a collision course with Sikorski's UFAS; both hoped to seize power at the critical moment.

The third party to hang fire were the National Democrats, a major party of property owners and some of the nobility, who were, as ever, at loggerheads with their traditional opponents, the Peasant Party and the Socialists. They declined to subordinate their expanding fighting force to Colonel Rowecki's command because they might need it in defence of their interests were the Allies to defeat Germany, and peace come. Not until late 1942 did they bring over their force of seventy thousand underground soldiers to Rowecki's command.

To give more force to the call for unity and to strengthen the will to keep silent under Nazi torture, Sosnkowski devised with the help of a priest a solemn religious oath. Every member of the Union for Armed Struggle from Rowecki down to messenger girls and boys swore:

Before God the Almighty, before the Virgin Mary, Queen of the Crown of Poland, I put my hand on this Holy Cross, the symbol of martyrdom and salvation, and I swear that I will defend the honour of Poland with all my might, that I will fight with arms in hand to liberate her from slavery, notwithstanding the sacrifice of my own

25

life, that I will be absolutely obedient to my superiors, that I will keep the secret whatever the cost may be.

The person swearing in the member responded sternly: 'I receive you among the soldiers of freedom. Victory will be your reward. Death the punishment of treason.'

Someone destined to play the most fateful part of all in the Warsaw Uprising now made contact with the UFAS. Colonel Komorowski, a cavalry officer who before the war had made a name for himself in the international show-jumping arena, lacked at this time either political or military ambitions. As one of the Polish minor nobility he was content in peacetime to farm his estate, ride his horses and take part occasionally in cavalry exercises with the Army. Thin, balding, pensive-looking, with a melancholy expression and a small clipped moustache, he was a strong upholder of the 'two enemies' doctrine and right-wing in politics; while not a leader of Rowecki's calibre, he was at the same time respected, likeable, fair and determined.

After the September defeat Komorowski began to make his way secretly to join thousands of others who were flocking to the banner Sikorski had raised in France, but friends in Cracow persuaded him otherwise. 'We must fight in this country as well,' they insisted. Komorowski agreed to stay and assume leadership of a military group which was planning to sabotage the Germans in south-west Poland.

3/   Plans for an Armed Rising

An envoy of General Sikorski entered Poland secretly from Hungary in March 1940, with instructions to Komorowski in Cracow to place himself under the command of the Warsaw GHQ of the Union for Armed Struggle. Komorowski decided to visit Warsaw first and meet there the man in command. He and an aide travelled with carefully forged identity papers in a railway compartment reserved for Nazi businessmen. They posed as timber merchants from Germany buying wood for coffins.

In Warsaw a liaison girl — a young housewife — escorted Komorowski to a private flat. He waited alone in a comfortable sitting-room, wondering who the UFAS commander might be, for as yet he knew him only by his alias, which was Grot. He heard a German patrol march by outside. The Nazi genocide policy had started, and Himmler had visited the capital at the end of March. Ludwig Fischer, Governor of the Warsaw District, reported afterwards to Hans Frank, Governor-General of Poland: 'The Reichsführer-SS has ordered 20,000 Poles to be committed to concentration camps.'[1]

The manhunt for people of influence had been speeded up. Those seized, Komorowski knew, were either transported to the camps, whose commandants Himmler had[2] reminded on 15 March 1940 that their chief duty was to liquidate all Polish leaders; or were shot in Parliament Gardens near the Vistula river by the 301 Battalion Security Police.[3]

Hearing the harsh commands and the steady tramp of Wehrmacht units outside, Komorowski thought of the herculean task — the formation of a secret army to fight the Nazis — he and others had taken on. No chain is stronger than its weakest link. They all of them depended upon each other's strength to stay silent under torture. In coming here he had put his life into the hands of someone about whom at the moment he knew nothing.

He sat waiting. Then the door opened and closed quickly and he found himself walking forward to greet the burly smiling figure with its shock of cropped dark hair of the man to whom he would then have turned with most trust. His old friend Colonel Stefan Rowecki had commanded Poland's only motorised brigade in the September campaign. Komorowski assured him of his confidence and that he would willingly serve under him. There and then they planned the dangerous problem of liaison between Warsaw and Cracow, agreed on methods of sabotage, training and uniting the many secret military groups under one command.

It was an important meeting in the life of the Secret Army, for these two men were to be its chief architects.

Like many Poles, Komorowski had a passion for 'good conspiratorial practice' — false identity documents, disguise, daily changes of rendezvous in homes of sympathisers to whom they were complete strangers; a new password every day, a different sleeping-place every night, and a tiny phial of cyanide for staff members who knew the movement's secrets to swallow when all seemed lost.

The Gestapo were constantly active. Everyone feared finding his name in black print in their lists of wanted men. In streets, cafés, shops, all Poles, even adolescents, had to keep alert and watch what went on, for at any moment they could be seized in a street-raid, flung into a lorry and never be seen again.

The Secret Army moved quickly to active operations under the leadership of Rowecki and Komorowski. By early 1940 it had launched sabotage of railways, war material dumps and machinery in the new German weapons factories erected in Poland. Arms, for which the Secret Army had great need, were dug up out of the caches in which they had been buried after the defeat, reconditioned and stored ready for use. The manufacture of hand-grenades and other weapons was begun in secret underground workshops, laboriously burrowed out beneath city cellars. A special section of artists and printers accurately forged false identity papers in a subterranean printing works excavated beneath the entrance hall of a Warsaw mansion. At the cost of enormous effort and one or two lives courier routes were established for the carriage of money and messages via Hungary to the Government in France.

And then on 10 May 1940 Germany launched its western offensive. France collapsed four weeks later and the Polish Government fled to Britain, which pulled the remnants of its broken army back home across the Channel. It seemed as if the newly formed Secret Army, isolated in a continent dominated by the Nazis, was faced with extinction. For Soviet Russia was still bound by the alliance with the Nazis, still sending them war material at Stalin's insistence.

General Sikorski realised that the Germans would soon redirect thousands of troops to combat sabotage with even more savage reprisals against Polish civilians. The new situation called for a change of policy.

Therefore, on 18 June 1940, four days after the fall of Paris, he sent a telegram to Rowecki ordering armed action by the underground to cease; and two days later another forbidding even sabotage as 'pointless and provocative'.[4] Komorowski and Rowecki saw the sense of this, believing themselves that military action would involve heavy losses through reprisals. But they realised that faith in final victory over the Nazis and the Soviets might now waver in the ranks of the UFAS.

Nevertheless they switched for the time being to a policy of intelligence and espionage only. At that time Poland was cut off from all news of the outside world except for Nazi and Soviet radio bulletins, which were more or less identical in tone. Foreign Commissar Molotov, for example, in a speech to the Supreme Soviet of the USSR on 31 October 1939 and subsequently broadcast from Moscow *ad infinitum*, had declared that: 'Everybody should understand that an ideology cannot be destroyed by force, that it cannot be eliminated by war. It is therefore not only senseless but criminal to wage such a war as a war for the "destruction of Hitlerism" camouflaged as a fight for "democracy"...'[5]

In the face of this propaganda the underground set up secret radio receiving stations tuned into British and American news bulletins. They covered everything from Churchill's speeches to BBC news reports of British naval and air clashes with German forces. Sometimes these bulletins were the purest invention. Leaflets with a printed appeal by the RAF to Poland not to weaken, and promising an early bombing offensive on Germany, fluttered down on Warsaw one twilight evening. Seeming to have come from a high altitude reconnaissance aircraft they gladdened the Poles and infuriated the Germans. They were in fact printed by the Secret Army in Warsaw, lifted aloft by small balloons and automatically released at a suitable altitude.

But these measures lifted the spirit of the oppressed people only temporarily. And grave setbacks followed in the later months of 1940. Dr Surzycki, a Christian Democrat leader whose eloquence had persuaded Komorowski to stay to help build the Secret Army in Poland, had become one of the main helpers on the intelligence front. One day in the autumn his secretary was caught by the Gestapo copying German documents for him and under severe torture she spoke his name. He was seized and tortured, but though sick and weak from illness he kept silent. He managed to send a message through a Polish prison-warder that he had not betrayed the underground. Shortly afterwards he died in a concentration camp.

Next, the Germans discovered the Secret Army headquarters in Silesia. Starosta, the commander, burnt all documents, but was shot while jumping from a balcony and the organisation there was dormant until a new leader could be found. Meantime, in Cracow, headquarters of the Gestapo, even the well-disguised Komorowski, with perfectly forged German documents, felt a sense of danger as he walked from house to house for military staff meetings. For safety he lived apart from his wife Irena and their son, stealing a few hours alone with them only on Saturdays and Sundays. She had spread the word among

29

friends and acquaintances who were unaware of his underground role that he was serving abroad with Sikorski's forces.

Yet some curious instinct whispered to him that the Nazis were on his track, an instinct he would always obey and which would save him when colleagues ignored it and were seized. He looked for some way of avoiding public appearances, of being able to meet his military staff without suspicion. He hit on the idea of working in a newspaper shop belonging to a member of the underground and began work as an assistant there; he registered under the name of Wolanski with the Nazi labour authorities, and his documents were impeccable. Here his Chief of Staff and his liaison officers visited him daily in the guise of customers.

But all these circumstances – German military successes in France; greater zeal of the Nazis in hunting down Poles in the Secret Army; General Sosnkowski's élitist policy and General Sikorski's order to cease armed action and sabotage – combined to cause a decrease for the time being both in the anti-Nazi impetus of the Poles and in the underground membership. From June 1940 to the spring of 1941 this fell from 75,000 to 54,000: and the total of combat platoons from 2,190 in October 1940 to 1,466 in March 1941.

Yet the outcome of the fall of France was not wholly negative. General Rowecki – to which rank both he and Komorowski were appointed before General Sikorski left France for England – prepared the first detailed plan, with the aid of his military staff, for an armed uprising.

The plan analysed Poland's possible courses of action according to the doctrine of the 'two enemies', Germany and Soviet Russia.[6] It envisaged, with British and possibly US aid, the massive bombing of enemy bases, both Russian as well as German, the dropping of parachute divisions and the landing of armoured units on the Polish coast near Danzig.

Conceived before the outbreak of the German–Soviet war, it nevertheless presupposed this likelihood, but even without it Rowecki foresaw the eventual defeat of the Nazis by British Commonwealth forces aided by the Polish Army and sooner or later reinforced by American troops. He was less certain about Soviet Russia:

At the present moment it is difficult to foresee what the concrete position of the Soviets will be in the final stages of the war. There are several possibilities and they can be simplified to two basic ones: first, Russia will manage to maintain its neutrality almost to the last days, continually keeping a large army intact on its western boundaries ready to march out to conquer at the moment when Europe is in revolt. In this case a Polish insurrection, being unable to mobilise properly, and short of arms, would have little chance of success. We would merely oppose thousands of our best men to the motorised flood of the Soviet hordes in their westward march, not achieving any effective results bar the further destructon of our country and bloodshed on a massive scale. Secondly, Russia will be in a state of war with Germany and Japan, or Japan and eventually Germany. In this case it is most probable that the Germans will deal several heavy military defeats to the Soviets, penetrating deep into Soviet territories through the Ukraine. This will certainly shake the whole Soviet structure, weakening their cohesion and threatening their establishment, at the same time destroying the worth of an army already weakened by lack of success.

General Rowecki thus looked forward to launching a general anti-Nazi insurrection at the critical moment of Germany's defeat by the Western Powers; and, sooner or later, to achieving the same kind of coup against an exhausted Soviet Union.

The ultimate objective was to re-establish Poland as a great Power independent of either the Soviet Union or Germany. In the process parts of White Russia and the entire Ukraine were to be freed from Soviet control. He also considered the likelihood of a contrasting development:

We cannot exclude the possibility, however remote it may seem, that in the Soviet–German war the successes will be on the Bolshevik side, and that they will manage to push the Germans out of Poland. Obviously, it would be madness to attempt any action against such an army marching into Poland, strengthened by its victory over the German army. Our role would then be to keep the apparatus in hiding, carrying on the conspiracy, waiting for the moment when the Soviet side and system begin to crack.[7]

For this eventuality he prepared a scheme for a general uprising in Poland timed for the moment of collapse of a beaten German army, together with 'defensive action' against the Red Army, both, he assumed, with the full support of General Sikorski's Polish forces abroad.

If the Red Army entered Poland in pursuit of a retreating German army without consent Rowecki proposed counter-attacking along the line of the Bug river, with a final defence line along the Vistula river. This move was based both on an uprising which, through the element of surprise, would capture the necessary additional arms from the Germans; the arming of several more divisions by the Western Powers, and reinforcement by the Sikorski forces in time for a line to be held against the advancing Russians if necessary on the line of the Vistula.

General Rowecki's plan arrived in London by radio on 25 June 1941, three days after Hitler launched Operation Barbarossa against his former ally, the Soviet Union. Rowecki's forecast of 'several heavy military defeats to the Soviets' proved correct. However, the plan, which went far beyond the military strength of the underground army conflicted in any case with General Sikorski's own views on the Soviets.

Rowecki was an outstanding leader, but while he prided himself on his non-political approach he yet was strongly anti-Russian. The higher levels of strategy demand a clear awareness of international relations. Here Rowecki was far inferior to Sikorski, who was at once a military realist, a highly accomplished politician and a diplomat whose approach to the problem of Polish–Russian relations rose well above rigid anti-Sovietism.

Germany, in Sikorski's view, was Poland's first and main enemy, with whom no compromise was possible. The Soviet Union was its second enemy, towards whom its policy was also war, imposed by the Soviets. But co-operation with them against Germany would be possible when they again recognised Polish sovereignty within her pre-war frontiers. A year ago, in 1940, Sikorski had foreseen the likelihood of a Nazi–Soviet war which probably would bring about some kind of a Polish–Russian *rapprochement*.

He had suggested to the British Government on 19 June 1940[8] the formation of a Polish army on Russian soil from among the thousands of Polish prisoners-of-war there, a seemingly remote project which actually materialised. In July 1941, not long after Hitler's attack on Russia, he and an eager Soviet Ambassador Maisky were already arguing, with the good offices of Anthony Eden, British Foreign Secretary, the terms of a resumption of Polish–Soviet relations.

After the signing of the Polish–Soviet Agreement in July 1941, relations between the two countries turned sour over the thousands of Polish prisoners-of-war still in Russia, and the Polish children who disappeared after Russia invaded Poland. But Sikorski still exercised a restraining influence. In a special instruction to Rowecki[9] he confessed that the subject of the underground army's attitude to the Soviet Union 'is a subject of constant worry to me'. Referring to Rowecki's proposals should the Red Army enter Polish territory without consent in pursuit of the enemy, he warned:

> To wage an armed struggle by the Underground Army against Soviet troops entering Poland would be sheer madness. To keep secret the military organisation of whose existence the Soviet Government is well informed, would lead to an open fight of the Soviet troops against the Underground Army, a fight on which Communist propaganda would spread distorted views in the camp of the Allied Nations.

And later when relations with Russia were nearing breaking-point he was telling Rowecki that 'an understanding with Russia is essential'.

The advent of the Russo-German War changed Poland's situation greatly, seeming to point the way to a profitable alliance with Russia.

Germany advanced into eastern Poland, eliminating the Russian zone there, and General Rowecki took command over the UFAS throughout Poland. On 30 July 1941 Sikorski signed the Polish–Russian Agreement. This annulled the Soviet–German treaties of 1939 relating to Poland; restored mutual diplomatic relations; undertook mutual aid and support during the war and the formation of the Polish Army in Russia under General Anders, as well as granting an amnesty to Poles imprisoned there.

Unfortunately, at this time favourable for Poland, the issue of ownership of the eastern territories seized by Russia was not solved. Nevertheless Sikorski justified the agreement on the grounds that if Russia were defeated Hitler's plan was to drive the Poles into Siberia – 'the Poles will disappear as a nation'.

For Sosnkowski the agreement was an outrage. He resigned his Government post in protest, at which Sikorski dismissed him as C-in-C of the UFAS. It meant the end of Sosnkowski's small, élitist movement. 'I do not share the view that this organisation should be completely inactive during the war,' General Sikorski declared in a letter to General Anders, Commander of the Polish Army in Russia on 1 September 1941.

> I think that the home country must continue to play an active part in the struggle. Such action must be, however, carried out so as not to expose the organisation and home country to enemy reprisals. Enough Polish blood has been shed already, and there is no need to lavish it in order to mark Poland's active part in the camp of fighting democracies. We must preserve forces as big as possible for the time of the outbreak of an armed rising, and this moment is still far ahead.[10]

The new policy led to fresh hope and the influx of volunteers into the ranks of the Secret Army could not be stemmed. The number of platoons, which were the basic operational units of the Secret Army, rose from 1,515 in the summer of 1941 to 2,469 in the winter of 1941–2, platoons varying in strength from thirty to fifty. During the same period the number of officers rose from 4,012 to 6,316, and the number of NCOs from 15,975 to 26,370. In order to make clear beyond doubt the overall national status of the UFAS, Sikorski in February 1942 changed its name to Home Army, although it was still widely called the Secret Army.

Three categories of men and women composed it. First, the professionals like Rowecki, Komorowski and about 200 others who worked full time in one or other of its different branches, such as military operations, intelligence, financial control. Underground work was their entire life. They were paid, but only enough for subsistence.

Ordinary men and women workers in factories, railways, offices and farms were the next, and largest group. All of them, officers, NCOs and rankers, had taken the oath and were ready on call for assignments such as espionage and sabotage — placing a time-bomb in an important wagon load going to the Reich; the assassination of a traitor, or of a Nazi official prominent in ordering the execution of Poles. After achieving their tasks, which might take anything from an hour or two to a week or more, the members concerned went back to their day-to-day work.

The third group was made up of young men and former soldiers, who after 1942 were forming themselves into units under the command of Secret Army officers and living mainly in the forests, in Polish Army uniforms as partisans, ready to attack the Germans on General Rowecki's orders. But so severe were German reprisals — at least one hundred Poles shot for the death of one German — that for some time Rowecki held his men in check.

Between the Secret Army and the pre-war Polish Army the gulf was wide. The regular officers and NCOs who were the nucleus of the pre-war army formed a military caste within the nation nurtured on the anti-democratic, romantic nationalism of Marshal Pilsudski, and many regular officers still clung to these beliefs. But the Secret Army had called into its ranks men and women from all walks of life with every kind of political belief, some of them military reservists who had undergone routine training; others who had never used a gun, a grenade or an explosive device in their lives.

Rowecki realised that the standard military training of the pre-war years would be of little use in the task ahead, which would involve partisan and street fighting with many different makes and kinds of arms. But some training was needed quickly. He worked out a military doctrine adapted to the new conditions, with new tactical regulations and instructions, as well as special reorientation training for regular soldiers, some of whom were finding it hard to adapt to the new conditions.

Two forms of training were launched, one general and preparatory, covering drill, words of command, weapons and elementary tactics; the second dealing with specific insurrectionary problems only. Teachers in the first course taught recruits how to adapt normal infantry tactics to guerrilla action, as well as the theory and use of British, Russian, German and Polish infantry weapons, including stripping down, the elimination of jamming in automatic weapons and maintenance.

Shooting practice at first did not exist due to the shortage of instructors and ammunition and to the danger of attracting the attention of the Nazis. The Secret Army men made up for their lack of firing practice by their determination to kill their oppressors.

Training in the second course was based on the actual role the soldiers would fulfil in the operational plan of the uprising, which then was still thought of as a nationwide affair. It consisted of alarm, which meant immediate mobilisation; assembly of units at their specific rendezvous; distribution of weapons; reconnaissance; security; attack on the enemy-held objective; defence of the captured objective against counter-attack.

Rowecki set out his military doctrine for the guidance of his officers in a pamphlet called *The Bases of Our Insurgent Battle*[11] which read in part:

> The rising as a type of action falls into a category halfway between the action of regular troops and a military revolution. We must base our operations on both of these aspects, particularly in view of our lack of insurrectionary experience...Thus the uprising must be preceded by a long period of preparation, precise and detailed, followed by a violent, universal, synchronised blow, which, by staking all on one card by acting extraordinarily boldly should bring about a decisive solution after a few hours on the night of the rising.

In this desperate and optimistic plan, Rowecki stressed particularly how violent and well directed the first attack would have to be to be successful. Once embarked upon the plan could not be changed because senior commanders would be incapable of influencing these rigidly conceived operations at the decisive moment. Therefore he made it clear that units attacking a specific objective were on their own, could not depend on any directions from higher echelons and could not expect to be reinforced, because all Secret Army personnel would be fully involved simultaneously.

Guerrilla theory demands that units operating on their own but according to plan seize first districts from the enemy, then whole areas and finally regions until they occupy most of the territory; the enemy is defeated piecemeal, not according to a rigid timetable, but by the guerrillas' growing strength, military organisation and capabilities.

Rowecki's plan arose out of a contrasting military doctrine based on 'strictly understood principles of hierarchy, obedience and discipline', as laid down by General Sosnkowski in the UFAS Statute. Unlike guerrilla strategy and tactics, where operations arise out of the tactical situation, growing gradually stronger and more effective, Rowecki called for a sudden universal blow rigidly planned and precisely carried out with the utmost speed by troops disciplined and trained for their own specific tasks. It was to be launched when Germany was at its weakest, and the Soviets too weak or disorganised to clamp their iron hand on the country.

The operations section of Rowecki's headquarters drew up maps marked specially with vital objectives — airports, railway stations, telephone exchanges, broadcasting stations, bridges, barracks, ordnance stores. In addition they compiled a so-called 'atlas of destruction' upon which enemy strong-points, fuel, ammunition, petrol and supplies dumps, and vehicle parts were marked for attack. The Polish Army manual on defence against enemy armour, together with a series of new military publications for artillery and engineer officers, were secretly printed and circulated.

Throughout Poland, officer training schools were launched with primary courses lasting five months, each class consisting of between three and five officer-cadets. Courses were also set up for propaganda and information, communications, sabotage and motor engineering. Specialised training courses for women covered first aid, liaison, communications, weapons training and sabotage.

How was this ambitious scheme accomplished under the eyes of the Germans? With their highly developed conspiratorial sense, the Poles devised many ingenious stratagems — lessons held in the waiting-rooms of doctors' surgeries, on farms, in factories, in railway compartments. From 1941 to July 1944, just before the Uprising, more than 8,500 men and women had attended the officer-training courses.

But General Rowecki's 1941 plans for a universal and simultaneous uprising in Poland were not final. In a series of letters to Sikorski they were much elaborated during the next two years, as a result of the changing pattern of war in the west and east, and the unexpected likelihood that the Soviets, not the British and Americans, would liberate Poland.

From December 1941 onwards the war had changed greatly in character. Pearl Harbor, 7 December, brought in the United States. In May 1942, the RAF, starting their major air offensive against Germany, hit Ruhr industrial targets with massive blows. From August onwards the US 8th Air Force struck at airfields, aircraft factories and fuel plants in Germany. The Wehrmacht was tied down in Russia, and in the second half of the year lost the decisive battle of Stalingrad, while Anglo-American armies invaded North Africa.

In Poland the former slender hopes of an uprising grew real. General Sikorski in London and General Rowecki in Warsaw began to plan their strategy more precisely. Sikorski forecast that owing to climatic conditions and their stretched lines of communication the Germans would be fought to a standstill in the depths of Russia. When Germany was clearly exhausted by war with Russia and the Anglo-American bombardments, the Allies would land in France. As the Allied armies neared the Rhine, Hitler would begin to transfer reserves from east to west and at that moment the Polish and all other resistance movements in Europe should rise.

Sikorski's vision of the future development of the war in Russia became the foundation for all subsequent Home Army rising plans. The zero hour decision for it was left to General Rowecki, who would presumably know the best moment. The Uprising would begin by the complete destruction of all road and rail links along which the Germans would be starting to travel from east to west across Poland, so as to stop all but small numbers from reaching Germany. Thus the Allies, Sikorski argued, would more easily be able to take control, and the Soviets, heavily involved in fighting the Germans in the east, would, it was hoped, be excluded. Simultaneously, the Home Army would rise and take Central Poland, then liberate first the eastern and then the western regions, forming for the purpose larger infantry or cavalry units. But aid from Polish airborne units stationed in England could not be relied upon, Sikorski warned.

Rowecki worked out in 1942 two preparatory stages: *readiness* and *alarm*, which were part of the general plan. He wrote:[12]

Expecting the impending outbreak, I shall order a *state of readiness*. This period can last from four days after the rising to two weeks, and it can be cancelled. In this state of readiness all soldiers must remain in the locality of their unit, being ready to move towards their objective four hours after the issuing of the alarm. During this period all commanders must set in motion their communications network and review the readiness and organisation of all units under their command.

The *state of alarm* I shall order by radio over the whole area in a special code. It will last 48 hours and will end automatically with the outbreak of hostilities.

This period is ordered for the uncovering and distribution of arms, and the movement of units to take up their battle order. All this must be completed within 48 hours, so that commanders are ready to begin operations within the six hours immediately following. The exact hour of the outbreak will be given in the orders. All activities carried out during these two periods must be kept strictly hidden from the enemy, so that the maximum of surprise can be obtained.

Despite the 'two enemies doctrine', and the growing friction with Russia over Stalin's demand for vast areas of eastern Poland, Sikorski still insisted on planning military action against the Germans only. In a message to Rowecki on 28 November 1942[13] he ordered: 'The Home Army Commander will treat the Red Army as an ally and will not allow any operation against it. He will demonstrate the Polish claim to its pre-war territories by fighting the Germans there, by mobilising all the armed forces there and by setting up the administrative network.'

Sikorski knew that the Soviets would resist the setting up of a Polish administration in the disputed areas between Poland and Russia, but he hoped to convince them before that of the rights of the Polish case. 'Maybe the Polish Government, with British and American support, will eventually induce the Soviet Government to recognise our rights in the East...' he told Rowecki in his message of November 28,[14] adding that in the event of the Red Army entering Poland in pursuit of the Germans the Home Army should mobilise and come into the open.

Its strength should be as big as possible, and it should emphasise its sovereign status and its positive attitude to Soviet Russia. I pave the way for such an action of the Army and of the Home country in the international field; for that is where a decision of a political nature will settle our frontiers. It is also imperative that...the military organisations in particular, present their totally united front, and that Communist influence does not prevail among them.

Whether or not Stalin and the Soviets knew it, Sikorski was their number one enemy, a wolf in sheep's clothing who endlessly tried to alert Roosevelt and Churchill to the dangers of the spread of Communism to the West. But the last thing he wanted on the threshold of Poland's freedom was to involve her in a fruitless conflict with Russia. Sikorski had learned the lessons of Polish history.

For this reason he personally kept command over the place and timing of the Uprising. 'On account of the possible worsening of our relations with the Soviets,' he told Rowecki in a message later,[15] 'I am keeping in my own hands the power to decide on whether the rising is to be declared in the two eastern belts. If the Soviet attitude to us should show itself to be openly hostile, I will only order the coming out of the civil authorities, withdrawing all our armed forces to the heart of the country to avoid their destruction by the Russians.'

The rising against the Germans in the eastern territories would obviously depend upon the state of Poland's relations with Russia at that time. Any threat of hostilities between them would cause a withdrawal of the Home Army to Central Poland and the probable application of Rowecki's plan for defending the country.

But soon Poland would lose General Sikorski for ever and without his wise leadership her fortunes would begin to waver. For the Communists would return to Poland as an organised party determined, with the aid of Soviet bayonets, to seize power.

4/ Two tragedies: the Ghetto and Katyn

Early in January 1942 a Red Air Force transport aircraft flew westwards through the night over Poland. It carried a team of Polish Communist activists, members of a special 'Initiative Group' who had been making preparations in Moscow after training and studying at the Marxist–Leninist school at Puszkino there. Led by Marceli Nowotko and Pawel Finder, former members of the pre-war Polish Communist Party, they leapt out into the darkness and parachuted down on to the snowy plains some miles from Warsaw. They had orders from the Red Army Staff's 4th Department, and from the Comintern, to form a new workers' party to absorb and control the various independent Marxist groups in Poland.

Nowotko and company met at a prearranged rendezvous the Warsaw Communists and Soviet special NKVD agents. Before the end of January they had formed the Polish Workers' Party, which was to seize power after the war by Moscow-dictated shock tactics and rule Poland as a Soviet satellite. Its first manifesto, issued in January 1942, demanded a 'free and independent Poland in which the nation will decide its own fate...in which there will be no fascism, no landowners' rule of slavery, no concentration camps, no national oppression, no hunger, poverty and unemployment.'[1]

But behind this façade of political idealism the new party urged that Russia should be given the large slice of eastern Poland that she wanted, including the old Polish cultural cities of Lwow and Wilno; and that Poland should be compensated in the west by the ancient Piast lands, to be seized from a defeated Germany. The manifesto added that the foundation of Poland's security must be an alliance with the Soviet Union.

Most Poles, however, strongly disliked and mistrusted the USSR, who had invaded their country twice within the space of twenty years – in 1920 and 1939. The manifesto therefore failed in its object of rallying thousands of Poles of left-wing views to the new party's standard.

In the first months of 1942 the new party formed a revolutionary military arm, the People's Guard. Dedicated to systematic guerrilla warfare, and advised by a Soviet colonel whose name or alias was

Glebov,[2] it called for the speedy intensification of operations against the Germans so as to help the Red Army, a policy in stark contrast to that of General Rowecki and the Home Army.

Sikorski feared that premature large-scale operations against the Germans would cause them heavy losses and frustrate plans for an uprising at the moment of Germany's collapse before the entry of the Red Army into Poland. While Rowecki was therefore training and building up the Secret Army's strength he was ordered to limit it to sabotage and minor diversionary operations.

Small People's Guard detachments went into action during the second six months of 1942. Equipped with arms supplied by Soviet partisans or captured from the Germans, they derailed twenty military trains, destroyed seven bridges, freed a few hundred men and women from prisons and camps, and fought twenty-seven actions with Nazi units. Though not comparable with the extensive Home Army sabotage at this time, it was a beginning.

Throughout Poland, meantime, and in Warsaw especially mass arrests grew daily more frequent. Ever larger numbers of people were seized on the streets, never to be seen again. On the night of 27 May 1942, some 201 men and twenty-two women, arrested at random earlier, were herded into lorries at Pawiak prison and driven to the village of Magdelenka, twenty-five miles south of Warsaw. There SS firing squads shot them in a near-by pinewood. Villagers testified that the SS-men drove off singing.

On 11 June 1942 the underground *Information Bulletin* under the headline 'Mass Murder Continues' reported 'rumours circulating in Warsaw that some fifty prisoners were shot on Corpus Christi (*4 June*). This brings the total number of persons murdered within one week to over 250.'

In July 1942 the Nazis began the worst crime of all, the so-called 'liquidation of the Warsaw Ghetto,' that small area in the city surrounded by walls eight feet high guarded by German sentries, inside which some 400,000 Jews, collected from all over German-occupied Europe, were forced to live in horrifying conditions. Five thousand or more Jewish men, women and children were every day transported from there to the Treblinka concentration camp and the gas chambers. By 8 August 1942 more than 150,000 Jews had been massacred.

Stefan Rowecki ordered the chief of the Home Army section which arranged help for Jews to offer arms, ammunition and a diversionary attack on the city, to be co-ordinated with a Jewish rising. But the orthodox Jewish leaders, mostly elderly men, preferred appeasement, arguing that if they were obedient and docile the Nazis would kill fewer Jews. Confronted with this mistaken decision, Rowecki nevertheless set in hand sabotage of railway links with the German extermination camps, to try to delay the transports as much as possible. But the Germans used guarded road convoys, too. By 10 September 1942, as the

40

whole world was later stunned to hear, only about 30,000 Jews were left alive — officially — though in fact another 40,000 still survived in secret underground passages and rooms.

The survivors, young Zionists, Socialists and Communists, formed the Underground Jewish Militant Organisation, determined to fight the Nazis the moment they resumed their genocide policy.

Rowecki ordered Colonel Chrusciel, Home Army commander for Warsaw, to arrange for as much arms and ammunition as could be spared to be smuggled in to the Jewish militants together with a tactical plan for the Ghetto's defence and materials for the manufacture of anti-tank and hand-grenades.

On 16 February 1943 Himmler ordered the total destruction of the Ghetto and all its inhabitants. Just over four weeks later, at dawn on 19 April, Nazi troops commanded by SS-Oberführer von Sammern-Frankenegg, later relieved by SS-Brigadeführer Jürgen Stroop, marched in to remove the remaining Jewish residents. The Jewish militants met them with a hail of fire, routed an SS company in battle order, stopped two armoured cars with anti-tank grenades and forced two more to retreat.

But on Easter Monday evening the Germans brought in batteries of field artillery and with salvoes which rattled the city windows began systematically to shell the defended areas. For a week Jews fought Nazis in bitter house-to-house battles, retreating step by step as gunfire and flame-throwers razed their strong-points.

Picked Home Army units under Rowecki's personal command made diversionary attacks on the German rearguard to enable the Jewish defenders either to escape or to strengthen their positions, but without decisive effect. By Saturday almost all the young Jews had lost their lives in the struggle. Only isolated strong-points held out, fighting bitterly until 16 May 1943. Stroop then reported his assignment completed. Daily rail transports began to leave Warsaw again for the gas chambers. Some fifty-six thousand Jews died or were captured in this last operation, in burning houses, under the wreckage of blown-up buildings, in the fighting or afterwards in the gas chambers.[3]

The Secret Army did not take these Nazi acts of terror passively. Sabotage and armed diversionary operations were already on the increase and on 27 April 1942 General Sikorski in a radio message ordered the Home Army to make special efforts to inflict the greatest possible losses on the enemy.

On 19 May 1942 members of the Socialist Combat Organisation blew up with a time-bomb a casino frequented by German officers near the Gestapo Headquarters in Szuch Avenue. On 17 June a number of Gestapo were wounded in a gun-fight when they raided the premises of the secret weekly *Rampart* in a plumber's shop. On the night of 24 May the Home Army blew up a building into which the German *Kriminalpolizei* were moving. A sabotage squad set afire a petrol and lubricants depot in the Praga district, burning some 300,000 litres of fuel for the Wehrmacht. A few nights later on 23 July 1942 fifteen army lorries were destroyed by fire in a Warsaw garage on Jagiellonska Street. On 30 September, Home Army sabotage groups burned to the ground a factory in the Warsaw Zoliborz district making airscrews for the Luftwaffe.

There were also larger-scale operations. Not long after midnight on 8 October 1942 Warsaw was shaken by a series of heavy explosions rumbling around the city's suburbs. Many people took refuge in cellars and shelters in the belief that the Red Air Force was bombing the city. In fact, seven Secret Army, including two women's squads, all commanded by Captain Lewandowski, had simultaneously blown up every one of the railway tracks leading out of Warsaw, derailing several trains, paralysing transport to the Eastern Front and stopping an urgent German supply and ammunition convoy destined for Stalingrad.

The Nazis intensified their reprisals. In revenge for the Secret Army's sabotage of the railway lines fifty suspected Communists were hanged. Then during four days of January 1943 alone more than 35,000 men and women were seized and packed off to concentration camps, or to work as slave-labourers in Germany. Even boys and girls were dragged out of trams or railway waiting-rooms into waiting lorries. Often armed SS detachments surrounded entire blocks of houses, paraded the inhabitants, picked out the most useful-looking ones and marched them off.

The Poles were thirsting for revenge, but Rowecki and the Secret Army command were still held back by the order to conserve their forces. 'Terror should be answered by terror and violence by an armed fight,' shouted the Communist underground paper *Freedom Tribune*. But the Home Army's *Information Bulletin* Number 29 warned that the time would come for a great Polish guerrilla action, 'not when it suits the purpose of our Communist neighbour, but at a time when it will be purposeful from our own point of view'.

Underground fighters of two opposing factions were now at the beginning of a struggle in Poland against both the Nazis and each other. The Home Army, commanded by General Rowecki, backed by the Government-in-exile and the majority of the Polish people, was conserving its strength for an uprising with the object of installing a parliamentary government loyal to the London Polish Government and the West. The Communists, the Polish Workers' Party, and the People's Guard, then only a few thousand strong, had launched small-scale partisan warfare in aid of the Red Army. They intended to seize power with its help and set up a workers' dictatorship loyal to the Soviet Union.

For General Stefan Rowecki the situation was becoming critical. Already in August 1942 he had reported to Sikorski[4] that the Nazi policy of terror was causing heavy casualties and was sending many young people to join the ranks of the People's Guard. He suggested

42

that he should increase armed resistance and start regular guerrilla warfare in eastern Poland. 'German terror has aroused in the community the desire for active self-defence, thus confirming for a large part of public opinion the correctness of the slogans of the Polish Workers' Party—armed defence and immediate struggle against the occupiers[5],' the Information Bureau of the Home Army said in a report to London.

With its slogans and methods of fighting 'K' (the Communists) has outshone the Polish liberation organisations, winning a strong propaganda argument...To the People's Guard in all districts there has been an inflow of volunteers, especially among non-organised youth. There have also been frequent cases of whole groups going over to it discouraged by the passivity of the Polish organisations—from the Polish Socialist Party, for instance, and the General Sikorski Military Organisation...*

Rowecki sent Home Army units into action. They blew up railways and bridges leading to the Zamosc area, attacked German military units, burnt down the villages into which the German immigrants had moved and sabotaged enemy lines of communication. Terrified, the German settlers abandoned the farms and homesteads, and caused the Nazis to give up this plan for mass German immigration.

During 1943 tension between the Home Army and its associated political parties on the one hand, and on the other the Communists and the People's Guard increased to breaking-point. In November 1942 Marceli Nowotko, the Secretary-General of the Polish Workers' Party was assassinated on the orders of one of his colleagues. Pawel Finder became Secretary-General and authorised Wladyslaw Gomulka, one of the secretariat, who later succeeded him, to try to negotiate a common front, including military co-operation, with the Home Army.

'We the Polish Workers' Party, the youngest party of the underground Poland,' Gomulka wrote, 'hold out our hand to all the political parties of Poland, inviting them to co-operate and to organise together with us the struggle of the whole Polish nation against the Nazi occupier.[6] Gomulka also argued that the anti-Nazi struggle would be most effective if it was waged on the basis of an alliance with the Soviet Union.

Conditions for collaboration as stated by Gomulka were: (1) increased anti-German operations by Home Army units. (2) People's Guard representatives to be stationed at the Home Army headquarters and regional staffs to form a joint operational command. (3) The People's Guard to retain its own communist form of organisational structure and the right to its own political decisions. (4) Renunciation of the

* One of the independent resistance groups allied to the Home Army.

Polish Constitution of 1935. (5) The creation of a new government in Poland to supersede the London Government.

Gomulka added that if these conditions were unacceptable, limited military collaboration would still be worth undertaking. He pointed out that if the London Government were to turn down these proposals entirely it would give the Polish Workers' Party a free hand in the future.

On behalf of the London Government, the new delegate, Jan Jankowski demanded from Gomulka first a clear statement that his party recognised the Polish Government in London; secondly, that it had no links with international communism; thirdly, that it would defend the country against aggression from any quarter, and finally that it recognised the inviolability of Poland's pre-war frontiers. Gomulka had to reject conditions which would destroy his party's links with the Soviets; Jankowski therefore turned down any form of collaboration.

It was a milestone in Polish–Soviet affairs. Even before the talks had failed, Stalin began early in 1943 a campaign against the London Polish Government. His policy was to extend Russia's western frontiers into territory granted to Poland in 1920 by the Treaty of Riga between the two. Marshal Pilsudski's 1920 rout of Bolshevik Russia's invasion of Poland when Stalin was a young political commissar had never ceased to rankle.

Perhaps he had waited patiently over the years for the chance to revise Russia's western frontiers. When it came, with the Nazi–Soviet Pact, he seized it quickly enough. In January 1942 he had tried unsuccessfully to persuade Sikorski in Moscow to discuss the issue.[7] In his report of a talk at the Foreign Office on 26 January 1942, Sikorski quotes Sir Stafford Cripps as remarking that Russia had established certain principles in the matter of State frontiers which she considered beyond discussion.[8] He added that in unofficial Russian circles the Curzon Line had even been mentioned. Sikorski never officially gave up Poland's claim to the 1939 frontiers, though as a political realist he might well have compromised on the basis of keeping the Polish city of Lwow.

The issue of the frontiers was first raised in a Russian newspaper on 19 February 1942, and on 2 March a Tass communiqué[9] declared that the Polish denial of rights to the Ukrainians and the Belorussians – up till 1939, Polish citizens – was 'contrary to the Atlantic Charter...' It then uttered what became the constant Soviet refrain – that the Polish Government in London was 'not representative of the Polish people'.

A Polish newspaper appeared in Moscow, *Wolna Polska* (Free Poland), which declared that it was the organ of the Union of Polish Patriots, a new body devoted to 'uniting all Polish patriots living in the USSR'. Its aim, the paper said, was to 'regain for Poland every inch of Polish ground, but not to claim an inch of other people's land'. President was Wanda Wasilewska, communist daughter of a Polish colonel, at the time a member of the USSR Supreme Soviet and third wife of Alexander Korneichuk, a Ukrainian playwright.

Colonel Berling, one of the handful of Polish officers who had opted to stay with the Soviets rather than leave Russia with General Anders and the Polish division for the Middle East, was one of the founders. The formation of the Union of Polish Patriots now put at Stalin's disposal an organisation for furthering his plans for Poland. These began with Berling's move in March to form two or three divisions from the numerous Polish soldiers still in Russian prison or transit camps. At the same time, Tass, the Moscow Kosciuszko radio station, the *Free Poland* newspaper there and the Communist Warsaw paper *Liberty Tribune* all began a synchronised campaign denouncing the London Polish Government and the Home Army.

In April 1943 the conflict between the two governments reached breaking point. The cause was the Katyn Forest massacre of Polish officers. Ever since the restoration of relations between the two countries in 1941, Generals Sikorski and Anders, Ambassadors Kot and Romer, had persistently inquired of Stalin, Molotov or Vyshinsky where the 10,000 Polish officers were who had been taken prisoner by the Russians on the Eastern Front in 1939. No satisfactory answers were ever received.

In the Kremlin on 3 December 1941 Sikorski and Stalin in the presence of Molotov, Polish Ambassador Kot and General Anders, had discussed the issue:[10]

Sikorski: I have with me a list containing the names of approximately 4,000 officers who were deported by force and who presently still remain in the prisons and labour camps. Even this list is not complete since it contains only names which we were able to take from memory ...These people are here. Not one of them has returned.

Stalin: That is impossible. They have escaped.

Anders: Where then could they escape?

Stalin: Well, to Manchuria.

Anders: It is impossible that all could escape...I know that groups of Poles were already prepared for release and departure but they were retained at the last moment...

Stalin: Surely they have been released, but as yet have not arrived.

Sikorski: Russia is immense and the difficulties are great. Maybe the local authorities did not carry out the orders.

Stalin: I want you to know that the Soviet Government has not the slightest reason to retain even one Pole. I released even Sosnkowski's agents who attacked us and murdered our people.

Such unsatisfactory discussions gradually changed Polish irritation to anger. Then in April 1943, came the climax. The Germans announced the discovery of mass graves in Katyn Forest near Smolensk, containing the bodies of thousands of Polish officers in uniform. They had, it was said, been discovered by the German Intelligence Corps, who had been puzzled by birchwood crosses erected by Polish villagers. The facts of the existence of the graves had already been verified by responsible Poles taken there by the Germans.

From Berlin, the Germans announced that they had set up a Committee of Inquiry, which had 'proved' that the Russian NKVD had shot the Poles in 1940. Nothing perhaps could have been better timed to strain still more the already threadbare relations between the Soviets and the London Polish Government and its Home Army. Komorowski observed the tremendous impression made upon the people. 'No one asked who was responsible. Grief and sorrow plunged thousands of families into mourning. All other thoughts were swept away. The men had been the élite of the Polish nation...who had all been mobilised as reserve officers in 1939.'[11]

The facts were revealed to the Russian public on 16 April in an official Soviet statement:

Goebbels' gang of liars have, in the last two or three days, been spreading revolting and slanderous fabrications about alleged mass shootings by Soviet organs of authority in the Smolensk area, in the spring of 1940. The German statement leaves no doubt about the tragic fate of the former Polish war prisoners who, in 1941, were in areas west of Smolensk, engaged in road building, and who, together with many Soviet people, inhabitants of the Smolensk province, fell into the hands of the German hangmen, after the withdrawal of the Soviet troops from Smolensk...

This announcement told the Poles for the first time that their officer-prisoners had spent the years from their capture in 1939 onwards road-making in the Smolensk region.

On 17 April the issue came to a head. General Kukiel, Polish Minister of National Defence, declared that his Government had applied to the International Red Cross for an impartial on-the-spot investigation of the massacre. The Germans soon after announced that they, too, were seeking such an investigation through the German Red Cross.

But the Soviets refused the Red Cross permission to examine the graves at Katyn, on the grounds that it would be held under German terrorist auspices. And on 21 April in a message to Churchill, Stalin accused Sikorski's Government of 'striking a treacherous blow at the Soviet Union to help Hitler tyranny...and adopting a hostile attitude to the Soviet Union'. The Soviet Government, he said, had therefore decided 'to interrupt relations' with that Government.[12] And none of the arguments against it that Churchill set out in two long and eloquent messages persuaded Stalin not to do so.

The final break must, from Stalin's point of view, have been a godsend. The main obstacle to his plans for a Polish Government allied to Soviet Russia had gone with this break with the London Poles. He did all possible from then on to undermine international confidence in them. The very next day in a *Pravda* article, Wanda Wasilewska forecast the creation of a Polish Army in Russia to fight by the side of the Red Army. And this army she said, would not be under the jurisdiction of the Polish Government in London, which was preventing active resistance to the Germans.[13] It was a significant forecast of a new Soviet-sponsored regime in Poland. Two weeks later, on 9 May, it was officially announced that the Council of People's Commissars had authorised the formation of the Polish Kosciuszko Division, and that this had begun.

Meanwhile, the Soviet radio broadcasts to Poland intensified the campaign against the Sikorski Government: 'The Polish Government has taken the treacherous step of an understanding with Hitler, foe of the Polish and Russian people, foe of all peace-loving people'; and 'The Polish Government's aggressive lust has led it to agreement with the Hitlerite Government, which is tearing asunder the Polish nation', were typical attacks.

Received in Poland at a time when the Nazis were intensifying their campaign of repression against the Polish people and the Secret Army, these attempts to discredit Poland and deprive her of material aid from her allies, roused fury against both the Soviets and the Polish Communists.

Rowecki reacted by informing General Sikorski that in view of the Russo-Polish dispute he had now cut down operations against the Germans, especially their lines of communication leading to the East.[14]

He again proposed an 'offensive reaction' by the Secret Army against the Soviets were they to enter Poland in pursuit of the Germans without first reaching an understanding with the Government. It included sabotage in the eastern territories, destruction of the Red Army's lines of communication between the rivers San and Vistula; battles against the Soviets wherever success was likely; or staying underground to wait for a suitable chance to strike.

But General Sikorski refused to change the order that the Secret Army should co-operate with the Red Army. He realised the Soviet danger, but his military realism led him to try to win a favourable solution through diplomatic action.

But in mid-1943 destiny, accident or conspiracy snatched both of these two leaders away within three days of each other. Ever since November 1939, Rowecki had been saved from the enemy by the Secret Army's vigilance. Suddenly, on 30 June 1943, the Gestapo sealed off a whole street, arrested him in one of his hideouts and flew him to Berlin at once for interrogation. The loss of this leader who had united and trained the Secret Army was immense, yet his lack of realism – his failure to win a useful understanding with the Communists – cost Poland dear.

Three days later General Sikorski died in an RAF aircraft crash in Gibraltar harbour, so mysterious that it has never yet been properly explained. In him Poland lost a truly great leader, both statesman and soldier.

The unity of purpose Sikorski had imposed on the Secret Army to guide its attitude to the Soviets went with him. His death opened the way to the tragedy of Warsaw. Destiny, accident or design, had played into Stalin's hands again. He was now able to exploit underground Poland's despair by a move in direct opposition to the Secret Army.

5/   Stalin shows his hand

German loudspeakers in Theatre Square and beside the ornate fountain in the leafy Saxon Gardens triumphantly blared out the death of Poland's trusted leader. Crowds wept in the sunshine. People had hoped that Sikorski would unite the nation and lead it to freedom and social justice after the war. Now that he was dead, emotions ranging from bitterness to hopelessness and despair temporarily overcame it.

In London President Raczkiewicz appointed as Prime Minister Stanislaus Mikolajczyk, one of the Peasant Party leaders, and General Sosnkowski, whom Sikorski had sacked, as C-in-C of the armed forces, including the Secret Army. Strongly as Mikolajczyk opposed this appointment it went through; the 1935 Constitution made it the President's choice alone; and to him, not to Parliament, or the Government, was the C-in-C responsible for his conduct of the war. The right-wingers in the Government-in-exile valued Sosnkowski's known anti-Sovietism, and insisted on the appointment. Winston Churchill accepted it reluctantly.

One of Sosnkowski's first moves was to appoint Komorowski, Rowecki's Deputy Commander in Warsaw, to the post of Commander-in-Chief of the Secret Army. Opposition to this appointment also was strong. Komorowski had not attended the Polish Staff College before the war. As a cavalryman, he lacked the necessary infantry experience. Politically he was well over to the right, and probably the main reason for his appointment was that he saw eye-to-eye with General Sosnkowski.

By October 1943, nearly four months later, the Red Army in a rapid advance had inflicted heavy defeats on the Germans at Orel, Kharkov, and the lower Dnieper, and had retaken Smolensk. Komorowski realised that soon it would pursue the Germans into Poland and gradually occupy the country. He sent messages to Sosnkowski and Mikolajczyk again raising the vexed question of the Home Army's attitude to the Red Army entering Poland without agreement while driving back the Wehrmacht.

Sosnkowski saw his freedom from responsibility to all but the President as entitling him to lay down the Secret Army's political line. In two blunt directives to Komorowski[1] in October 1943 he said that the

Secret Army should regard the Soviets as enemies unless they recognised the Riga Line of 1920 as the post-war frontier of Poland; agreed that the London–Polish Government's representatives should administer Polish territories liberated by the Red Army; agreed that mixed Allied commissions should act as observers; and allowed Polish divisions formed in Russia to be transferred to Polish control, or be disbanded. In addition, he proposed that the Western Powers should safeguard the 'lives, rights and property of our citizens' and refuse to recognise territorial changes brought about by armed force. He remarked at the same time that Britain and the US were clearly reluctant to promise aid for an uprising, most likely for political and geographical reasons. Like Rowecki, Sosnkowski was driven by his fanatical anti-communism to call for hopelessly unrealistic policies.

He now agreed in discussions with fellow ministers that there should be no nationwide uprising without Anglo-American aid, but with the strange reservation that 'acts of despair are sometimes unavoidable in the lives of nations, owing to the feelings of the nation, the political symbolism of such acts and their moral significance for posterity'.[2] He realised that such an act of desperation might bring about the 'wholesale slaughter' of civilians by German troops in furious retreat through Poland.

The Government, having to some extent reaffirmed its authority over Sosnkowski in the conduct of the war, eventually formulated its own plans of action for the Secret Army if the Red Army entered Poland without consent. These included an uprising shortly before the Russo-German front rolled into Poland, but only if the Anglo-Americans were advancing deep into Europe and could guarantee substantial aid, including air cover. If this was not guaranteed, intensified sabotage and diversionary operations were to be launched instead as the German armed forces retreated, an operation code-named *Burza* (Tempest).

If Russo-Polish diplomatic relations had been re-established Tempest should be launched in liaison with the Red Army. But if relations were still broken and the Red Army entered Poland without consent, the Home Army should launch Tempest against the Germans, but, together with the civil authority, remain underground until further orders, undertaking self-defence if necessary.[3]

These vague and hypothetical instructions, ordering the Secret Army to attack the retreating Nazis, then run back into hiding in face of the Russians, caused impatience, if not contempt in Warsaw and Komorowski decided to assume the prerogative of the man-on-the-spot. He issued his own orders and informed the Commander-in-Chief in a message:

> I have given all commanders and units orders to come into the open after taking part in operations against the retreating Germans. Their task will be to avow the presence of the Polish Republic.

50

My order is at variance with that of the Government. I see no reason to create a vacuum on Polish territory as a result of military inaction in face of the Russians by the Army, which represents Poland and her legal authorities. To conceal our mass organisation under the Soviet occupation would be impossible. I will limit to an indispensable minimum the number of commands and units which disclose their existence. The remainder I will try to safeguard by formal demobilisation. In case of...Russian occupation, I am assembling in the utmost secrecy the skeleton network of a new clandestine force unconnected with the Home Army, to be at your disposal.[4]

Komorowski had thus gone far to win freedom of action from the Commander-in-Chief and the Government.

His order to province and district commanders, given instead of the Government order, on 26 November 1943,[5] stated clearly that the main battle task was action against the Germans, and that self-defence only would justify armed action against the Soviets entering Poland in pursuit of the retreating Nazis. The fighting would take the form of either a universal and simultaneous uprising, or of intensified diversionary operations (Tempest) throughout Poland. He went on:

Tempest operations shall take the form of intensive harassing of the retreating German rearguards, together with strong diversion of the whole area, particularly against rail and road communications. A special radio message in code will order the start of Tempest, and receipt of it by province and district commanders is equivalent to an order to make ready for action. Main intention: to start action when the German forces can be attacked with maximum effect. Avoid friction with Soviet partisan detachments. After completing operations against the Germans local Polish commanders should declare their identity to the local Red Army commander. The Polish authorities always remain the rightful rulers, with due consideration to requests by the Soviet commands. Attempts to incorporate Home Army units into the Soviet or Berling's forces should be resisted.

This order gave Secret Army provincial and district commanders the enormous responsibility of deciding when and where to launch their units into action. Painstakingly Komorowski met them all during the winter of 1943–4, and discussed the situation with them to help them realise what they were up against, so that as far as possible he could be certain they would 'find the right moment and place for bringing their detachments into action'.

Not until February 1944 was he to receive the Government's approval for his decision to reveal the Home Army to the Soviets, with the proviso that in doing so commanders should make it clear that their unit was part of the Polish armed forces, under the orders of the Polish

Government, the C-in-C and the Commander of the Home Army. This Komorowski had already done.

Meantime, in a message to London Komorowski declared that the Polish Workers' Party and its military arm, now called the People's Army, were strong enough to start a premature uprising. In late 1943 the Polish Workers' Party had throughout Poland no more than 12,000 members, although its People's Army had nearly 40,000, and weapons for only about a quarter of them.

Komorowski nevertheless told London[6] that they must be prepared for a struggle against the Communist organisations, who were probably planning to set up a government obedient to Moscow. He suggested the formation of a special security corps 'to maintain law and order' in the liberated territories before the administrative organs of the Polish Government were in operation.

At the same time, October 1943, he ordered Secret Army guerrilla formations to 'combat brigandry' and suppress 'plundering and subversive brigand elements'. Komorowski claimed later that the object of this order, ambiguously expressed, was simply to deal with the bands of brigands who were living in the forests and terrorising the peasantry. The Communists, who had no doubt suffered in clashes with Secret Army formations, protested that the order was directed against them. They procured a copy of the order and sent it to Moscow. Stalin used it at Tehran to buttress his argument that the Government-in-exile's Secret Army was more eager to fight Communists than Nazis.

The affair caused suspicion and disquiet in London. Defending himself, Komorowski assured Mikolajczyk that he had no desire to launch civil war in Poland. He requested the Government to issue a political and social manifesto—the ideological banner of the Secret Army—guaranteeing the introduction of the constitutional, economic and social reforms for which the people had been waiting for so long.

Preparations for the Tempest operation began in December 1943. Commanders of large partisan formations deployed their men in areas which straddled the German lines of communication; and in the eastern provinces—those disputed by the Soviet Union where Tempest would begin—all Secret Army men were mobilised. Commanders were supplied with their own code and a short-wave transmitter; arms and ammunition, boots, caps, short topcoats and medical equipment, all made in secret workshops and smuggled to the forest rendezvous.

Still anxious, Komorowski again ordered unit commanders to do all possible to avoid trouble with Soviet partisan deatchments operating in Poland. He received from Volhynia, in eastern Poland 'alarming reports' in reply. On 7 November 1943, 'Bomba', one of his best commanders, in charge of a formation of 640 men, was invited by the leader of a Soviet partisan unit to meet to discuss combined action against the Germans. The Polish officer set out for the meeting with fourteen men. They did not return and were never seen again. Bearing in mind the vigilance of German troops in the vicinity this in itself was not evidence that the Russians had wiped out the Poles; or indeed, that this foreshadowed a hostile policy towards the Secret Army.

At the same time, however, again in Volhynia, the leader of another Soviet detachment invited the Polish captain of a partisan unit and his adjutant to their camp to 'co-ordinate mutual action against the Germans'. They, too, did not return and some time later their bodies were found at the site of the Russian camp.[7] The evidence was slender, once again, but it was enough to make the Secret Army wonder what the future held when the Red Army poured over the frontier into Poland.

Meanwhile, collaborating closely with Moscow, and reacting to the swift advance of the Red Army, the Polish Communists set about the formation of a secret underground state in opposition to the one formed in 1940 loyal to the Government-in-exile. They began talks with small left-wing splinter groups of the Peasant Party and the Polish Socialist Party about the formation of a united political organisation to be called the National Home Council.[8]

Its first meeting, under the chairmanship of Wladyslaw Gomulka, who had succeeded to the party leadership, took place on New Year's Eve in a house on Twarda Street, Warsaw. Boleslaw Bierut, a veteran Polish Communist, was nominated president of the newly formed organisation. Without delay it issued a manifesto claiming that the 'National Home Council of Poland' was 'the factual political representation of the Polish people' until the war ended.

Challenging the authority of the London Polish Government, it claimed the authority to issue legislative decrees and set up throughout central Poland embryo provincial, county, municipal and rural peoples' councils staffed by Communists – but none, of course, in the eastern territories claimed by Stalin.

In response to this challenge to its authority, the Government-in-exile branded the National Council of Poland as 'a fraud and an agency of a foreign power'.

Three days later, on the night of 3 January 1944, the first Red Army spearheads crossed the frontier of the province of Volhynia and entered Poland. What the Polish Government-in-exile both feared and expected had now taken place. It issued a declaration pointing out that if a Polish–Soviet agreement had preceded the crossing of the Polish frontier it would have enabled the underground Polish army to co-ordinate its action against the Germans with the Soviet military authorities. The Polish Government still 'considered such an agreement highly desirable'.[9]

On the same day, Prime Minister Mikolajczyk broadcast to Poland from London: 'We are entering a turning-point of history. We should have preferred to meet the Soviet troops not merely as allies of our allies, fighting against the same common enemy, but as our own allies as well.' With this statement the split between Moscow and the Polish Government grew even wider.

The diplomatic battle had also been joined over the issue of the frontiers of Poland. Stalin stuck to his demand for eastern Poland as far as the Curzon Line and the north-eastern part of East Prussia, including the ice-free port of Konigsberg. Churchill supported him by bringing pressure on the London Poles to accept these demands and the extension of their territories in the west as far as the Oder-Neisse Line.

Stalin[10] also demanded in letters to Churchill and Roosevelt that Sosnkowski and other 'pro-fascist imperialist elements' should be removed from the Polish Government and be replaced by democratic-minded people, which would, 'one is entitled to hope, create the proper conditions for normal Soviet–Polish relations, for solving the problem of the Soviet–Polish frontier and, in general, for the rebirth of Poland as a strong, free and independent state.'[11]

Stalin's attitude to the legitimate Polish refusal was one of outraged innocence, expressed with menace that grew stronger with each Soviet defeat of the Nazis. 'I am more convinced than ever that men of their type are incapable of establishing normal relations with the USSR,' he wrote to Churchill on 3 March 1944. 'Suffice it to point out that they, far from being ready to recognise the Curzon Line, claim both Lwow and Wilno. As regards the desire to place certain Soviet territories under foreign control...the mere posing of the question is an affront to the Soviet Union.'

Churchill, who had tried to settle these frontier issues before the Red Army entered Poland knew well enough that only compromise could save her independence.

In a declaration of war aims in Warsaw on 15 March 1944, the Council of National Unity stated that Poland's eastern frontier should stay as established by the Treaty of Riga in 1920, and not be moved westward to the Curzon Line; that all East Prussia and the port of Danzig must be Poland's and that vital Polish economic interests should be permanently secured along the Oder river in Germany.

Even if Stalin had any goodwill towards the Secret Army and the underground civil authority in Warsaw, little of it could have remained after this challenge to his territorial demands. Three days afterwards, on 18 March 1944, the Council of People's Commissars of the USSR authorised the expansion of the First Polish Army Corps in Russia into the First Polish Army. Stalin would soon have a military force apart from the Red Army in Poland which could help him to impose a puppet government.

On 15 March 1944, a delegation of the Communist Polish Workers' Party and its civil organisation called the National Home Council, headed by Edward Osobka-Morawski and Marian Spychalski, were called to high level talks in Moscow. Making their way across the German–Soviet front with the help of a group of Soviet partisans, they crossed the Bug river, were in due course picked up by a Soviet transport aircraft and flown to Moscow.

Here on 22 May 1944 they met Stalin, who told them he was ready to recognise the National Home Council of Poland,[12] once it had established an executive organ. It would be useful to him in his negotiations with Churchill and Roosevelt, who wanted him to recognise the London Polish Government, which in its existing form he had no intention of doing. Stalin agreed with the delegation that the National Home Council and its supporters should form the nucleus of the new Polish Government and head the ministries. He also promised to supply the underground People's Army in Warsaw with arms.

He had now all but cleared the way for the establishment in Poland of a Communist government. Only General Komorowski's Home Army stood in his way. But Stalin was a veteran in the art of luring his enemies to their destruction.

6/   Tempest fails

Komorowski and the Secret Army staff had reached an important
turning-point in January 1944. The question: whether to stop all
military action against the Germans until Stalin agreed to renew diplomatic relations with the London Polish Government; or no matter
what Stalin's policy was towards this Government, to go on fighting
the Germans in Poland and to launch Operation Tempest as they retreated into the country's eastern areas?

To Komorowski, who believed that he held the trump card of the
Secret Army, the choice in this issue was clear. Not to come out into the
open and fight the Germans would, he believed, be fatal to Poland's
cause, because the Soviets would seize on the fact as 'proof' of their
argument that the Secret Army was hostile to them. Furthermore,
public opinion in Poland would turn against the instigators of such an
order. It would have been looked on as next to capitulation. Therefore
he was quite certain that the army must risk coming out into the open
as the Soviets advanced into Poland, even without liaison or contact
with the Soviet command, or even any clue as to what action the Red
Army might take against a non-communist force emerging in the battle
area. 'We had to take up battle — it was a matter of principle; once again
we faced questions of our freedom and independence.'[1]

General Sosnkowski, whom Stalin hated so much and whose
dismissal he was then vigorously urging upon Churchill and Roosevelt,
argued that the issue should depend strictly upon the resumption of
Russo-Polish diplomatic relations and the Soviet acceptance of Poland's
Treaty of Riga eastern frontiers. He believed that without this all Poland's
sacrifices and losses would be in vain, because Stalin was determined to
smash the old Poland and set up in its place a communist satellite state,
perhaps even a new republic ruled from the Kremlin.[2] Prime Minister
Mikolajczyk, however, overruled Sosnkowski and so Komorowski's
momentous policy of fighting the Germans whatever the circumstances
went ahead, with all its grim implications for the future.

Unfortunately, both the London Government and Komorowski
still believed that Prime Minister Churchill and President Roosevelt
would recognise Poland's contribution to the Allied cause, and would

56

therefore bring diplomatic pressure or even military force to bear on the Soviets to prevent Polish territory being seized and the nation's freedom crushed. Cut off in beleaguered Poland and dependent upon the not very illuminating radio messages of his London colleagues, how could Komorowski know the whole truth—that the two Allied leaders hoped for Stalin's aid in the war against Japan? Roosevelt, caught in the electoral web which periodically paralyses US foreign policy had set himself the impossible goal of offending neither Stalin nor the seven million Americans of Polish descent.

In secret, at Tehran early in 1943, he had told Stalin that 'as a practical man' he did not wish to involve the US publicly in the Russo-Polish dispute, but he agreed that Poland's eastern borders should be moved to the west and the western border even to the River Oder.[3] It was as good as an invitation to go ahead. Stalin told the President that he 'understood'.

Komorowski had not been informed by his Government of the bitter arguments about the frontier issue then being pursued in the diplomatic field between Prime Minister Mikolajczyk on the one hand and the British Government on the other, acting in support of Stalin.

So Komorowski was shocked when early in February Mr Jan Jankowski, the Government delegate in Warsaw, received from Prime Minister Mikolajczyk a message[4] asking for reaction to the proposal that the Curzon Line should be taken as a basis for negotiations with the Soviets about Poland's revised eastern frontier. 'Will you please state the position of the home country on Poland's eastern frontier in the event of Germany's total defeat...taking into account the decision of England and America not to fight for Poland's eastern frontier, and the possible danger of the Soviets creating "faits accomplis" in the remaining part of Poland,' the message ran. It also mentioned Stalin's demand for the dismissal of the Commander-in-Chief, General Sosnkowski, and of General Kukiel, Minister of Defence.

Jankowski, in an uncompromising reply[5] on behalf of the Council of National Unity representing the four main parties, strongly objected to any talks with the Soviets about the revision of the eastern boundaries, because they were already settled by the 1920 Treaty of Riga:

In spite of our terrible sacrifices, the Polish nation is determined to fight the new Soviet aggression for its own independence and Europe's freedom. The Polish nation believes that the Allies and the world will understand its attitude and actively support it...We shall not give in or bend; on the contrary, there will be a breakdown and anarchy in the Polish nation if there should be submission to Soviet demands. Knowing the real aims and methods used by our eastern neighbour, we do not attach any serious importance to agreements regarding the functioning of our authorities in the Soviet occupied territories, because we do not believe that they would be loyally kept. The

Polish people are fully aware of the seriousness of the present moment—and the unity of their views and firm will to fight for the freedom, integrity and independence of the Mother Country is complete.

The Red Army was then embattled with the Germans in Volhynia, eastern Poland. Komorowski, in a special order reminded area and sector commanders[6] that Tempest should start from the eastern boundaries, without special orders, at the moment of German retreat 'as in this way we can make it quite clear that the eastern boundary provinces belong to the Republic...It must be carried out regardless of the behaviour of the Soviets towards us.'

If ever military commanders faced fatal pitfalls over and above the normal hazards of war, Komorowski's Secret Army commanders in eastern Poland were so confronted. He warned them of the dangers of premature mobilisation. 'They could easily be annihilated by the retreating Germans.' Should the Soviets, on the other hand, try forcibly to disarm them or compel them to be absorbed into General Berling's Communist People's Army, the commander was authorised to order his troops to refuse and to go into hiding. Before going to meet Red Army commanders to discuss liaison, Secret Army commanders must appoint a second-in-command ready to take over, 'under conspiratorial conditions' in case the commander were arrested—in which case he was likely to be shot. If a unit commander's proposals for military liaison with the Red Army were refused the unit should hide its weapons and disband, so as to avoid fighting with the Soviets. When fighting the Germans in these disputed territories alongside Soviet units, commanders must reveal themselves to Red Army commanders: 'At the command of the Government of the Polish Republic, I am reporting as a military commander, with proposals for arranging military co-operation against the common enemy with Soviet Armed Forces entering the territories of the Polish Republic.' He was then to add that Home Army detachments belonged to the Polish Government and were under the orders only of its Commander-in-Chief.

In other words, on top of all the other hazards, commanders were ordered to risk their lives and liberty by throwing down the gauntlet to Red Army officers and Soviet commissars. They were to tell the Soviet giant which had destroyed the German military machine and driven it back all the way from Moscow: 'These lands are Polish! Here we rule!' even though Stalin's commissars had already begun confiscating estates and establishing collectives in these lands he had decreed were Soviet.

But as the eleventh hour neared there was not much else left to Komorowski except to stake all on a few desperate throws of the dice, to try to raise the White Eagle of old Poland again.

58

The first throw occurred in March 1944 when the Polish 27th Division, commanded by Lieutenant-Colonel 'Oliwa' launched Tempest in the Kowel and Wlodzimierz regions of Polish Volhynia, territory claimed by Stalin. About half the strength of a normal infantry division, at 6,000 strong it was composed only of two regimental battle groups, the 50th and 24th Infantry Regiments; it also lacked the normal heavy weapons.[7]

On 20 March for the first time the Home Army's 27th Division and the Red Army fought side by side as allies and engaged the Germans in the battle for Kowel.[8] The battle was hard, the losses heavy.

Six days later, on 26 March, Colonel 'Oliwa', O.C. 27th Division, went to a meeting with the Red Army's General Sergeyev and Colonel Kharitonov to discuss military co-operation. The Soviet officers, having already 'ascertained the views of the Central Soviet authorities, expressed their readiness to enter into co-operation with the Polish Underground Army'. The conditions were:[9]

operational subordination of the Polish Forces to the Soviet Command locally and also beyond the Bug River: recognition of the Polish Forces as a division under Polish authorities in Warsaw and London: the Division to be absolutely free to maintain contact with them: a regular Polish division to be formed out of the existing Polish partisan detachments: no partisan activity in the rear of Soviet Forces: full field equipment and armament for the Polish Division to be supplied by the Soviet authorities.

The terms were fair and generous, even though they prohibited partisans behind the Red Army lines supporting the emergence of a Polish administration in the disputed eastern territories. But Komorowski, who received them by radio from 'Oliwa', turned away from the path which could have led to a limited agreement with the Soviets. Like Sosnkowski, he was only interested in full-scale diplomatic *rapprochement* based on recognition of the old frontiers in the east. A few days earlier, in a message to London dated 23 March, he had argued that 'because of the failure to re-establish diplomatic relations...it is not advisable hastily to contract liaison with the Soviet Command on our own initiative. It would be better to implement Tempest independently for as long as possible.'[10]

He therefore composed a reply which differed from the Soviet conditions in insisting that the Division would be subordinated to the Soviet Command only temporarily until the problem of its tactical dependence was settled differently by a Polish–Soviet agreement. Secondly, it ordered that the division should be organised with drafts from Volhynia and that the conscription of these men should be regulated by the Division itself in agreement with the Soviet authorities. Komorowski also reserved for himself the right to appoint officers above the rank of battalion commander, leaving the divisional commander powers of promotion below this rank. The Division was to pursue war aims defined by the 'Central authorities of the Polish State'. It was not to be transferred to Russia and all soldiers in it were bound to take the Secret Army loyalty oath.[11]

Polish Prime Minister Mikolajczyk welcomed the Soviet offer. He sent Ambassador Raczynski to tell the British Government that although they were by no means certain as to the future attitude of the Soviet authorities they were none the less ready for their part to contribute with full energy to a further development of friendly relations.[12]

General Sosnkowski took an entirely different view. 'I doubt whether the Soviet Command's promises will be fulfilled...and even if they were I do not believe there will be a favourable outcome of this experiment,' he said in his reply to Komorowski. 'The subordination of the Division to you and me would probably be completely illusory. It would be useful if it might procure a quantity of arms and save at least a part of these men and units. I expect that at a certain stage attempts to include the division in Berling's army will be made.'[13]

Komorowski agreed. 'We appraise the Soviet attitude to us realistically,' he replied to the Commander-in-Chief on 19 April 1944.

> We expect nothing good from that side, nor do we delude ourselves that they will loyally co-operate with the independent Polish units...We regard it as necessary that our every move should be consistent with the sovereign rights of the Republic...
>
> Hence, my instructions to the Commanding Officer of the Volhynian Area included conditions of a kind which the Soviets would certainly refuse to honour. I have in a separate order instructed that if this should happen, the Commanding Officer of the Volhynian Area must break through the German rear to the territory under my direct command.

Komorowski added that the military situation strongly indicated a Soviet victory, though a slow one, and that the occupation of all Poland was likely. As a result, he said, 'We must be prepared for an open collision between Poland and the Soviets, and on our part we should have to demonstrate to the full, in this collision, the independent position of Poland.'

Komorowski was reviving the plans outlined by General Rowecki in 1942–3 for resisting the Soviets should they enter Poland without consent, an attitude which General Sikorski had called 'suicidal'.

On 10 April 1944 the Germans counter-attacked in the Kowel region and after hard fighting temporarily seized the military initiative and drove back the Soviet forces. The Polish 27th Division and the Soviet

56th Cavalry Division were encircled during fighting near the Turia river. Colonel 'Oliwa' was killed, Major Zegota, his second-in-command, withdrew to regroup and rest his troops in the forests west of Kowel. He clashed with the Germans once more then radioed Komorowski to ask whether he should try to break out west or east, and was ordered to come west. In the end one column broke out to the east, traversed the Russo-German front and was absorbed into General Berling's People's Army; the other went west and crossed the Bug river to link up with Home Army detachments.[14]

Komorowski meantime had not taken up the Soviet terms for military co-operation. For this, the Secret Army men, and in the end, Warsaw too, paid dearly. Komorowski's policy warned the Soviets of his plans, and their policy too hardened. It was another turning-point.

Henceforward, Soviet commanders agreed to Polish–Soviet military collaboration during the fighting, but afterwards demanded the Secret Army's incorporation into General Berling's Polish divisions under Red Army command. Officers who refused faced shooting; men, forcible enrolment in Berling's army or detention in camps in Russia. No Home Army formations were tolerated behind the battle front.

Operation Tempest had thus failed in its brave and hopeful political aims of raising the Polish flag in Volhynia until the emergence of the underground civil authority, acting temporarily on behalf of the London Polish Government.

The failure pushed Komorowski and the Warsaw GHQ into a still more uncompromising stance towards the Soviets in eastern Poland. Hitherto towns had not been included in Tempest operations, on the not very convincing grounds that in this way Tempest would be distinguished from the 'general and simultaneous uprising'; and to avoid civilian losses. But on 1 June Komorowski decided that if their political aims were to be achieved cities and towns must be captured before the Soviets' arrival — except Warsaw, where there was to be no fighting. Indeed, the Government-in-exile and its delegate in the capital, Jan Jankowski, had already begun to discuss arranging through the Vatican for Warsaw to be declared an open city.[15]

The underground civil authority, meantime, was preparing for the task of government it hoped and expected to undertake while Poland was in the process of being liberated. By Presidential decree dated 26 April 1944 Jan Jankowski was appointed Deputy Prime Minister. In this capacity he nominated a Council of Ministers made up of himself and three men from each of the main political parties, the Peasant, Socialist and National parties. Their task was to direct the main fields of the country's underground administration, apart from military affairs.

The Communist Polish Workers' Party was not invited to take part. Was another chance missed of establishing some degree of eleventh hour co-operation? Even though the Polish Communists were in concert with Stalin, had not Sikorski stressed that an understanding with Russia was essential, and would this not have been a step in that direction?

For the same reasons the Communists were not represented on the Council of National Unity, an advisory body set up in January 1944, composed of three men from each of the four main parties, one from smaller parties, as well as Church and Co-operative representatives. No political decisions were made without the agreement of this body. An executive committee of five members called the Praesìdium deputised for the Council. Komorowski attended its sessions once a month to brief it on the military situation.

In the military field Komorowski and his staff in Warsaw called the tune, even though their actions directly affected the people's lives. War, Clemenceau once remarked, is far too important a matter to be left to generals. Komorowski and his staff were in precisely that position of having a free hand in a potentially disastrous military situation.

Making and getting enough arms was one of the Secret Army's major worries, apart from staying out of the Gestapo's clutches. Normal infantry weapons were most needed — Sten and Bren guns, hand grenades, revolvers, Piat anti-tank guns as well as plastic explosives, fuses and detonators. The RAF supplied a total of about 49 tons of weapons from August 1942 to 30 April 1943, relatively little, due to the flight problems involved. This supply increased during the period 1 August 1943 to 31 July 1944 to 263 tons,[16] including uniforms, medical equipment and blankets, still extraordinarily little, considering that only sixteen aircraft were lost during these operations.

But the Home Army's Quartermaster Department had during the past three years organised its own secret arms production remarkably well. Groups of technicians throughout central Poland supplied blueprints for both standard weapons and new developments, including time and incendiary bombs, railway bombs and detonators.[17] Production of all arms needed was carried out in German-controlled and inspected workshops and secret Polish workshops. None of them knew which others were involved.

Ironically, the favourite workshops for the purpose were those controlled by the Germans, because the best Polish workmen and the most sophisticated machinery were available there. These workers made the parts — gun barrels, trigger mechanisms, magazines — either covertly during night-shifts, when German supervisors were not so much in evidence, or else by modifying official factory drawings and producing the parts openly.

When the Secret Army could not obtain specific parts or materials anywhere in Poland, it arranged for Poles employed in German-controlled factories to send orders for them to parent industrial establishments in the Reich. The consignments would then be intercepted on arrival at the Polish factory. German plants who unknowingly sent material to assist the Polish underground included Magdeburg Werke, Zeiss of Jena, Bruhn Werke of Brunswick and Stock of Berlin.[18]

The Secret Army employed many small Polish workshops for the production of automatic rifles, light automatic weapons and flame-throwers, though it was complicated by the need to provide secretly the necessary metal, which had first to be stolen from German stocks. Having captured some of these weapons, the Germans decided that they could only have been produced in large, well-equipped plants by expert technicians. The Gestapo therefore searched these big plants, and fortunately ignored the small ones. Home Army technicians themselves assembled and tested the weapons in secret workshops, of which there were seventeen, including two completely proofed against the sound of firing.

Materials were bought on the open market, bought or stolen from German plants, seized in armed raids on warehouses or transports; by adaptation of less effective materials and fictitious orders to German plants.[19] For the production of the explosive cheddite the Secret Army needed 120,000 kg of potassium chlorate, a chemical which the Germans had placed under special guard. Polish directors of a matchworks factory therefore over-ordered substantially and in due course the Secret Army cleared the warehouse in a night raid. When more was needed, the staff of a German-controlled factory ordered several tons from the Reich. It was secretly intercepted under the noses of the German supervisors on arrival and transported to the Polish workshops. Other materials were similarly obtained. A large foundry in Germany unknowingly supplied sixteen tons of iron sheeting for making flame-throwers. The German firm of Bruhn-Werke in Warsaw imported a rush order of special steel wire by air from Sweden which the Secret Army needed urgently for Sten-gun springs.

Instead of storing these arms and ammunition in Warsaw where they might easily be discovered by the enemy, and in any case were considered unlikely to be used there for fighting, the Home Army secretly transported them to the eastern regions for use in the Tempest operations there.

On 22 June 1944 Stalin launched the Soviet summer offensive with 124 divisions and nine rifle brigades on four fronts, against the German Central Army Group commanded by Field-Marshal Ernest Busch. Within seven days the German defences had crumbled along a 350-mile front. The German 4th and 9th Armies centred around Minsk virtually ceased to exist, while the 3rd, further south, was routed. On the northern flank Soviet General Bagramian's 1st Baltic Front and General Chernyakhovski's Third Belorussian Front surged forward north and south of Vitebsk, taking the city on 27 June and destroying five German divisions. General Zakharov's Second Belorussian Front overran Mogilev on 28 June and Rokossovsky's First Belorussian Front destroyed a force of 33,000 Germans at Bobruisk the next day. The Moscow–Smolensk highway was cut in two places west of Minsk, which fell on 3 July with some 50,000 captured, and by 5 July Rokossovsky had taken Kowel. By 15 July the Soviet armies had knocked out twenty-five German divisions.

Thus the moment approached for the final stages of Tempest in eastern Poland. On 12 June General Komorowski and his staff had decided independently of London to concentrate Secret Army partisan groups about 10,000 strong, though still under-armed, in the Rudnicka Forest and elsewhere near the city of Lwow, in the Ukraine. Colonel 'Wilk', who was in command, received orders from Komorowski at the end of June to launch Tempest and capture the city at the approach of the Red Army by means of a full-scale attack by two brigades, supported inside the city by additional Secret Army units. He gave this order independently of London.

But on 7 July 1944 General Sosnkowski, in a message to Komorowski, warned that Stalin had decided to proceed with regard to Poland by the method of 'accomplished facts'.[20] Pointing out that in these circumstances a general armed rising would have too slender a chance of success, he ordered Komorowski to go ahead with Tempest, which he was of course already doing. But he prudently recommended: 'If, owing to a happy conjunction of circumstances, in the last days of the German retreat and before the entry of Soviet troops, a chance should arise for us to occupy, even temporarily, Wilno, Lwow, or any other important centre or a circumscribed small part of land, we should do so, in order to appear as the rightful masters.'

Sosnkowski was no doubt thinking of the casualties the Secret Army might face without the heavy weapons needed for a full-scale attack. But it was too late. Two brigades of the Home Army, about 5,500 men, attacked Wilno from the south on 6 July. Despite their fierce courage the Germans, with heavy mortars and machine-gun nests in defended strongpoints, flung them back. Colonel 'Wilk' reported to Warsaw in the early hours of 7 July: '...Home Army forces attacked Wilno. Fighting went on for twelve hours. City not taken. Heavy losses...'[21]

On 7 July Red Army units attacked the town and military liaison was established, but even so not until 13 July were the last German strongpoints overcome. The Commanding Officer of the Nowogrodek Area reported Wilno's capture to Komorowski – 'with the considerable participation of the Home Army, which entered the city. Relations with the Soviets temporarily correct. Wilno experienced a brief, but joyful moment of freedom.'[22]

But relations with the Soviets worsened almost at once. Red Army men next day turned back Home Army units trying to enter the city to

Above. Warsaw falls: Hitler reviews his victorious legions in the defeated city at the end of September, 1939. (*Prasa Agency*)

Right. General Bor-Komorowski, Commander of the Polish Home Army from 1943. (*Polish Library*)

Above. Five o'clock on the afternoon of 1 August 1944; the beginning of the Uprising. Civilians flee from the Germans across barricaded Marzalkowska Street. (*Prasa Agency*)

Left. Polish barricade on Chlodna Street, scene of the first major German counter-attack on 6 August. (*Prasa Agency*)

Left. The Telephone Exchange on Zielna Street in flames. (*Interpress*)

Above. The capture of the Telephone Exchange by the insurgents,
21 August 1944. (*Interpress*)

Top. On 26 August, after a desperate battle, the SS stronghold in Warsaw falls to the Polish Home Army. One hundred and fifteen SS-men were taken prisoner. (*Prasa Agency*)

Bottom. Young girls served as liaison officers for the Home Army. They passed through the sewers to bring orders to far-flung outposts. (*Prasa Agency*)

Above. The Polish flag flying from the 'Prudential' building in Napoleon Square during the Uprising.

Left. Soldiers of the Polish Home Army after capturing the Church of the Holy Cross on Krakowskie Przedmiescie Street. (*Radio Times Hulton Picture Library*)

Below. Polish soldiers of the Harnasie group defending the ruins of the Church of the Holy Cross. (*Prasa Agency*)

Right. Battle for the Old Town. German soldiers run past a burnt-out tank on Zakroczymska Street.

Left. Polish insurgents work feverishly to build anti-tank trenches in the narrow streets. (*Radio Times Hulton Picture Library*)

Above. Streets became graveyards during the Uprising. The burial of a fallen relative. (*Interpress*)

Below. German troops of Ukrainian origin sheltering behind the colonnade of Warsaw's celebrated Opera House in Theatre Place. (*Radio Times Hulton Picture Library*)

Top left. A German tank advances through the burning City Centre.

Above. The Germans advance, September 1944. A Wehrmacht officer on a captured barricade shouts orders to his men. (*Radio Times Hulton Picture Library*)

Bottom left. German troops advancing through the ruined houses of the old town. (*Radio Times Hulton Picture Library*)

The last days of the Uprising. The wounded Poles were without food, water or medical aid. (*Prasa Agency*)

The final capitulation. General von dem Bach, at his headquarters near Warsaw, witnesses the signing of the document of surrender by (*left*) Colonel Iranek-Osmecki and (*right*) Colonel Dobrowolski. (*Prasa Agency*)

After the surrender, the citizens of Warsaw are forced to leave their city before its final destruction by Hitler's demolition squads. (*Prasa Agency*) stress its Polish character and support a Polish administration. The NKVD arrested Colonel 'Wilk' and his staff of thirty officers when they attended a conference with the Soviet General Cherniakhovsky. Polish units 6,000 strong retired towards the Rudnicka Forest, pursued by Soviet units. Some obeyed Soviet orders to lay down their arms, others resisted and were shot or disarmed and transported to Russia; still others accepted conscription into General Berling's army as the lesser of two evils. A few escaped to the West. And so Tempest in Wilno also failed.

So far Komorowski had harvested only bitter fruit from the seeds of the policy of 'no compromise with the Soviets' which he and Sosnkowski had consistently sown. The Soviets were determined to annex all the territory up to the Curzon Line, and by vainly trying to set up a Polish administration Komorowski was courting failure and tragedy. Komorowski and his staff seem to have been either unable or unwilling to understand this. Ignoring the dead Sikorski's earlier instructions that in face of such a situation in the east they should withdraw from this region across the Bug river, they now prepared for a third attempt.

Perhaps at Lwow the dice would fall in their favour and they would be lucky.

But meantime Komorowski wished to steel his troops against the Soviet armies, prepare them morally for the clash he had envisaged in his sombre message of 19 April to Sosnkowski. Accordingly, on 12 July 1944 he issued a special order[23] to all Secret Army province and district commanders on relations with the Soviets. Reminding them that the Soviets did not recognise the Polish Government and tried in all possible ways to undermine it, he declared that this was the policy of an enemy of the Polish Republic, whose independence they were trying to defend. 'Thus, on the one hand the Soviets are a powerful ally in our fight with the Germans, and on the other, a dangerous usurper, striking at the very roots of our independence.'

Only in the battle against the Germans were they to co-operate with the Soviets; politically they must resist them, and to counter the Soviet argument that the Polish people supported them, they must stress the entire obedience and loyalty of the people and the Home Army to the Government and the Commander-in-Chief. Commanders must fight the Germans independently for as long as possible without contact with the Soviets, entering into co-operation with the Soviets only if tactical factors made it imperative.

They should give them information about the Germans on request, but not tell them about the wider deployment of Polish units, not co-operate outside the military field and refuse to undertake any operation for the Soviets or to fight in any other place without authority from General Komorowski. Home Army soldiers must show a dignified attitude towards the Soviets, avoiding superiority or servility, and due to the wide gulf between the two sides should avoid political discussions with Red Army soldiers. They should simply declare that they fight for Polish independence and for freedom to decide themselves the social system they want after the war. They must avoid incorporation into the Berling army or the Red Army, defend themselves if Soviet forces attack them and if necessary temporarily disband.

Komorowski's main fear, the above order makes clear, was destruction of the Secret Army through coming to blows with the Soviets or by being forced piecemeal to join Berling's Communist army. For even at this eleventh hour he believed that German military disintegration would offer the chance of a successful uprising, and with it the seizure of power in Poland by the London Government. But yet he warned against it in a realistic military analysis two weeks before the uprising. 'The Soviet summer offensive, directed mainly at the centre of the German front, has achieved unexpectedly rapid and effective results,' he reported to Sosnkowski, the Commander-in-Chief, on 14 July 1944.[24]

The defence of the German centre front has been broken, and the retreat has all the look of a defeated army. German losses must be enormous, if only judging by the numbers of generals killed or captured. The westward advance of the Soviet army threatens the entire German northern front with being cut off from their retreat into East Prussia and being pinned down against the sea. The road to Warsaw lies open. As long as the Soviet army's advantages are not ruined by lack of supplies there is no way in which it can be stopped without a major offensive by German units in reserve...According to our information, the Germans have suffered a defeat on their central front which it will be impossible to repair without bringing in more important reserves. It looks as if the Germans will have to take a long step backwards to regain control of the situation.

Komorowski then forecast that the Soviets intended to launch an uprising throughout Poland with the People's Army, the military wing of the Polish Workers' Party. 'They believe that the Polish community, tired of war and thirsting for vengeance, will be ready for battle. The Soviets intend to call out the uprising at the moment they cross the Bug river. They are planning to drop paratroop units and arms for the people. For some weeks they have been dropping leaders and instructors.'

Prudently, he then contended that 'with the present numbers of German troops in Poland, and their anti-insurrectionary preparations, consisting of turning every building held by them, and even offices into fortresses with bunkers and barbed wire, the *universal* rising would have no hope of success. It may only be successful in the event of the collapse and disintegration of the Germans...In the present conditions the carrying out of the rising, even with excellent supplies of arms and the co-

66

operation of allied air forces and paratroops, would involve very high losses.'

It was a sound assessment. But Komorowski then concluded that nevertheless the Secret Army must testify before the entire world Poland's will to fight the Germans, so as to destroy the Soviet propaganda charge that they were silent allies of the Nazis, or neutral towards them. No mention of an uprising in Warsaw occurs in this sober appraisal.

A four-day battle for Lwow began on 23 July. When Red Army artillery began thundering in the distance, Colonel Filipowski led 3,000 Secret Army troops in an attack on the city. He declared himself to the Soviet commander next day and offered liaison. But the Soviets turned down the offer on the grounds that the Polish units were 'untrained and badly armed, which combined with great zeal had been causing them heavy losses'.[25] Filipowski and his troops nevertheless fought on, entered the town when it fell on 27 July and staged a patriotic demonstration to support an emergent Polish administration.

It met with a sharp rebuke. The Russian General Gruszko gruffly warned Filipowski: 'Lwow is Soviet and Ukrainian for the time being... A Polish Government led by Morawski exists and the Polish Army, commanded by Zymierski, is fighting against the Germans. Home Army units fighting the Germans will be absorbed into the Polish Army. The Polish administration...will be subordinated to the Soviet organs.'[26]

Next day, 28 July, he was again summoned to the Soviet headquarters. General Gruszko ordered him to instruct his men to lay down their arms within two hours and disband. 'Soviet authorities here will proclaim general mobilisation,' Gruszko declared. 'The Poles will have the choice of joining either Berling's army or the Red Army. Home Army officers who are exempted from the mobilisation order may retain their arms and voluntarily join Berling's army.'[27]

Filipowski returned to his headquarters, ordered his troops to disband at once and informed Komorowski by radio. The Home Army commander replied with an order to all troops east of the Curzon Line receiving Soviet mobilisation orders to enlist instead in Berling's forces.[28]

Komorowski's quixotic policy of trying to seize large towns in the disputed areas east of the Curzon Line before the advent of the Red Army had failed. Warsaw had now become his only hope. The failure to raise the White Eagle of old Poland in Volhynia, Wilno and Lwow had convinced him and his senior commanders that 'an effort was needed which would stir the conscience of the world'. Only a successful uprising in Warsaw could do this. Towards it Komorowski and his staff during the second half of July 1944 were moving.

The bells toll for Warsaw

During the Warsaw winter of 1943–4 Nazi ferocity raged without check. State-Security-Police Chief Dr Ludwig Hahn conscientiously carried out the Hitlerian terror policy. Mass executions to terrorise the people had taken place almost daily in the streets from 16 October 1943 onwards. The death toll averaged 280 a week, some of the victims being Secret Army men and women, usually tortured before execution.

Nevertheless, people tried to lead as normal an existence as possible, though they never knew whether they would ever come home again if they ventured on to the streets, or whether they would be seized in one of the massive house-to-house searches were they to stay at home.

But from 15 January 1944, not long after the Soviet forces had entered Poland in pursuit of the Germans, Hahn ended mass street executions. The last occurred when forty men were taken from the Pawiak prison and shot outside 6 Senatorska Street, making the total for that day, 15 February, no less than 250.[1] A possible reason for the change was the underground's reprisal killing of the German SS and Police Leader Kutschera. Mass executions were still to take place, but secretly, in Palmyra Forest and amid the grim ruins of the Ghetto. Bursts of firing echoed nightly across the capital. Some eight thousand four hundred Polish men, women and children were killed in Warsaw from October 1943 to 31 July 1944. 'People like me, ordinary people, picked up off the streets,' wrote the Polish poet Zofia Nałkowska then, in her journal. 'There is fear, there is shame, racking the heart, sucking at the entrails...They are just the same as I when I walk down the street...It is sheer chance that they are not me, that they are not any of the ones who have escaped...Take me tidying a desk drawer where the papers have been soaked by the drips from the skylight.'

A beautiful and attractive city had become a giant and terrifying death-trap.

It was against this background of continuing Nazi killings that Komorowski and the Secret Army staff planned their moves in July to restore the old Poland after the political failure of the Tempest actions.

They feared both a spontaneous uprising, which could easily happen in this city where hatred had reached an inflammable point; and an uprising launched by the Communist Polish Workers' Party.

But events began to overtake and push them into precipitate action in mid-1944, when serious military and political blows weakened the Germans. First came the Allied invasion of Normandy on 6 June, the break-out from the bridgehead of St Lô on 26 July; second, the renewed Soviet offensive in Poland on 18 July by Marshals Koniev and Rokossovsky from the line of the Bug river, which drove the Germans back pell-mell; third, the attempt by Colonel von Stauffenberg to kill Hitler on 21 July, and its effects on the higher echelons of the Nazi Party.

The Secret Army command still intended at this time that Warsaw should take as little part as possible in the fighting during the general uprising elsewhere in the country. The plan[2] was for a small but adequate number of troops, like a Home Guard, to protect the city's population from last-moment Nazi atrocities. Main traffic arteries from east to west were to be left clear of obstacles, so that the retreating enemy forces would have uninterrupted movement westwards. But to satisfy the Polish wish for revenge and to do as much damage to the Germans as possible, a well-armed Secret Army force, about four thousand-strong, was secretly to leave the city when the front neared Warsaw, assemble some miles to the west and there launch a strong attack on the retreating and presumably demoralised Germans.

In the event, the consequences of this plan were serious for Warsaw. Throughout July, weapons made in the capital or dropped nearby by the RAF were transported at great risk by Secret Army helpers to the areas of eastern Poland where Tempest was under way. On 7 July Komorowski ordered 900 sub-machine-guns and ammunition, and during the last fourteen days of the month another sixty such weapons with 4,400 rounds were sent to the east.[3] It brought the weapon strength in the capital dangerously low in the event of any sudden outbreak of fighting.

Thus he had clearly no intention of ordering an uprising in the capital at least up to 21 July. But unknown to him the most influential members of his staff, General Pelczynski, Chief of Staff, General Okulicki, Chief of Operations and Colonel Szostak, Chief of the Bureau of Operations, during their daily meetings in the second half of July had privately debated the problem of whether or not an uprising should be launched there.[4] They agreed together that this had become necessary and that General Komorowski and Mr Jan Jankowski, Government Delegate and Deputy Premier, should be persuaded of the need for it.

On 21 July Generals Komorowski, Pelczynski and Okulicki, entering separately by password, as always, the home of a sympathiser where they had not met for several weeks, assessed the swiftly-changing military situation. Of the three only Leopold Okulicki had attended the Polish Military Staff College, and Pelczynski reputedly deferred to his opinion. Then aged 46, Okulicki was a somewhat impetuous, action-loving, hard professional soldier who had parachuted into Poland some months earlier from Britain as General Sosnkowski's special representative on the Secret Army staff. Unlike Komorowski, he was born of peasant stock, joined Marshal Pilsudski's Legions at the age of 16, fought with distinction in the Polish–Russian War of 1920, became a regular soldier, and was soon commissioned. Okulicki, who had played a notable part in the defence of Warsaw in 1939, was one of the small original group of organisers of the Secret Army. He was arrested by the Russians in Lwow in 1941, spent eighteen months in a Soviet prison and was then released to help General Anders organise Polish forces there. He left Russia together with Anders and the Polish Army, with whom he fought in the Middle East.

Okulicki now submitted a proposal to his two fellow-generals at the 21 July meeting[5] that at the crucial moment of the expected German collapse they should launch the Secret Army in an uprising to take Warsaw and establish the independence of the Republic in its capital before the entry of the Soviets. Despite the shortage of arms there this did not seem to them too hazardous, if the right moment was chosen. Pelczynski was already won over. Komorowski, too, let himself be convinced by the ebullient, aggressive Okulicki.

For after the meeting on 21 July Komorowski sent to London a new optimistic appraisal of the up-to-date military situation in direct contrast to his sober report of 14 July. He forecast that the Soviet advance south of the Pripet Marshes would be rapid, would quickly arrive at the Vistula—which flowed through Warsaw—would cross it without effective German counter-actions and continue its westward drive.[6]

'Generally, it seems certain that on the Eastern Front the Germans are in no position to regain the initiative from the Soviet army, or even to offer any effective resistance,' he wrote. 'In the last few weeks we have seen the growing disintegration within the German army, which is tired, and has no will to fight. This last attack on Hitler, together with the German military situation, could lead to their collapse at any moment. This imposes on us a constant readiness to rise.'

Already, on 19 July, Komorowski had ordered a twenty-four-hour stand-by for Secret Army forces throughout Poland. Now, he told London in this 21 July message: 'I have given the order for a state of readiness for rising on July 25 at 01.00 hours, but I have so far not stopped the current (Tempest) tactics.'

A momentous change of policy was concealed in this message. It meant that Warsaw, in which hitherto there was to be no fighting if it could be avoided, might now become a battleground within the framework of either the general uprising or Tempest. Commanders and their troops would now, from 25 July, be covertly standing by in readiness for the general uprising, avoiding German observation as best they could. But Komorowski had yet to convince Jan Jankowski and the leaders of the four political parties of the need for this plan.

The arguments for it, upon which the senior commanders of the

70

Home Army agreed, were threefold, according to the *History of the Polish Armed Forces*,[7] semi-official post-war publication of the former London Polish Government: Militarily there seemed little doubt that unless the Germans brought in enormous reinforcements, which they did not possess, they could not hope to prevent the Soviet armies from crossing the Vistula in the very near future. Home Army Intelligence studies showed that Red Army offensives on the Eastern Front advanced by hundreds of kilometres at a time. The Soviet summer offensive from the Bug had a mere 200 kilometres to reach the Vistula and Warsaw, which suggested that it would cross the river and leave the capital far behind, securing an extensive slice of territory all along the western bank as a final launching pad for a decisive attack on Silesia, Pomerania and Berlin. A decision had therefore to be made about Warsaw.

The three generals believed that one of two situations would develop. Either the Germans would fail to organise an effective defence of Warsaw, abandoning it after the first Soviet attack. Or, in accord with their known policy of defending communications centres, especially those situated on rivers, they would try to hold it as an aid to holding east Prussia and southern Poland. To Okulicki especially, both of these alternatives indicated the need for an uprising. The first involved no problems, for the Home Army command believed it would be easy enough to seize the city before the advent of the Soviets. The second meant that a Nazi–Soviet battle would very likely take place, with ruinous effects upon the city; and the sole way, it was argued, of shortening this was by an uprising which would seize it and thus push the front out of the city. 'The Home Army Command,' says the *History*, 'was well aware of the fact that the C-in-C in London and the western Allies were at this moment unable to help them substantially, but this did not have a direct bearing on the decision, for if all went well there should be no great immediate need for airborne help.'[8]

Their main motives for staging an uprising in the capital were political. They, and the London Polish Government, were determined to restore the old Poland, though some of them conceded that social and economic reform was desirable. Soviet Russia, on the other hand, was marching into Poland, they believed, ready to impose a social system that contravened the Republic's independence and sovereignty. A battle for Warsaw by the Home Army to capture the capital would therefore echo throughout the world and expose Stalin's policy of sovietising Poland. This was additionally important because Soviet Russia was trying to foist on the world a picture of a nation plunged in apathy and resignation, liberated entirely by the Red Army and the Communist People's Army. Finally, it was held that only by taking part decisively in the fight against the Germans would Poland be morally entitled to share the fruits of victory and a place among the victorious powers.

Apart from political and military reasons there were pressing psychological factors to be taken into account by the Home Army chiefs. Not only the Home Army men, but probably the whole nation in July felt, together with an obvious desire to take revenge on the Germans, the need to achieve some victory in the allied cause. The population of Warsaw, keenly aware of the city's glowing tradition of independence struggle and its role as centre of underground Poland, felt this more keenly than anyone.

Komorowski, Pelczynski, Okulicki and other senior staff officers of the Secret Army ended on 22 July their talks on the need to launch an uprising in Warsaw. Komorowski at once told Jan Jankowski and asked for his support. Jankowski, who already believed that possession of Warsaw was vital for the Government, agreed that they must try to capture it before the entry of the Soviets.[9] He arranged a meeting with the delegates of the four main political parties forming the kernel of the underground state, so that Komorowski could find out their opinions of the plan.

Jankowski asked Komorowski to let him have a draft of questions first, adding that he should 'formulate the questions very concisely and say very little'. Jankowski was the Deputy Premier of a substantially right-wing Government, even though the Prime Minister, Mikolajczyk, was himself a moderate Peasant Party leader. In Warsaw, many members of the Polish Socialist Party had moved during the occupation far to the left, and though anti-Soviet were at the same time suspicious of both the London Government and the Home Army leadership. Hence these two leaders knew they had to take care if they were to carry the politicians with them.

Komorowski and Jankowski therefore drafted two simple questions and personally submitted them to the politicians.[10] The first was: whether the representatives of the Committee of National Unity believe that the entry of Soviet troops into Warsaw should be forestalled by the seizure of the capital by the Home Army? The second: what minimal period should, in their opinion elapse between the seizure of the capital by the Home Army for the civil authority, and the entry of the Red Army?

The politicians unanimously said yes to the first question; and to the second agreed that at least twelve hours would be needed to allow the civil authority to start functioning.[11]

Komorowski had thus secured full agreement on the need to launch the uprising in Warsaw, but only by disallowing free discussion and imposing two rigidly formulated questions which over-simplified the grim realities underlying the problem. None of the vital military issues were raised in these questions, such as the fact that the Western Allies could not bomb German-held airfields or drop parachutists; that there was to be no operational liaison with the Red Army; that both food and ammunition stocks were enough for five days' fighting only, or at what moment in the presumed German retreat the uprising

72

would be launched. Komorowski merely gave the politicians an analysis of the current military situation on the Russo-German front, so far as it was known to him.

At this time Home Army units under the command of Colonel Tumidajski were co-operating closely with the Red Army in the fighting in the Lublin district about 140 miles south-east of Warsaw, where they had captured several small towns and destroyed a number of heavy enemy tanks and self-propelled guns. Chelm was taken by combined Home Army and Soviet forces on 21 July; Lublin the next day.

On the evening of 22 July an event of great significance for the London Government and the Home Army became known in Warsaw. At 8.15 p.m. Moscow Radio announced in Polish[12] that a Polish Committee of National Liberation had been set up in Chelm, the first large town freed from German occupation in Polish territory not claimed by the Soviets. It declared that the London Government and the civil authority in Poland were illegal and that the Communist National Council of the Homeland in Moscow was 'the sole legal source of authority in Poland' as the 'provisional Parliament of the Polish Nation'. The Committee of National Liberation was described as the *de facto* though provisional Polish Government. At the same time it was announced that the National Council of the Homeland (KRN) had assumed authority over the Communist People's Army and appointed General Rola-Zymierski as its Commander-in-Chief.

This open challenge of their authority at once strengthened the resolve of Komorowski and the Home Army staff to launch the uprising. They and Jan Jankowski in a reply published in the official Home Army paper[13] dubbed the Committee of National Liberation a Soviet puppet, renewed their insistence on complete obedience to the legal independent Polish Government in London, forbade any negotiations with the Committee or its agents, and warned against the Communist People's Army for its sworn allegiance to a foreign power.

Meanwhile, the Russo-German battle to the east, north-east and south-east of Warsaw grew almost hourly more of a factor in the decision of when to begin fighting in Warsaw, and from 22 July onwards the impact of the German reversal in Normandy, the attempt on Hitler's life, and the rout of their armies in Poland hit Warsaw with dramatic effect. German civilians, of whom there were thousands there, besieged the railway stations for tickets to Germany, and when unable to get them offered the Poles small fortunes for horses and carts. From the Gestapo offices in the former Polish Ministry of Education and Religious Instruction in Szuch Avenue clouds of smoke arose as frightened officials hurriedly burnt incriminating documents and prepared to leave. The Nazi Governor of Warsaw, Dr Fischer, and the Mayor, Herr Leist, unceremoniously fled.

Komorowski, now under strong pressure from the fire-eating General Okulicki to launch the uprising at once, walked through the hot and dusty city to check for himself the reports he had received about the German rout. Wearing glasses, his military moustache shaved off, and purposely stooping slightly, he looked in his threadbare suit more like an ageing professor than a general with all the Home Army's secrets in his head.

Over the hundred-yard long Poniatowski and Kierbedz bridges across the Vistula he saw German military vehicles of all kinds flowing east to west in endless columns. Tanks, self-propelled guns, and armoured troop carriers with weary soldiers clinging to them clattered along both sides of the roads, interspersed with small groups of demoralised infantry, civilians, horses and carts.

Komorowski noted how the spectacle of the Germans actually beaten and running away in a chaotic rout caused Polish men and women whom the Nazis had terrorised for five years past to shake their fists or to break out in exclamations of joyful wonder. In a crowded tram he heard a conductor raise a laugh by shouting: 'Ladies and gentlemen, please hurry up! The firm is departing, the firm is closing down and going into liquidation!' Everyone was certain that these were the last days of the fiendish Nazi regime.

Komorowski's intelligence reports claimed that the German armies had suffered still another major disaster in the east. But aware of the shortage of arms and uncertain when the Soviets would be entering the capital, he prudently rejected the next day, 22 July, General Okulicki's and Colonel Rzepecki's demands that the Uprising should be launched at once.

A sharp conflict of opinion now developed among Komorowski's staff over the issue of when to launch the Uprising. Colonel Iranek-Osmecki, Chief of Intelligence, remembers that a fierce argument developed during the 24 July (Monday) meeting, and that it went on during the next day's meeting. In a talk before General Komorowski arrived, Okulicki and Rzepecki argued that that day, Tuesday, 25 July, was the last possible day for a decision in view of the German disintegration and the almost uncontrollable desire of the citizens to fight. They told Iranek-Osmecki that they wanted to persuade Komorowski to issue the order then, but Iranek-Osmecki urged extreme caution in view of the temporarily uncertain Russo-German military situation.

During the full-scale staff meeting that day these two officers again pressed Komorowski to give the order, arguing that the present, with the Germans in full retreat, was the right time. Once again he said no, but cautiously took one more step nearer the brink with a cryptic message to the Government in London:

> We are ready at any time to launch the battle for Warsaw. The participation of the Parachute Brigade (then in Britain) in this battle would have immense political and tactical significance. Be prepared to bomb airfields around Warsaw at our request.[14]

The message overturned the accepted policy of avoiding fighting in the capital, yet General Komorowski and Deputy Premier Jankowski did not state their case. What were their objects in abruptly announcing that they 'were ready to launch the battle for Warsaw'? Were they presenting the Government with a ready-made decision to rise, a *fait accompli* in which only the timing had to be decided? Or abruptly forcing the Government either to rubber-stamp the decision taken in Warsaw or to countermand it? They knew that a refusal by the Government would inevitably raise again the Russian doubts of the Secret Army's commitment to the struggle.

The Government and the C-in-C were now at loggerheads over the Home Army's course of action. Komorowski's telegram reached the C-in-C's staff in London during the evening of 26 July. Sosnkowski was then visiting General Anders' Polish II Corps in Italy; the message was sent on to him on 28 July.

But Sosnkowski had already decided upon a quite different plan, the details of which on 25 July he sent on to General Kopanski, his Chief of Staff in London, for onward transmission to Warsaw. In it Sosnkowski directed that when Soviet occupation of Warsaw was imminent the Home Army Command and Staff should divide into two groups.

The first should stay in hiding in Warsaw, together with Deputy Premier Jan Jankowski and the underground civil authority and 'organise resistance to the Soviet policy of *faits accomplis*'. He said that it would be senseless for this group to come out into the open in the face of the presence of the Soviet-backed Committee for National Liberation. And he warned of the likely arrest of all declared Polish authorities by the Soviets.

The second Home Army Command group should withdraw in a south-westerly direction and continue to conduct the battle as a whole even if Warsaw were to be captured before the entry of Soviet forces. He said that these directions were to be sent on to Komorowski as soon as possible.

The essence of Sosnkowski's plan was the involvement of the Home Army in anti-Russian as well as anti-German action, the 'two enemies' folly once more. But on 29 July Kopanski telegraphed the Government's refusal of the plan, saying that it had given full freedom of action in Warsaw to Jankowski.[15]

Another event of importance influenced the Government. Prime Minister Mikolajczyk was about to visit Stalin in Moscow. It was a mission largely engineered by Winston Churchill and imposed upon Mikolajczyk in a last-moment desperate attempt to renew Russo-Polish diplomatic relations and establish military liaison. But it was vital for Mikolajczyk to arrive with some arrows to his bow. He must be able to refute Stalin's argument that the Home Army was encouraging the Germans by taking too little part in the war; and to demonstrate that his Government, not the Communists ruled Poland.

If he arrived having just ordered the Secret Army to rise against the Germans in Warsaw both these arguments would be won. Better still, if it had successfully captured Warsaw before the advent of the Red Army, or was then battling victoriously for it, he would have an argument that Stalin could not ignore. On 26 July therefore, before flying via Gibraltar, the Mediterranean and Persia to Moscow, Prime Minister Mikolajczyk ordered a message to be sent authorising Vice-Premier Jankowski to allow the uprising to be launched when needful. It said:

At a session of the Government (Cabinet) of the Republic, it was unanimously decided to empower you to proclaim the insurrection at a moment which you will decide as most opportune. If possible let us know beforehand. Copy, through Army, to Home Army Commander. *Signed* 'Stem'. Minister of the Interior.

Since Deputy Premier Jankowski usually accepted Komorowski's decisions in the military field, the Home Army Commander was now effectively free to launch the Uprising at will. He hoped a few more days of Soviet victories and German defeats might cause the total disintegration of the German armies, so that the Uprising would be almost certain of victory.

It was the act of a prudent commander, which so far he had shown himself to be; but it was too late.

On the very day, 26 July, that the southern wing of Marshal Rokossovsky's forces reached the Vistula between Deblin and Pulawy, 75 miles south of Warsaw, the German retreat through Warsaw ended. Governor Fischer and the entire Nazi administration began to stream back into the city. Home Army Intelligence did not know that Hitler had decided to defend Warsaw and that he had on 21 July ordered General Guderian to take over command of the Eastern Front, reorganise the defence and halt the Red Army offensive.

Guderian appointed General von Vormann to command the 9th Army, in the middle sector of the Vistula, including Warsaw. By 26 July these two commanders had stopped the German rout, while transports bringing the 'Hermann Goering' SS Panzer and Paratroop Division and the SS 'Viking' Panzer Division began to detrain south of the city. But Komorowski's preparations for the Uprising continued.

On 26 July General Pelczynski,[16] Chief of Staff, informed Colonel Chrusciel ('Monter') Commander of the Warsaw Region, that 'it might be necessary to begin the battle for Warsaw at any time'.

The HQ [he continued] will issue the order to start the struggle, perhaps at your command. You will have to be ready to attack within eight hours from the moment of decision...

To gain the information necessary to make the decision I instruct you immediately to undertake adequate reconnaissance in the direction of Modlin, Wyszkow, Tlusczcz, Minsk Mazowiecki, Garwolin, Gora Kalwaria-Warka (i.e. on the east, north-east and south-east approaches to Warsaw). You are required to find out:

1) If the Germans intend to defend Warsaw.
2) Which German forces from the above sectors are withdrawing to Warsaw.
3) Where there is contact between Germans and Soviets.

This information is necessary to estimate the moment of German withdrawal from Warsaw.

Komorowski and the small group of senior officers surrounding him, now holding the whole future of the city and its inhabitants in their hands, were meeting twice daily so as not to be overtaken by events. Reports came that the Soviets were disarming Secret Army troops in eastern Poland and shooting officers who refused to join the People's Army. 'It will compel us to resort to self-defence,' Komorowski warned, in a message to the Government on 27 July.

To this small group of officers an uprising seemed as much an act of self-preservation against Soviet ruthlessness as vengeance against the Germans – a gamble certainly, but one which offered a chance of saving the Secret Army from certain destruction and Poland from the Communism which they abhorred.

At another full-scale staff meeting on 26 July, General Pelczynski emphasised that they still had insufficient data upon which to base a decision to take up arms, but that it was essential to remain in constant readiness. There were disagreements on the timing. Colonel Pluta-Czachowski, Chief of Signals, pointed out the lack of operational liaison with the Red Army and argued that the uprising should only be launched when it was known to be actually forcing the Vistula at Warsaw.

Colonel Iranek-Osmecki, head of Intelligence, emphasised that the Germans had reinforced the Warsaw sector with three Panzer divisions during the last three days. He knew furthermore that the Germans were concentrating a powerful force at Wyszkow, thirty miles north-east of Warsaw on the Bug river, for what appeared to be a possible counter-attack in a southerly direction against Rokossovsky's forces. He argued that they should be prudent indeed about a decision to fight, because the Soviets could well be temporarily pushed back from their present positions near the Vistula. Colonel Bokszczanin and Lieutenant-Colonel Muzyczka supported him. Several others, including Okulicki and Rzepecki, argued forcefully for an uprising without delay.[17]

Colonel Chrusciel then gave the meeting a report of their weapon-strength. This, according to Colonel Jan Rzepecki, had an obviously depressing effect. In silence they listened to the pathetic list of weapons with which they were to begin war against Germany's armoured divisions ...Thirty-nine machine-guns, 130 light machine-guns, 608 sub-machine-guns, four Piat anti-tank weapons, twenty-one anti-tank rifles, four mortars, 36,429 hand grenades, 5,000 petrol bombs. There were no heavy weapons — recoil-less guns, heavy mortars or artillery — so essential for an attack on the well-fortified German objectives.

Lack of ammunition was even more discouraging. Chrusciel argued that there was enough to keep on the offensive for three to four days, after which he counted on using captured German arms and ammunition and air consignments dropped by the Allies or the Soviets. By going on to the defensive he could last up to fourteen days. He said that German discoveries of arms caches during the last few days, and the unexpected dispositions of German troops near to others accounted for the low weapon and ammunition strength.

He explained that his plan of action was to launch surprise attacks simultaneously at all German-held objectives, his main effort being directed at seizing the city centre, the railway stations there and the Vistula bridges. He would keep strong reserves in hand and deploy them as the situation demanded.[18]

In August, the Secret Army in Warsaw numbered 600 platoons, or about 40,000 men, and the Communists People's Army some 400 men. Sublimely disregarding the alarming fact that he had arms, small arms at that, for barely 6,000 men, apart from hand-grenades, Chrusciel had improvised an operational plan which four infantry divisions fully equipped with heavy weapons and supported by field and anti-aircraft artillery would have found a hard test against the city's German forces.

Meanwhile, tension in the city was rising almost hourly. Crowds of half-starved Warsaw citizens, anticipating the enemy collapse, began looting German-owned food shops and warehouses,[19] and were shot down by the military police. Units of the Hermann Goering Division marched across Warsaw in full battle order in an obvious attempt to impress the population with the renewed German strength. The German 73rd Infantry Division detrained outside the city and manned the Praga defences.

In a message to London on 27 July Komorowski[20] informed the Commander-in-Chief, who was then still in Italy, that he had decided to fight in Warsaw pending the outcome of the Russo-German battle on the Vistula's east bank. 'After the panic evacuation of Warsaw from 22 to 25 July, the Germans have recovered. German administrative authorities have returned and have started to function again,' he added, in what must have seemed an ominous tone to the Government, which had authorised him to begin the fighting when he wished.

On 27 July came an event which added to the city's tension and the state of nerves beginning to wear down the resilience of this group of generals and colonels who held in their hands the fate of so many.

The Germans announced that Warsaw would be defended against the Soviets and Governor Fischer issued a proclamation over the loud-hailer system that one hundred thousand Warsaw citizens aged 17 to 65 must report next day at 8 a.m. in six places for work digging defences. Colonel Chrusciel interpreted this as the start of a German move to evacuate Warsaw and to destroy the Secret Army. It spurred him into issuing at 1900 hours, without consulting Komorowski, a potentially dangerous order: 'Alert! On account of today's German orders, issued over the loud-hailers, I hereby order: 1) All troops must assemble at readiness posts and there await the announcement of X-hour. 2) Action against the Germans may only be undertaken before X-hour (*the order to start fighting*) in exceptional circumstances.'[21] By dawn on 28 July the mobilisation of some thousand Secret Army troops had been almost completed without catching the eye of the Germans.

General Komorowski's morning meeting of the military staff on 28 July was faced with both Chrusciel's unauthorised mobilisation and Governor Fischer's demand for 100,000 able-bodied people. Tension was now worsened by confusion.

Chrusciel said that he thought immediate action was needed both to prevent spontaneous fighting by Secret Army troops and to stop the Communist People's Army ordering an uprising. But by midday, when nobody turned up it was clear that the citizens had ignored Fischer's order. Komorowski therefore ordered Chrusciel to counter-mand his mobilisation, which was done. This ignominious outcome testified to the measure of disorganisation and tension prevailing at GHQ which was now spreading to the rank-and-file. Awaiting the long-expected order, many of the troops stayed instead in their assembly areas in a state of prolonged nervous alert.[22]

The Staff finally agreed during the meeting that the Uprising should be launched when the Soviets were known to be in Praga, the Warsaw suburb on the Vistula's east bank, and had also attacked from their newly-won bridgehead near Deblin, south-east of Warsaw. The decision was a setback for General Okulicki, who had called for it while the Germans were retreating, and who still wished for it at once.

Henceforward Komorowski and his staff waited and watched for the right moment. Then on 28 July, as the thunder of artillery in the east echoed over Warsaw, they changed the hour of the Uprising to 1700 hours on any given day, instead of dawn, when the German guards were often relaxing before handing over to the day guard and were less quick and less aggressive in their reactions. It was a fateful decision.

Chrusciel ordered it[23] on the grounds that it would be easier during this rush hour for the troops to rendezvous at their assembly points without being noticed; and that after four hours' fighting in daylight he would expect them to have cleared the Germans from the city centre. They could then reorganise their positions, form a perimeter and dis-tribute arms captured from the enemy, so that by the next morning an organised army would be ready for another day's fighting. And this, despite their initial lack of arms. The defects of this new plan were to become painfully clear when the shooting began.

On the same day, 28 July, Komorowski received a message from London stating emphatically that Deputy Premier Jankowski was to decide precisely when the rising should be launched. It was a last-moment ineffectual attempt to take the initiative out of the hands of the generals.

Colonel Jan Rzepecki noted on 29 July in his diary: 'Bursts of firing echo sporadically throughout the city, mainly caused by secret army men, who noting their lack of arms are trying to seize them from the Germans. In houses in several parts of Warsaw the Germans discovered groups of them which led to a number of local gun fights. German infantry, motorised and *Panzer* units patrol the city day and night. Tanks and machine guns have been sited at all cross-roads and we are expecting reprisals for the total disregard of Fischer's order to report for defence works, as well as an attempt to forestall any kind of uprising by a great combing through of the city.

'The lack of reprisals, far from calming us, leads us to suppose that Warsaw might suddenly face forced evacuation as the Russo-German battle for it explodes. And in these conditions it seems likely that if we do not keep a tight rein a spontaneous outbreak of our battle may occur.'

Komorowski decided on 29 July that General Okulicki should be his deputy and should take over in the event of his becoming a casualty, or being arrested by the Russians on their entry into the city.

Every event of which it was aware now pulled or pushed the Home Army Command nearer the abyss. In a message sent from London on 26 July which arrived on the 29th they learnt of Mikolajczyk's journey to meet Stalin. The need to support him by an uprising weighed heavily with them. They felt that Mikolajczyk could not face Stalin empty-handed.

On the same day, at 8.15 p.m. over the Moscow radio station named after the Polish national hero Kosciuszko came the first of those fateful broadcasts in Polish calling on the citizens of Warsaw to rise:[24]

No doubt Warsaw already hears the guns of the battle which is soon to bring her liberation. Those who have never bowed their heads to the Hitler power will again, as in 1939, join battle with the Germans, this time for decisive action.

The Polish Army now entering Polish territory, trained in the USSR, is now joined by the People's Army to form the corps of the Polish Armed Forces, the armed arm of our nation in its struggle for independence.

Its ranks will be joined tomorrow by the sons of Warsaw. They will all...pursue the enemy westward, wipe out the Hitlerite vermin from the Polish land, and strike a mortal blow at the beast of Prussian imperialism.

For Warsaw, which did not yield, but fought on, the hour of action has already arrived. The Germans will no doubt try to defend themselves in Warsaw, and add new destruction and thousands of victims. Our houses and parks, our bridges and railway stations, our factories and our public buildings will be turned into defence positions.

They will expose the city to ruin and its inhabitants to death. They will try to take away all the most precious possessions and turn into dust all that they have to leave behind.

It is therefore a hundred times more necessary than ever to remember that in the flood of Hitlerite destruction all is lost that is not saved by heroic effort, that by direct active struggle in the streets of Warsaw, its houses, factories and stores we not only hasten the moment of final liberation but also save the nation's property and the lives of our brethren.

Poles, the time of liberation is at hand! Poles, to arms! There is not a moment to lose!

A Soviet manifesto[25] signed by Foreign Commissar Molotov and Edward Osobka-Morawski, head of the Moscow-sponsored Committee of National Liberation, echoed this appeal. It began: 'Poles! The time of liberation is at hand! Poles, to arms!...Every Polish homestead must become a stronghold in the struggle against the invader...There is not a moment to lose.'

These appeals for immediate armed action were also printed on leaflets and dropped over the city by Russian aircraft. Their note of urgency suggested that the Red Army's attack on Warsaw was imminent. For, reasoned the Poles, there could otherwise be no object in urging the citizens to start an uprising which, unsupported, would be bound to end in carnage, with no gain to the Red Army. 'No one in the city doubted for a moment,' Colonel Rzepecki noted in his diary on 29 July, 'that the Russian front had arrived at the gates of Praga and that a great battle would start any day now, the battle for Warsaw. But the military situation is still very unclear and this is only the beginning of a battle whose end cannot be foreseen. Monter (Chrusciel) claimed on the 29th that Russian armoured reconnaisance units had actually entered Praga. He reported that the German bridgehead was only held very weakly and that there are no proper defences on the Vistula line.' Rzepecki also noted that the Globe Reuter news service on 29 July quoted its Moscow correspondent as reporting that Soviet units 'are probing the outlying regions of Warsaw and that a heavy battle is starting near by.'

During the afternoon of 29 July another event pushed Komorowski a few steps nearer the brink. The people were surprised to find the city walls plastered with posters signed by Colonel Julian Skokowski, commander of the Communist People's Army in Warsaw, stating that

Jan Jankowski, the Government delegate, the Home Army Commander, Komorowski, and his staff had fled the city. Skokowski was taking over command of all Secret Army units and would mobilise them to fight the Germans.[26] Following the declaration of the Moscow-sponsored National Committee of Liberation repudiating the London Government it seemed to indicate the Soviets were trying to gain control of the planned uprising.

Komorowski was determined this should not happen. He at once instructed Colonel Chrusciel to order his troops to be ready for the Uprising from 1700 hours the next day, 30 July.[27]

But the fortune of war was no longer with Komorowski. 'In Central Poland, Marshal Rokossovsky's tanks, motorized infantry and Cossack cavalry, powerfully supported by the Red Air Force, pressed on towards Warsaw and were heavily engaged about 20 miles south-east with German lorry-borne reinforcements rushed to the front to stem the advance,'[28] a Soviet bulletin said on 29 July.

A German counter-attack against Rokossovsky's 2nd Soviet Tank Army was about to begin.

8/   Soviet defeat in the suburbs

From 29 July onwards the boom of artillery across the Vistula and the bombing of German targets in Praga rattled the windows of Warsaw day and night. Several times on 30 July Moscow Radio broadcast another urgent appeal from the Polish Communists to the men and women of Warsaw to rise against the Germans. 'Warsaw is shaking in its foundations from the roar of cannons, the Soviet armies are violently attacking and approaching Praga,' it began, on a high note of excitement.

They are coming to bring you freedom. The Germans will try to hold Warsaw when they have been pushed out of Praga. They will destroy everything. Bialystok they destroyed in six days. They murdered thousands of our brothers. We must do everything in our power not to let them repeat this in Warsaw. People of Warsaw! To arms! Let the whole population stand up as a wall around the National Council of the Homeland, around the Warsaw Underground Army. Attack the Germans. Arrest their plans to destroy all public buildings. Help the Red Army in its crossing of the Vistula. Send information, indicate routes. May the million inhabitants of Warsaw become a million soldiers who will expel the German invaders and win freedom.[1]

Komorowski and his staff were fairly well advised of the Soviet pressure towards the end of July on the German forces defending the Praga approaches although they lacked precise knowledge of the Red Army's whereabouts. On 30 July one of Colonel Iranek-Osmecki's intelligence officers had talked with officers of a Soviet tank patrol at Radosk, within ten miles of the capital. They confidently expected to enter it any day.

At the 30 July morning staff meeting Komorowski maintained that there were still no grounds for starting fighting the next day; the Germans were not retreating from Warsaw and the Soviets were not yet in Praga. Colonel Bokszczanin contended that 'until the Soviets open artillery fire on the city we must not make a move'. Colonel

Pluta-Czachowski stressed the lack of operational liaison and argued that only when the Soviets were crossing the Vistula bridge should they start the fighting.[2] Any chance of joint military action with the Communists had ended finally after the Skokowski attempt to gain control of the Secret Army.

On that same day, 30 July, Colonel Iranek-Osmecki told two of his intelligence officers, Lieutenant-Colonel Herman and Captain Muszczak, that the Uprising was imminent and might start at any time. Herman argued that in view of the strength of German forces in the region it would be madness to do so. Iranek-Osmecki refused to discuss this senior staff decision with two subordinate officers. He requested Captain Muszczak to inform the Polish Workers' Party leaders in Warsaw as an act of courtesy that fighting was about to begin. The Communists were not to be consulted and there was no question of liaison with them.[3]

Meantime, both the troops and the civil administration needed to be protected from future possible German or Soviet reprisals. Komorowski and Jankowski therefore jointly requested the Government in London to obtain recognition of the Home Army as an integral part of Allied Forces, and of the civil administration as part of Allied Military Government.

Lieutenant Jan Nowak, a courier, parachuted in from London on 30 July with an important message from the Polish Government stating that the Home Army was unlikely to receive the large-scale British help requested in Komorowski's 25 July message. This asked for German-held airfields near Warsaw to be bombed; for Polish RAF squadrons to fly to Poland, and for the Polish Parachute Brigade to be dropped near the capital.

Count Raczynski, Polish Ambassador, had requested Mr Anthony Eden to arrange for these operations to be undertaken, but Sir Orme Sargent, of the Foreign Office, informed the Ambassador on 28 July that 'operational considerations alone preclude us from meeting the three requests you made for assisting the rising in Warsaw'.[4]

It would not be possible to fly the parachute brigade over German territory as far as Warsaw without risking excessive losses. The despatch of fighter squadrons to airfields in Poland would also be a lengthy and complicated process which could, in any case, only be carried out in agreement with the Soviet Government. It could certainly not be accomplished in time to influence the present battle.

As regards bombarding Warsaw airfields, Warsaw is beyond the normal operational range of Royal Air Force bombers and the bombing of airfields would in any case be carried out much more appropriately by bombers operating from Soviet-controlled bases.

Insofar as your authorities may have had in mind shuttle-bombing...

this is carried out by the American Army Air Force and not by the Royal Air Force. I am afraid, therefore, that there is nothing that His Majesty's Government can do in this connexion.

The London Polish Government now knew without any shadow of doubt that the aid which they had requested was impossible. But apart from sending the British refusal on to Warsaw in a less categorical form they made no attempt to restrain Komorowski and the Home Army GHQ by, for example, making the uprising conditional upon the actual crossing of the Vistula by Soviet forces. No doubt they had Mikolajczyk's visit to Stalin in mind.

Komorowski was still keeping a cool head, refusing to be jockeyed into starting the fighting prematurely, and for the time being during these momentous days holding a tight rein on his more impetuous staff members. Reports were received at the staff meeting on the morning of 31 July of the Soviet force's advance towards Wolomin and Radzymin, twelve and sixteen miles respectively north-east of Warsaw. Some of the officers present — Pelcyznski, Chrusciel, Okulicki, Rzepecki, Iranek-Osmecki, Pluta-Czachowski, Szostak and Bokszczanin — saw this as a reason for starting the fighting at once; others good cause for further waiting. Iranek-Osmecki warned strongly of the danger of a German counter-attack.

Komorowski therefore asked everyone to say in turn whether or not they believed the moment had come. Four of them, Colonels Chrusciel, Bokszczanin, Iranek-Osmecki and Pluta-Czachowski favoured waiting, while General Okulicki and Colonels Szostak and Rzepecki demanded an immediate uprising. Neither Komorowski nor Pelczynski stated their views, but the meeting ended at noon with Komorowski concluding that 'the struggle will not be undertaken on August 1 and it is not very likely that it will be the next day either'.[5]

The politicians had to be told of this decision, and in the early afternoon Komorowski met Jankowski, Deputy Premier and Government Delegate, with the four members of the Council of National Unity, led by Kazimierz Puzak, the Socialist chairman. Komorowski gave them a very bleak analysis of the situation. On the one hand there were altogether an estimated twelve German divisions in the region; on the other, his shortage of ammunition, and the improbability of capturing very much now that the Germans had removed most of it out of the city westwards, meant that he could depend on keeping on the offensive for only one and a half to four days.

He therefore believed that the operations planned for the last days of the German retreat from the capital were not a realistic proposition[6] in the very near future. It was a categorical statement and hearing it, the politicians, especially Kazimierz Puzak, strongly emphasised the need for maximum caution.

Thus, at noon on 31 July, the Secret Army C-in-C and the underground political leaders were agreed not to make a battleground of Warsaw for the time being. It was an important change of policy.

Colonel Iranek-Osmecki left before the meeting ended, to meet at a house in Napoleon Square various members of his intelligence department who were returning from reconnaissance in the Praga district, One of them, Captain Jozef, arrived late with the important news of a German counter-attack about to be launched, he was reliably informed, by units of four Panzer divisions – the 'Hermann Goering' Division, the Fourth Panzer Division, the 19th Panzer Division, and the SS Panzer Viking Division. The Germans were for the time being stronger and were likely in the battle that was developing to throw the Soviets back temporarily.

Colonel Iranek-Osmecki knew that this information made further postponement of the Uprising absolutely imperative. For if GHQ were to launch it now, when the Soviets in the Praga sector were about to receive the full weight of von Vorman's armour and could not come to their aid, the outcome would be disastrous.

He left the house in Napoleon Square at about 16.45 hours, expecting to get to the staff meeting with this vital piece of news by the time it began, at 17.00 hours. Fusillades of shots broke out and died away here and there in the city. Ahead of him near a railway bridge he saw a crowd of people and heard loud commands shouted in German. The Gestapo and the Schutzpolizei had set up a cordon and were arresting anyone who approached. Iranek-Osmecki turned quickly in the opposite direction. He realised with a sense of alarm that he would have to make a detour of two or three kilometres and might not get to the meeting in time.[7]

Punctually at five o'clock, an hour or two after Komorowski had said that an uprising was not a realistic proposition, the afternoon staff meeting began. Apart from Komorowski, only Pelczynski, Okulicki and Rzepecki attended, because nothing of note had occurred – no Soviet advances, for example, which could precipitate a decision. Nevertheless, tension and anxiety weighed heavily on these weary wanted men, faced now with the onus of a terrible decision. Chrusciel was due later, but he arrived suddenly a little after five. Subduing his excitement he said he had received a report that Soviet tank forces had entered Praga. He insisted that his report was correct and argued that they should start fighting at once.[8]

Alarmed at this report, according to Rzepecki, but without checking it in any way Komorowski at once sent for Deputy Premier Jan Jankowski and briefly put the situation before him. He said, in contrast to his clearly stated opinion that morning, that he believed it was the right time to begin the fight.

Something strange had happened to Komorowski since the morning's meeting. Gone was his caution, his prudence, his realism. On the foundation of this single, unchecked report and without even waiting for the return of Colonel Iranek-Osmecki, who he knew had been gathering information from his agents in the field, he was ready to order now an immediate uprising.

Launched in Warsaw at this moment it would turn the German defeat into complete disaster, he told Mr Jankowski. It would cut their supply lines to their troops in the entire Warsaw sector, prevent them reinforcing their 73rd Division before Praga and guarantee an easy success for the Soviet out-flanking movement to the east, north-east and north of Warsaw he thought was then beginning.

He admitted that even if the Secret Army managed to overthrow the German garrison and seize the city with its first onslaught, they had only enough arms and food for at the most seven days. He also knew, although he did not seem to make this very clear to Jankowski, that he could not count on any substantial aid from Britain. 'So far as we could foresee, our success depended upon not striking too soon. The Red Army must enter Warsaw within a week after we struck the first blow.'[9]

General Komorowski was about to try to secure the capital for the London Polish Government before the arrival of the Soviets, yet militarily he depended on them for its accomplishment. Instead of a prudent, realistic general, he had somehow become in the space of one morning a desperate political gambler.

Jankowski listened to him 'and then put questions to various members of the Staff'.[10] What those questions were, to whom they were put and what the answers were, neither Komorowski nor anyone else has ever stated.

Upon this brief discussion with Jankowski the existence of an ancient city and its million inhabitants depended. Yet all we have from Komorowski is: 'Having completed his picture of the situation, he turned to me with the words: "Very well, then. Begin."'[11]

Komorowski told Chrusciel, upon whose report the decision rested, and who was in command of the fighting: 'Tomorrow, at seventeen hours precisely, you will start operations in Warsaw.' Chrusciel at once left the room for his own operations HQ.

Thus, in half an hour, the final decision was made on the foundation of evidence which General Komorowski had not checked and which ran counter to the advice of his own intelligence chief. Certainly it is easy to be wise after the event, but the desperate haste with which the insurrection was launched after ten days' marking time has a sorry sound to it.

Iranek-Osmecki arrived breathless half an hour later. He brought the even more dramatic news that the Germans were about to counter-attack and that their troops defending the outer ring of the Praga sector were holding on. Komorowski simply looked at his watch and said: 'Too late. It's done. Stalo-sie! We have decided to fight tomorrow.'[12] That was all.

Iranek-Osmecki insisted that the information he had just received from Praga made it clear that Chrusciel's report was optimistic or exaggerated at least. Fresh German reinforcements were still concentrating for the tank battle with the Soviets.

Just after 6 p.m. Colonel Pluta-Czachowski arrived. He brought reports that the German counter-attack had actually begun. Komorowski now had clear evidence that tomorrow's uprising would be premature. Yet he repeated what he had already said – the orders to fight were issued and it was too late to countermand them.[13]

In fact, Chrusciel had still not issued the battle order and did not do so until an hour later, at 7 p.m.[14] It had then to be coded and given to the messenger girls for distribution to area commanders. On 31 July this was impossible because the Germans had that day brought the curfew forward to 8 p.m. So it was just possible that Komorowski might have been able to repeal the order, or could at least have tried to do so, but he refused. 'It's too late now,' he contended.

Colonel Szostak then arrived and heard news of the order and his colleagues' objections. He had earlier urged an immediate uprising; now he had doubts. He asked Komorowski why he had heeded neither his chief of Operations nor his chief of Intelligence before deciding. Komorowski's answer was hardly convincing in view of his earlier realism. He said that had he waited it might have been too late to have started the fighting before the Soviets entered the city.[15]

Their long five years' struggle to keep the organisation intact had ended. The leaders of the Secret Army left for their separate tasks with an inevitable deep sense of foreboding.

How were these brave and able men like Komorowski, Pelczynski, and Chrusciel, when the longed-for moment arrived and the liberation for which they so much thirsted seemed at hand, unable to carry out what Colonel Adam Borkiewicz, another Secret Army officer, rightly calls 'their rationally and carefully prepared plans'? Why were they unable 'to keep cool heads, and why did they lack will enough to stand by their original decisions'?

The Uprising was the culmination of 'five years of unparalleled nerve-racking torture', which affected the older generation, and especially the age group to which these men belonged, far more than the younger generation. By 31 July all of them were in a state of hardly bearable nervous exhaustion. Komorowski himself had for five years been the quarry of an unrelenting manhunt. He had seen many of his comrades one by one caught, tortured and killed; he had slept briefly somewhere different every night, he was shorn of his true identity and his personal possessions. He did not even know the hiding-place of his wife, who was then expecting a child, or even whether she was alive.

Now, while the Secret Army, its morale at fever pitch, was assembled in a state of readiness at its rendezvous points, he and his staff were torn by dissension. His own military realism on the one hand held him back, while on the other impetuous officers and eager troops pushed him forward. 'It seemed unthinkable that the Home Army...should stand passively by and not attack the retreating and demoralised German armies,' wrote the Peasant Party leader Stefan Korbonski, who attended many of these late-July meetings.

National dignity and pride required that the capital should be liberated by the Poles themselves, and that was accepted without any discussion. Moreover, we had to think of what the Western world would say if the Russians were to capture Warsaw unaided. In that event Stalin would have no difficulty in convincing the Allies that the Home Army, the underground Government, and the Polish underground movement as such were a fiction. What kind of an army would it be, what sort of a Government, that, being in the capital, failed to take part in the battle for the liberation of the city? Finally, the Germans were spreading the report that on Hitler's order Warsaw was to be razed to the ground whatever happened.[16]

During the last days of July too, the Gestapo had considerably increased the arrests of Secret Army officers and had, as well, destroyed numbers of Polish arms dumps. It pointed to a large-scale police attack on their military formations. Three days before the Uprising, on 29 July, machine-gun posts were simultaneously set up in the streets, while at a few key points, such as the Zoliborz viaduct, tanks were positioned.[17]

Then on the evening of 31 July, after reports of the Soviet advances a few kilometres north-east of Warsaw, came Chrusciel's report of the breakthrough – Chrusciel, an able Polish tactician, who had lectured at the Staff College before the war, and who right up till that morning had staunchly supported Komorowski in his refusal to launch the Uprising prematurely.

It turned the scale. Komorowski could not hold out any longer though perhaps one ally at the crucial moment would have helped. 'If I had been present and had told him what I knew, I think Komorowski would not have decided to fight. I knew that the German bridgehead on the east side of the Vistula was not broken,' Colonel Iranek-Osmecki[18] says today.

What was the precise Russo-German battle situation in the sector east of Warsaw at this time, and what chances had the Soviets of coming to the aid of the uprising if they wished to? On 28 July Marshal Stalin ordered General Rokossovsky, Commander of the First Belorussian Front armies, to occupy Praga (opposite Warsaw) between 5 and 8 August, and to establish a number of bridgeheads south of Warsaw on the western bank of the Vistula.[19]

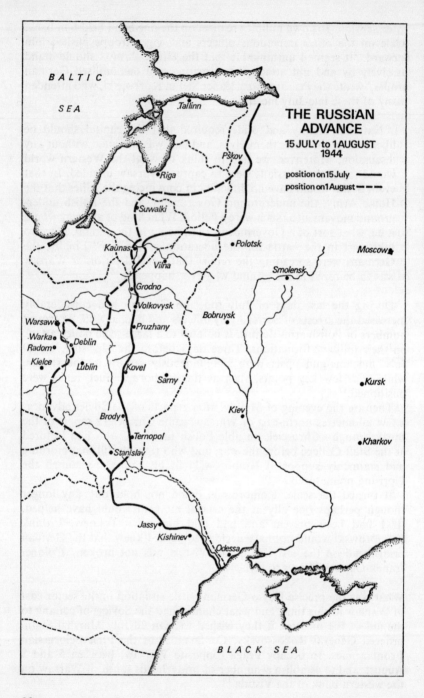

BALTIC

SEA

.Tallinn

THE RUSSIAN ADVANCE

15 JULY to 1 AUGUST 1944

Pskov

position on 15 July ——————

position on 1 August – – – – – –

• Riga

• Suwalki

• Polotsk

Kaunas

Moscow▪

• Vilna

• Grodno   Smolensk•

• Volkovysk

Warsaw•   Pruzhany   Bobruysk•

Warka•
Radom•   Deblin

Kielce•   Lublin

Kovel   • Kursk

Brody   Sarny

Kiev•

Ternopol

Stanislav   • Kharkov

Jassy•

Kishinev•
Odessa•

BLACK SEA

The Red Army's infantry initially had a three to one superiority and its armour and artillery one of five to one over the enemy. Rokossovsky's First Belorussian Front comprised nine armies: one tank army, two tank corps, three cavalry corps, one motorised corps and two airborne armies. German forces comprised the 2nd Army of four Panzer divisions and one of infantry; and the 9th Army's two divisions and two brigades of infantry.

In the early hours of 27 July the Soviet 2nd Tank Army and the 8th Tank Corps attacked westward along the Warsaw–Lublin road in the general direction of Praga.[20]

The next day spearheads of infantry corps of the Soviet 69th Army of Marshal Konev's more southerly 1st Ukrainian Front struck through to the east bank of the Vistula near Pulawy,[21] eighty miles south-east of Warsaw. At dawn on 29 July spearheads crossed the river north of Kazimierz and after fierce fighting with enemy detachments seized a bridgehead near the Janowiec area. Other bridgeheads were seized and linked up despite strong German tank and infantry counter-attacks. After this hard fighting the 69th Army then went temporarily on the defensive.

On 31 July the 1st Polish (Communist) Army was ordered to force a crossing on a wide front at Pulawy and to seize bridgeheads on the west bank of the Vistula in order to help similar operations by the Soviet 69th Army and 8th Guards Army, which began crossing near Magnuszew, about twenty-five miles nearer Warsaw. The Polish 1st and 2nd Infantry Divisions crossed the river in several places on 1 and 2 August, and, continually engaged in heavy fighting, held on until 4 August, when orders were given to withdraw to the left bank, which was done on the night of 4 August. The Polish Communist Divisions lost more than 1,000 killed and wounded. The Russian 8th Guards Army however, successfully crossed the river and established a bridgehead between Magnuszew and Warecko.[22] The Polish Divisions were assigned the task of defending the northern part of this bridgehead.

Meanwhile units of the Soviet 2nd Tank Army renewed their advance in a north-west direction towards Warsaw. They were opposed in the Garwolin area, about forty miles south-east of Warsaw by two advance-post battalions of the German 73rd Infantry Division, deployed in a single line along the north bank of the Swidra river. The main forces of the 'Hermann Goering' Division were in reserve, centred in the Rembertow–Okuniew sector, twelve miles east of Praga. Warsaw's approaches were held by the German 3rd, 5th, 19th and 4th Panzer Divisions. The 73rd Infantry Division, about 10,800 strong, was commanded by General Fritz Franck.

Soviet forces now launched an all-out offensive in the Praga sector, the 2nd Tank Army units attacking the outposts of the 73rd German Infantry Division. Spearheads of the Soviet 3rd and 8th Tank Corps clashed with the German outposts, including 'Hermann Goering'

Division reconnaissance units near Garwolin after midday on 27 July. Despite stubborn resistance the German units were gradually forced back towards Kaluszyn.

Garwolin was partially taken during the night and the main body of the German 73rd Division fell back to the strong Siennica–Kolbiel–Latowicze Line. On the morning of 28 July the German 9th Panzer Division HQ and detachments of the 'Hermann Goering' Division arrived in the sector and at once engaged the Soviet 8th Tank Corps. A fierce tank battle followed. By noon on 29 July the 8th Tank Corps had driven the Germans back and occupied Kolbiel and Siennica, in the outer ring of Warsaw's German defences.

Detachments of the Soviet 3rd Tank Corps, breaking German resistance to the north of Minsk Mazowiecki about twenty-six miles from Warsaw, pressed on to Zielonka, capturing General Franck, Commander of the 73rd Division, together with some of his staff and important documents. They revealed that a reconnaissance unit of the German 5th Panzer Division, the 'SS Viking', was operating near Minsk Mazowiecki. Detachments of the 'Hermann Goering' and of the 73rd Infantry Divisions were defending the Cechowa and Otwock sector of the outer ring of Warsaw's defences. The approaches to Praga were defended by the 19th Panzer Division and the 3rd 'Totenkopf' Panzer Division in the suburban areas of Okuniew and Pustelnik.[23]

At dawn on 30 July, the retreating Germans held a line comprising Zielonka, Cechowka, Minsk-Mazowiecki and Otwock. The 2nd Tank Army's 16th Tank Corps attacked along the Lublin road towards Otwock; and despite a German counter-attack with a regiment of infantry and forty tanks of the 19th Panzer Division, seized Otwock by the evening and took villages near Milosna Stara, about fifteen miles east of Warsaw. An assault on the key-point of Okuniew in the outer ring of the Warsaw defences was now feasible. The 8th Tank Corps launched an attack in the afternoon but were halted by German artillery and air attacks.

The Soviet 3rd Tank Corps, by-passing strong enemy positions in the Zielonka district from the north-east in the evening, now drove the enemy from the towns of Wolomin and Radzymin, only twelve and sixteen miles north-east of Warsaw, and took up defensive positions along the Dluga river. But this unit's situation on the night of 30 July was perilous. Far ahead of the main body of the 2nd Tank Army, it was running short of ammunition and fuel, while units of the 39th Panzer Corps still fought on in Wolomin and Radzymin. More serious, five German armoured divisions were now converging in the direction of Radzymin-Wolomin.[24]

Early on 31 July, the 1st Armoured Paratroop Regiment of the 'Hermann Goering' Division attacked from Praga towards Wolomin. The main forces of the 19th Panzer Division lunged at Radzymin from the south-west along the Warsaw–Wyszkow road; and from Wyszkow the 4th Panzer Division hit out to support it. The main body of the SS Panzer 'Viking' Division was moving from Wegrow to attack Wolomin on the following day; while strong forces of the 'Death's Head' Panzer Division were on the march from Siedlce towards Stanislawow in order to cut off the Soviet units on the north-east bank of the Dluga river.

Thus, just as the Uprising in Warsaw was about to begin, the approaches of the Warsaw suburb of Praga became the scene of one of the biggest tank battles fought in Poland in the summer of 1944. Some 450 tanks and self-propelled guns were deployed by the Germans. The most that is at present known of Soviet strength is that twelve days earlier on 18 July 1944 the 2nd Tank Army put 808 tanks and self-propelled guns into the field.[25]

In order to aid the hard-pressed 3rd Tank Corps the 2nd Army Commander ordered an artillery and air bombardment on the German positions at dawn, 31 July, followed by an all-out attack by 8th Tank Corps, and under the weight of it the enemy withdrew towards Okuniew. Fifty tanks of the 'Death's Head' Division then counter-attacked in a westerly direction from the Stanislawow area to try to link up with the 'Hermann Goering' Division and the 19th Panzer Division, then engaged in a tank battle with Soviet units at Okuniew and Ossow.

Despite powerful air support this move was narrowly defeated and on the evening of 31 July 8th Tank Corps took Okuniew, but its attack later in the day on the German strongpoint of Ossow near by was driven off with heavy losses. Later that evening the initiative began to pass, in this, the Praga sector of the front, to the Germans. The Soviet 3rd Tank Corps was still isolated north of 8th Corps and like 16th Corps had spent the day opposing numerous heavy attacks by German armour, artillery and infantry.

The Soviet 2nd Army Commander was faced with heavy casualties, a growing shortage of fuel and ammunition and an immediate threat to his rear. His all-out effort to comply with the Soviet Supreme Command's orders, break through on the fifty-mile ring of German defences and enter Praga between 5 and 8 August was not feasible. At 4.10 a.m. on 1 August he ordered his units to break off the attack.[26]

The first Soviet offensive against Warsaw had failed when its spearheads were at some points within six or seven miles of the city's eastern suburbs. By 1 August—the day the Warsaw Uprising began—the initiative had passed completely to the Germans and it stayed with them for several days.

General von Vormann brought up more artillery, infantry and two armoured trains from the 2nd Army's reserves and launched a strong counter-attack. Detachments of the 'Viking' and 'Totenkopf' Panzer Divisions, advancing from the forests to the east of Michalow, battered their way into Okuniew, drove out the Soviet 8th Tank Corps at 21.00 hours on 1 August and linked up with General Sauchen's 39th Panzer Corps from the west.

On the morning of 2 August the 19th Panzer Division thrust into Radzymin from the north-west. A simultaneous attack by 4th Panzer along the southern side of the Radzymin–Wyszkow road was delayed, but they too entered Radzymin towards the evening and joined forces with 19th Panzer. Several hours later after bitter fighting, the Soviet 3rd Tank Corps was thrust back from Radzymin towards Wolomin, eventually taking up defensive positions along the Czarna river.[27]

Thus, by the evening of 2 August General von Vormann's Panzer units had battered and thrust back the Soviets in a well-directed counter-attack. The Soviet armies now lost mile by mile, at no less cost, the Warsaw approaches which they had gained at great sacrifice.

In the afternoon of 3 August the 'Hermann Goering' Division, attacking from the north-east, recaptured Wolomin. But from the evening of 4 August onwards, although the Germans maintained a withering artillery and mortar fire on the Soviet 2nd Army's groupings they ceased their tank attacks and the battle on the Praga approaches finally ended at noon on 5 August.[28] The Germans were transferring two divisions to Warka, thirty miles south to deal with enemy pressure there. The Soviet forces had by this time lost 425 tanks and self-propelled guns out of the 808 with which they began the battle.[29]

Exhausted by the fighting, which for them had begun about thirty-five days earlier, the Soviet 2nd Tank Army units handed over their defensive positions to units of the 47th and 70th Armies and withdrew to re-equip and await reinforcements.

Not until 25 August was Rokossovsky to inform Stalin in a telegram that he was ready to stage a new attack on Warsaw.[30]

What did this ancient and glorious city mean to the Poles, Germans and Russians about to become involved in so bloody a struggle for it? The citizens, the men and women of the Secret Army, loved it of course because it held their homes, families and work, also for its cultural heritage of scholarly museums, historic libraries, resplendent churches and gilded palaces. But especially they revered it for its 150-year-old role of struggle for national independence against those predatory neighbours Tsarist Russia, Prussia and Austria. The will to play a part in this historical tradition and fight the Nazis cemented the Secret Army's diverse social character, giving a temporary unity to men and women whose visions of post-war Poland were alarmingly out of joint.

Warsaw, the visible symbol of freedom and unity, had thus become in great part the inspiration of the five years of struggle against the invader. From pragmatists no less than idealists it called forth a readiness for total sacrifice.

To the Nazis and the Soviets, on the other hand, it figured as an important strategic and tactical cockpit. Seven communications arteries lunged through it, crossing the Vistula over three road and two railway bridges. For the Germans, fighting defensive battles in the area, the bridges and roads across the city were all-important. They had to be kept open for the free movement of troops and supplies to the Eastern Front.

To the Red Army, on the other hand, Warsaw's communications network was vital for the Berlin offensive, although the bridges, which it knew the Germans would destroy, were of less account.

A fairly large city, Warsaw extended over some 15 kilometres from Bielany in the north to Czerniakow in the south; and eight from Praga on the east bank of the Vistula to Wola in the west. The City Centre stretched approximately from the Royal Castle in the north, on the southern confines of the Old Town, to Lazienki Park in the south – a wooded parkland surrounding the exquisite eighteenth-century Lazienki Palace built by King Stanislav Poniatowski. The Vistula, varying from three hundred to five hundred yards wide, hemmed in the City Centre on the east, while the western limits of this district lay along the outskirts of the working-class suburb of Wola.

The fearsome ruins of the Ghetto lay like a monument to evil between Bonifraterska, Leszno, Okopowa, Stawki and Miranowska streets. They were surrounded by a high wall and armed police. Among the ruins rose the infamous Gestapo torture prison, the Pawiak; and the Gesiowka, where Jews were held before transportation to Nazi death centres.

North of the Citadel, a fortress built by Tsar Alexander III to reinforce Russian rule which dominated the river bank north of the Old Town, lay the new northern suburb of Zoliborz, mainly villas and apartment blocks in tree-lined streets, leading to the suburbs of Marymont and Bielany. They were separated from the Old Town by a railway track which ran west through Wola and adjacent Ochota, where it turned east and traversed the City Centre before crossing the Vistula and passing through Praga. The Old Town and the City Centre were thus virtually surrounded by railway, a decisive fact in the battle to come.

The western suburb of Wola, mainly composed of old wooden houses, was cut by two main motor roads leading to the west, while south of them lay the suburb of Ochota, astride the main road for Radom and Lodz. Here were situated the German police barracks. Mokotow, a residential district of new tallish buildings to the south, was cut off from the City Centre by Mokotow Field, a large open space once used both as a racecourse and a parade ground.

Hemmed in by the river bank to the east, two vital east–west arteries north and south of it and a third artery running from north to south, was the partly medieval Old Town, just north of the City Centre. Thus, to hold the City Centre, the Old Town and the roads that bordered them was effectively to command Warsaw, for the road leading to the

Kierbedz Bridge ran between the Old Town and the City Centre, whose southern districts were bounded by the main road to the Poniatowski Bridge.

Warsaw drew its water supply from the Vistula, through the water works between Ochota and the City Centre. The power station dominated the Vistula embankment between the Poniatowski and Kerbedzia bridges. Gas came from a works in southern Wola. All three of these public utilities swiftly became targets for attack and counter-attack by Poles and Germans alike.

A lifeline for the Poles as the struggle for the city grew in intensity was the dark and labyrinthine sewage system, built as much as a hundred years ago to carry rainwater and sewage to the river. The outflow reached the Vistula north of the city in the Bielany area, where the two main sewage tunnels met, both running in a north–south direction. The tunnel running from central Mokotow in the south, beneath the City Centre, the Old Town and Zoliborz to Bielany was used by the men and women of the Secret Army as a subterranean communications route.

Other smaller systems, still more frightening, made roundabout circuits like rabbit warrens before reaching the main collector systems. The larger tunnels varied from about five to seven feet in diameter, the smaller from about two feet to four feet. The rush of drainage water sometimes filled these completely. Pitch black, foetid, twisting and turning for miles, choked with sudden niagaras of water, the sewers were to become the Secret Army's only means of communication between beleaguered districts.

This, in brief, was the city with its 1,200,000 inhabitants which Komorowski's Secret Army was now to try to wrest from the Germans, in the belief that the Russians were about to fight their way in from the east. All was now to be staked on seizing control of it before the Soviets entered, in an effort to forestall a communist takeover.

What kind of operational plan had the Secret Army? How was this force of mostly untried and poorly-armed soldiers to set about overthrowing the German garrison? Generals Rowecki and Sikorski between them had drawn up operational plans for the intended Uprising in 1942–3, and this included Warsaw; its role in this plan became substantially the plan for 1 August 1944.

Airily, the plan ordered the destruction of all German security and administrative units, the disarming or, if necessary, annihilation of German army and police units; the capture of military stores and warehouses; the occupation of the city and its immediate surroundings, especially communications centres, railway stations, Vistula bridges, radio stations, telecommunications centres and public utility buildings. It was a task that would have tested a well-armed force of two or three divisions, let alone a citizen army short of bullets and guns.

No less ambitiously the plan ordered that defence lines were to be organised on two perimeters, the first on the eastern outskirts of Praga, the second on the west bank of the Vistula, from Bielany to Siekerki, so as to seal off the city in the east and stop the entry of more German forces. At the same time the Secret Army was to secure the safety in the capital of the London Government's provisional administration, which would start to function at once.

Rowecki counted on Anglo-American aid when he drew up the plan, as well as the participation of Polish forces in the west. With this in mind, he stated in detail how the above aims should be achieved, ordering that the most important tactical objectives as well as secondary nests of resistance must be destroyed by simultaneous surprise attacks. 'Strongly defended objectives, on the other hand, should be isolated,' he commanded.

The manoeuvre must be carried out in such a way, that after the reduction of the primary objectives and the capture of arms, the stronger positions may be annihilated with the help of better armament. The central and skirting railway lines must be sealed off so as to prevent German movement into or out of the city.

Strong pickets must be placed at the end of all the main communication arteries out of the city, as well as the most important routes on the outskirts so as to hinder and prevent any troop movements by the enemy in any direction.

As the main forces finish their fighting within the capital, they must be used to organise the defence of Praga and of the western bank of the Vistula, while a reserve must at the same time be assembled in readiness for action to the north or west of the city.

On the basis of this plan Komorowski's staff worked out their own more detailed operational instructions, including orders for the erection of adequately manned anti-tank barricades at all important road junctions and city access roads to stop German forces entering the city after the start of the fighting.

Strangely, they entrusted organisation of the western defence perimeter to the commanders of the Zoliborz, City Centre and Mokotow forces 'at the moment when the forces of these sectors are freed from the initial fighting'. Commanders of the City Centre and Zoliborz sectors were also, with the co-operation of the Praga forces, on the Vistula's east bank, to capture the all-important road and railway bridges across the river. The chances of their being free to help set up the western defence perimeter to stop the Germans entering from that quarter seemed a little remote.

The Praga sector was to organise the defence of the east bank, but in the event of heavy German attack, to cross the river into the City Centre and there form a reserve for the defence of the river's west bank.

To the independent Okecie sector was given the heavy task of capturing the strongly garrisoned airport and Luftwaffe base, after which it was to organise its defence and prepare for the landing of British, American and Polish aircraft.

The commander of the forces in the suburban sector of Marymont, north of Zoliborz, was to capture Bielany airport and Raszyn radio station, then capture and mine all the railway stations and bridges in this sector. In addition, his forces were to erect anti-tank defences and strong-points on all city access roads in their sector and be permanently ready to march to the City Centre with reserve troops should they be needed.

To the Sappers was given the task of laying mines in the hours before X-hour along the railway lines to be blown at the outset of the Uprising. A special plan dealt with the destruction of the Warsaw railway system, vital for stopping both German troop movements and shelling by heavy artillery from armoured trains. The Sappers were also to send three platoons to Praga to build anti-tank defences on the approaches to the bridges: and to allot the remainder of their units to the City Centre, Wola and Zoliborz districts to help in strengthening the defences along the surrounding railway lines.

Comprehensive though the plan tried to be it was nevertheless unrealistic to a marked degree, conceived as though the Germans were weak and the Poles strong and well-armed; and indeed, for the operational tasks allotted them they would need to be.

Of course, before he was persuaded otherwise, Komorowski had made German collapse in the Warsaw sector of the front a condition of the Uprising. Now he was about to attack a strong, well-armed, well-disciplined force of seasoned troops with an untried army devoid of heavy weapons, weak in small arms and with ammunition for only about five days.

All therefore hinged on the men of the Secret Army being able to overwhelm the German units and arm their unarmed comrades with captured weapons. Just as in the Trojan War, about 1250 B.C., it was vital not only to kill or disarm the enemy but also to seize his weapons. Thus, the Uprising was first and foremost an 'equipment action'; and only secondly a battle for vital objectives. Even the best operational plan was little more than provisional in face of this.

Colonel Chrusciel received the order for the insurrection at 6 o'clock on 31 July, but to take it to his headquarters from Komorowski's headquarters, then to code and prepare orders for dispatch to the group commanders was impossible that evening before the 8 o'clock curfew. Distribution of the order to start fighting at 5 o'clock began at 7 a.m. the same day, thus leaving commanders less than ten hours to inform their workaday troops — even if they themselves received the order at once, which was impossible.

Under the eyes of SS and police patrols scores of messenger girls arrived at the headquarters one after the other and somehow without attracting attention were sent off on their vital errands. At this point Chrusciel's timetable came to grief.

Warsaw subsector commanders received the order at about 8 a.m. on 1 August, the district commanders at about 10 o'clock, commanders of the fighting formations at midday; their platoon commanders at about 2 o'clock, or three hours before it was due to begin, and suburban commanders only an hour before, or even later.

The outcome on this first vital day was incomplete mobilisation. In some platoons, even though the troops were standing by in a state of readiness, as much as half the strength failed, for one reason or the other, to rendezvous on time. Many decided to leave work and make one final visit home to their wives and families and were trapped there by premature outbreaks of fighting. Suburban commanders with important perimeter defence tasks received their orders last of all and had the poorest turn-out. Even in the highly trained 'Radóslaw' and 'Bastion' groups, both of whom had crucial assignments, the turn-out was not much more than half owing to late orders.

On the way to the Home Army Staff GHQ in the early afternoon, Komorowski walked through streets full of young men and women carrying rucksacks and bulky parcels. 'Overcoats bulged with hand grenades, or did not quite conceal from my eyes a tommy gun or a rifle. Though I knew that only a person in the street would notice these things, I could not repress an irrational anxiety. I passed German patrols at every few paces, and armoured cars were moving ceaselessly through the streets.'[31]

As well as the intermittent rumble of artillery on the Russo-German front, the deep crump of detonations near at hand could be heard as the Germans blew up railway equipment near Praga.

Still looking like ordinary civilians, the Secret Army men entered their posts in houses, offices or factories commanding German barracks, vital street crossings, railway stations or bridges, all of which objectives they were ordered to seize in their first surprise attacks. For upon surprise greatly depended whatever chance of victory they had.

They barricaded entrances and posted sentries. From out of deceptive wrappings or from under their clothing they took their scanty weapons. They put on their red and white arm bands, the proud badge of Polish troops on their native soil.

Then they awaited the moment for which they had longed so devoutly for five grim years, when together they would hurl themselves at the Nazis. And by the tragic delusion that the Red Army had cracked the German defences and soon would fight its way into Warsaw to aid them they gained courage and hope.

9/ The Uprising flares

On that hot morning of 1 August 1944 when tree-lined, grassy Warsaw already looked parched and yellow, the German authorities were sharply divided about the likelihood of a Polish uprising in the city at that time. Colonel Geibel, commander of SS and Police, had learned of the possibility owing to the conscientious savagery of his SS torturers in their interrogation of Secret Army men and women in the corridor of cells on Szuch Avenue. On 15 July he began fortifying all the city's main objectives more strongly with concrete and barbed-wire and brought in his outlying police pickets. He also reported to his superiors that owing to lack of troops he would not be able effectively to oppose an uprising.

At 11 o'clock on 1 August, convinced now that something was afoot, he tried to persuade Dr Fischer, Governor of Warsaw, to withdraw into the strongly fortified police headquarters in Szuch Avenue in the City Centre. Fischer did not agree that an uprising was likely and refused.

Lieutenant-General Reiner Stahel, appointed by Hitler on 27 July to command the Warsaw garrison Wehrmacht troops because he was reputed to be a commander especially reliable in time of crisis, arrived in the capital on 31 July and went straight to the Wehrmacht HQ in Brühl Palace, Theatre Square. There in rude and unmannerly fashion he took over command from Major-General Rohr.[1] He then shut himself up inside this charming Empire-style residence with its walled-in courtyard facing the city's most beautiful square; he could not therefore sense the highly inflammable atmosphere outside in the streets.

He had observed that the city seemed calm on his arrival, but his intelligence department was less confident, for recently, believing that the Poles had been subdued, Himmler had seriously cut down the garrison strength. The Germans, it must be remembered, had not thought it necessary to draw up a defence plan against an uprising in Warsaw. For internal defence they had simply divided the city into five sectors, each with its own supplies and forces, and had instituted an alarm system with three degrees of urgency, the first two for disturbances and riots, which the Police and the SS would handle; and the third for an insurrection, when the Wehrmacht would take over.

100

For this purpose Stahel should have had a force of fifteen thousand Wehrmacht troops, thirteen thousand Luftwaffe troops, four thousand Waffen SS and four thousand armed police, apart from about four thousand station and factory guards, a total of forty thousand men.[2] He discovered, however, that on 9 July Himmler had transferred a battalion of the Hermann Goering SS Regiment to Grodno, thus weakening the garrison by several hundred first-class troops specially trained in street fighting, while to protect the German Governor of Poland, Hans Frank, in Cracow, he had drafted a police battalion. Worst of all, the army and air force had ordered to the collapsed Eastern Front nearly all the good fighting units available.[3]

Examining his fighting strength in the Brühl Palace on 31 July Stahel was dismayed to find it little more than a quarter of what it ought to have been. He had in all only about 5,500 good fighting troops, 4,300 SS and Police units, 1,300 Luftwaffe anti-aircraft troops, 800 Hermann Goering SS and two companies of Pioneers, about 12,000 troops all told, included among whom were about 900 renegade Ukrainians, Cossacks and Turkomen, former Soviet prisoners of war of doubtful value.[4]

He ordered into Warsaw at once several batteries of anti-aircraft guns from Okecie airport just outside the city.

Meantime, on 1 August, the Secret Army's poor communications, combined with the desperate haste with which Komorowski and his staff had triggered off the rising, quickly led to misfortune. About one-third of the already scarce arms were not issued because the underground conspiracy rules allowed only two men to know where the caches were hidden. The order to fight arrived at a group command some time during the day and had then to be taken to those in charge of the arms even before the problem of distribution could be solved. For this reason, and their proximity to enemy strongpoints which became involved in premature outbreaks of fighting, some caches were never even uncovered.[5]

In the almost unbearably hot and sultry afternoon both excessive zeal and carelessness caused the Poles at some points to start fighting too soon. In the northern suburb of Zoliborz at about 2 p.m. Secret Army troops were more or less openly carrying arms from the caches to the distribution centres. A carload of German gendarmerie drove up. The Poles opened fire and in the streets surrounding Wilson Square fighting broke out. The Germans sent in reinforcements, including several armoured troop carriers of parachute grenadiers, SS men and gendarmes. The Poles were crushed with heavy losses after three hours' combat.[6]

Lesser outbreaks flared too soon elsewhere in the city as well: in the district of Czerniakow at 3 p.m.; at 4 p.m. in Napoleon Square and Kercely Square; about half past four in Mirowski Square and Chocim Street, Wola, round Komorowski's GHQ.

Geibel ordered all police units in the city to stand-to immediately. Surprise, upon which the Uprising so much depended, was completely lost. But the insurgents still had a tactical advantage, for Stahel had not yet imposed the third-degree alarm. Having with savage vigour helped the police to put down the isolated outbreaks in the city, he did nothing more, displaying a characteristic lack of insight.[7]

Then at 4 o'clock one of those human incidents happened which sometimes influence in greater or lesser degree the course of history. An officer of the Luftwaffe telephoned Geibel to tell him that his Polish woman friend had a little earlier implored him to leave Warsaw at once because the whole city was to rise against the Germans at 5 o'clock. This warning, and what he already knew, finally convinced Geibel beyond any shadow of doubt.[8]

He notified General Stahel, Dr Hahn, the security-police chief, and Dr Fischer, again pleading with Fischer to come to the police zone and when he again refused sending him a crack police battalion.[9]

Alarmed, Stahel at once imposed the third-degree regime and took command of the whole garrison, army and police. Before 5 o'clock all the Germans were standing by throughout the city.[10] Stahel was clearly surprised. 'The appearance of the streets was quite normal, to anyone not aware of the events,' he wrote with rare simplicity a little later, 'when suddenly at about 16.30 the uprising flared up almost simultaneously in many places.'[11] Within an hour Stahel's GHQ in the Brühl Palace became the target of a headlong Secret Army attack. His communications were cut and he was pinned down. Worse still he lost all control of the fighting.[12]

Komorowski found himself in an almost equally dangerous situation. Originally, the Secret Army GHQ was to be situated in the Mokotow district on the city's southern outskirts because it was near to the radio station there, near to Okecie airport and handy for communications with Secret Army detachments in the west needed for attacks on the German rear. But on 29 July he and his staff decided to move to Wola, a working-class district right next to the City Centre, so that they would be in the heart of the strategic area.

In mid-afternoon on 1 August Komorowski made his way to the new headquarters in the Kamler tobacco factory, facing a narrow cul-de-sac named Pawia Street closed by the wall surrounding the Ghetto and its grim ruins. This headquarters was oddly situated next door to a building on the Ghetto side of the wall housing German troops and guarded by concrete pillboxes facing each of two access streets. According to the plan these troops were to be put out of action promptly at 5 o'clock by Colonel Radóslaw's group of Secret Army shock troops, but they were not mobilised in time.

In his shabby civilian clothes Komorowski shuffled down the untidy street towards the butter-coloured factory, passing within 15 yards of the nearest German pillbox, which he noted was held by a wideawake machine-gun team. Inside the factory he met Lieutenant Kamler, the owner, who informed him that the German garrison next door had been brought up to fifty men, with rifles, grenades and two machine-guns. Kamler had thirty-three men with fifteen rifles, forty grenades and a few of the highly destructive home-made Polish grenades called *filipinka*.

Already upstairs were the Secret Army general staff as well as Jan Jankowski, Deputy Premier and Government delegate, and Kazimierz Puzak, the Socialist chairman of the Council of National Unity. Technicians had set up radio transmitters and receivers for communicating with the world. Everyone was hopeful and excited.

Komorowski cautioned Kamler not to allow his troops to start action against the near-by Germans until the arrival of Colonel Radóslaw's seasoned fighters. But he had forgotten that the Polish sentry at the factory gate was armed with a rifle. A German military vehicle approached. Seeing, of all things, this armed Pole, a German guard in the truck immediately opened fire, but the Polish sentry shot him first. Kamler shot the driver and two German soldiers standing in the back of the lorry. Machine-guns in the two pillboxes opened up with a clatter, spraying the street and the buildings, loosing a burst into the room where Komorowski and his staff were assembled, filling it with plaster and broken glass, but hurting no one.

It was a quarter past four, forty-five minutes before the Uprising was due to begin. Germans in full equipment streamed into the house opposite. Kamler ordered both factory gates to be barricaded with timber, packing-cases, handcarts, anything movable. His fifteen men with rifles and the grenade-throwers were posted at commanding places from the roof to the gates. They reported that the Germans were preparing an attack with supporting fire from their machine-guns.

A Polish grenade-thrower up on the second floor, opposite the window fifteen yards away where the German machine-gunner was firing, threw a *filipinka* and silenced it, killing the gunners, but the Germans also then threw grenades and badly wounded two Polish soldiers.

German security police converged on the scene from their barracks in near-by Leszno Street. Some of them entered the narrow street in the back of an open lorry and drove towards the factory gates beneath the open window. Their comrades in the house opposite tried vainly with signals to urge them back, but too late. Two grenades flung down exploded among them, killing all thirty-five, and the lorry careered off the road, hit the wall and burst into flames.

From across the Ghetto ruins a police attack now began, too heavy for the small force in the factory to ward off while defending itself against the strong offensive from the house opposite. Komorowski was worried. It was nearly 5 o'clock and still there was no sign of Colonel Radóslaw and his men. It would be a calamity as well as the supreme irony if the Secret Army GHQ were to be overwhelmed even before the Uprising had properly begun. They were now pinned down by accurate fire from the security police and the troops opposite.

Suddenly, at 5 o'clock, with a wave of sound rising in a crescendo of rumbling explosions orchestrated by ear-splitting automatic fire the insurrection burst forth in a frenzied onslaught against the German arch-enemy.

Komorowski, cornered with his military staff and the nucleus of the provisional government, hardly dared to move, hoping desperately for aid, later depicted it as Napoleonic in the perfection of its timing:

> At exactly five o'clock [he wrote][13] thousands of windows flashed as they were flung open. From all sides a hail of bullets struck passing Germans, riddling their buildings and their marching formations. In the twinkling of an eye the remaining civilians disappeared from the streets. From the entrances of houses, our men streamed out and rushed to the attack. In fifteen minutes an entire city of a million inhabitants was engulfed in the fight. Every kind of traffic ceased. As a big communications centre where roads from north, south, east and west converged, in the immediate rear of the German front, Warsaw ceased to exist. The battle for the city was on.

Not often does military action achieve such mechanical precision of timing. Human nature intervenes and with a blend of fear and courage paralyses reason, so that someone falls short or exceeds his allotted task, or the enemy reacts uncharacteristically, or the objectives turn out to be too strongly defended, stay in the enemy's hands, and in part at least the day is lost.

On this tremendous first day of the insurrection, the fighting followed just such an uncertain course. During the attack on Komorowski's GHQ a Polish relief force counter-attacked from the rear and drove off the German police unit, but not long after 6 o'clock a shout of alarm and a burst of fire were heard above. Several Polish troops rushed up the narrow stair-case, two of them were hit by shots from the attic door at the top of the stairs and fell back in a heap to the bottom.

Invading the building through the roof the Germans had shot and wounded the sentry there and reached the attic before they were heard. They had to be eliminated quickly and new guards placed on the roof before more arrived. But the attic window and door gave them a commanding position over the narrow staircase up which only one man could pass at a time. Two more Polish troops fell in an attempt to rush the room before an accurately thrown *fillipinka* grenade killed all four of the enemy inside.

Two replacement guards were sent up to the roof, but by now the pace of the German attack had slowed as they were pulled out to reinforce their own positions elsewhere in the city under heavy Polish attack. They now simply loosed off the occasional burst at any window

104

that seemed a likely target. Half an hour later the first of Colonel Radóslaw's GHQ defence troops entered from the roof, the advance guard of the rest of the unit jumping sometimes from roof to roof while under fire, blasting a way through the walls of neighbouring attics when this was impossible.

Directly they were numerous enough to carry out their mission they began a vigorous attack against the German pillboxes and barracks. For the time being the GHQ was safe.

Shortly afterwards Komorowski again heard shouting from the roof, it sounded more joyful than alarmed. He went up the narrow blood-stained stairs with his aide to the roof, where one of the guards gave him a smart salute and a happy smile. 'The flag, sir! The Polish flag!' he shouted with great excitement.[14]

Komorowski looked in the direction the man was pointing towards the tallest building in Warsaw, the sixteen-storey Prudential Building, which dominated the City Centre.

There he saw the white and red flag of Poland floating bravely over the city. Gazing around from the roof-top he now spotted other Polish flags flying from the dome of the Town Hall, the Post Office Savings Bank tower and one or two other buildings.

It was a great moment. No Polish flags had flown there since 1939. Above them a blanket of smoke hung over Warsaw like a giant parachute reddened beneath by the forest of flames leaping from blazing buildings. The roar of the battle grew louder from minute to minute.

Komorowski went downstairs again to hurry the transmission of two important messages to London. The first, jointly from himself as Home Army Commander-in-Chief and Jan Jankowski, Deputy Premier, read:

To the Prime Minister and the Commander-in-Chief: The date for the beginning of a struggle to capture Warsaw was jointly fixed by us for August 1st at 17.00 hours. The struggle has begun.[15]

A surprising message, for even though the Polish Government had empowered Deputy Premier Jankowski to authorise the insurrection when he believed it opportune, it had clearly asked to be told before-hand 'if possible'. It was certainly possible; and the need must have been foremost in Jankowski's mind. Moreover, upon Komorowski lay the imperative duty of telling the Commander-in-Chief, General Sosnkowski, immediately the decision was taken.

But both of them failed to communicate not only until more than twenty-four hours after the fateful order, but also until after the fighting had started, when sending a message had become more complicated — shortly after it was set up the GHQ transmitter was damaged in the action with the Germans. Two Polish soldiers were killed bringing spare parts for it. So this absolutely vital information was not transmitted from Warsaw until noon on 2 August, nearly twenty hours after the fighting had begun, and almost two days after the order had been given.

Whatever the reason, in the light of the Home Army's dependence on outside aid this failure to inform the Allies is strange indeed. Even Komorowski goes some way towards admitting it. 'The fact that no one outside Warsaw knew what was going on made people at GHQ feel uneasy,' he wrote later[16] with careful understatement.

He sent out a message of faith and encouragement to the troops then embattled with the Germans:

> Soldiers of the capital! I have today issued the order which you desire, for open warfare against Poland's age-old enemy, the German invader. After nearly five years of ceaseless and determined struggle, carried on in secret, you stand today openly with arms in hand, to restore freedom to our country and to mete out fitting punishment to the German criminals for the terror and crimes committed by them on Polish soil.[17]
>
> *Commander-in-Chief, Home Army*

Komorowski makes no mention of aid from either the Western Allies or Soviet Russia. It was a significant omission. Was he letting the Secret Army know that they were fighting alone?

Still in Italy, Sosnkowski had reacted furiously to the telegrams he had had from London telling him that fighting in Warsaw was imminent. '...Any thought of an armed rising is an unjustified move devoid of political sense and capable of causing tragic and unnecessary sacrifice in the situation created by...the Soviet policy of violation and *fait accompli*,' he warned, in a message to President Raczkiewicz on 28 July, opposing the Government decision.

> In this spirit I am telegraphing the Home Army Commander. In my opinion the higher authorities of the Republic ought to have realised from the latest events that the experiment of public declaration and co-operation with the Red Army had failed, and should face the consequence of this by reverting to the original principles of the instruction of 27 November 1943...[18]*

In his message that same day to Komorowski, repeating the first part of his message to the President, Sosnkowski added a warning that if the aim of the insurrection was to take possession of part of the Polish territories the Home Army 'will be forced to defend the sovereign status of the Republic...against anyone who attempts to violate this

* It stated that if the Soviets entered Poland while relations between the two states were still broken off, the administrative authorities and the armed forces should stay underground and await further decisions from the Polish Government.

status. You can understand what this would mean in the perspective of the failure of the experiment at co-operation, on account of the ill-will of the Soviets.'

It was a blunt warning from the C-in-C not to launch an uprising at this time, but having received it on 31 July the Government decided to withhold it from Komorowski. Backing for Mikolajczyk in his confrontation with Stalin now outweighed even the C-in-C's condemnation. The telegram would of course not have reached Warsaw in time to stop the Uprising, but the Government were not to know this.

Alarmed by the course of events Sosnkowski again warned Komorowski in another telegram on 29 July, received in London on 2 August, Warsaw on 6 August, that 'the fighting against the Germans must be kept in the frame of the *Tempest* plan. In the present state of affairs I am unconditionally opposed to a universal uprising, the historical outcome of which would be the exchange of one occupation for another. Your assessment of the German situation must be clear and realistic. Any mistake in this area could cost a great deal. At the same time you must conserve all political, moral and physical strength and concentrate it against the annexationist plans of Moscow...'[19]

Sosnkowski, even though the bells of destiny had struck twelve, was continually stressing the doctrine of the 'two enemies'.

A bleak prospect indeed this telegram must have spelt out to Komorowski, then embattled with the Germans in the capital. It meant that there was to be no compromise with Moscow in exchange for military aid. And by now he must have known how great was his error in launching the insurrection at that time of military uncertainty.

From a tactical point of view as we have seen, the Germans were not taken by surprise when fighting flared throughout the capital. They held all their main positions against the Polish attacks—the Vistula bridges, the airport, the radio station, the police and the army headquarters. But General Stahel's predecessors had not drawn up any plan to contain and defeat such an uprising in the city, he had not enough troops to deal with it, he had ordered his units on to the defensive and by shortly after 5 p.m. he was pinned down by the Polish attack on his HQ.

Lacking leadership, the best the Germans could do was to hang on for dear life under the impetus of the initial Polish attacks. For the first few days they had no plan of action of any kind. Their reactions were slow, uncoordinated and lacking direction. All they could do was to fire back with everything they had against anyone, insurgent or civilian; and they were not short of ammunition.

The Home Army troops in their threadbare suits or working clothes kept the initiative at first, though their losses were considerable. If they had been mobilised properly, with a little time to spare and with all the available weapons, they might well in face of the German inactivity have succeeded in seizing some of their major objectives. Komorowski would then have had a different story to tell to London; and Mikolajczyk in Moscow a story that would have had greater impact upon Stalin.

Zenon Kliszko, a leading member of the Communist Polish Workers' Party had left a political meeting during the afternoon of 1 August, and was on his way home to his flat in the Zoliborz district with his ration of sugar for his wife and sixteen-months-old child. Quite suddenly, in the late afternoon, prolonged bursts of shooting echoed near by and he realised that the rumoured Uprising must have begun.

Kliszko felt angry with himself and his Communist political associates for not knowing what thousands of other men and women must have known for hours. In the streets young men, few of them armed, but wearing Home Army red-and-white armbands, were trying to keep order and persuading passers-by to take shelter in gateways. Bullets zipped through the air as heavy firing sounded from all sides.[20]

Kliszko – after the war he became a top member of the Polish Politbureau, but fell from grace in 1971 with Gomulka – took shelter for the time being in the gateway to the courtyard of the last house on Bonifraterska Street among a small crowd of people desperately anxious to get home to their families. Everyone there was talking excitedly and Kliszko heard joy, anxiety and worry about what the next day would bring. He spoke to one or two people, but no one seemed to know what was going on. Nobody guessed that the battle would last for two months and that some of them would never see their nearest and dearest again.

Time passed, it grew dark, the firing went on and the men and women sheltering there with him huddled in the courtyard and doorways of the apartment block and tried to sleep. Kliszko, propped up against a wall, saw the stars of the August night gradually fade as the dawn broke and the Uprising's first night came to an end. One at a time or in threes and fours people left the safety of the building for the empty street and with shoulders hunched walked or ran off in the direction of their homes.

Firing began again from the Citadel direction and now and again one of the running people fell down and stayed down. Kliszko began walking, trying to keep an even pace as the sound of shooting in Wola about a mile south grew suddenly louder, but in Zoliborz it was ominously quiet. He found his wife, mother and daughter free from harm at home. But this first night bore no relation to what was to come.

Irena Orska locked up her apartment early on 1 August and hurried off to Mass at the Church of the Holy Cross. She found it packed with solemn-faced men and women, resigned, but not frightened and so deep in prayer that their words and feelings were almost tangible. She herself was quite unable to pray, although like everyone there she knew what would occur that day. Looking at the statue of the Virgin, she tried in prayer to tell Her of the fate approaching them. She thought of her two brothers and two sisters, all in the Home Army, and then of her teenage daughter, and hoped that she would come to no harm.

After Mass she met Barbarka, her daughter, at Pomianowski's café for a cup of barley coffee. Barbarka told her that at 5 o'clock she was going to report for duty with the Home Army. Mrs Orska was stunned but would not refuse her daughter or try to send her away. Though she feared to lose her she had not the heart. She herself reported for special nursing duty with the Home Army at the Ujazdow Hospital and hurried to see Dr Christopher, a surgeon, and a Home Army medical officer. There were about twenty people in the room, mostly nurses and doctors. Christopher came in just after her, white-haired and nearly seven feet tall, bringing with him his own remarkable air of self-assurance.

He stood before his desk. 'I shall not be the one, my dear ones, to remind you of the long time we have lived under the German occupation or of what it has brought us,' he said. 'These years will not be easily forgotten, for their memory is engraved on our very hearts.

'Today is the great day. Today the people of Warsaw are rising to free the capital from oppression. This is our order, and we shall carry it out. We'll have to conquer the city and hold on for a few days. The Soviet Army is expected to enter Warsaw on the fourth or fifth day of our Home Army's struggle within the city. Is everyone ready? Is everything clear? In the future please report to Colonel Malin, or to myself. Or...wherever God will permit you to report.'[21]

Outside in the bright sunshine Warsaw looked tired but festive. Mrs Orska went back home and had lunch with her daughter. It was a quiet, hot summer afternoon. Suddenly, at a quarter past three, a burst of gunfire shattered the stillness. It must have begun. She ran downstairs, hoping to get to her Red Cross post in time, but the Germans were covering near-by streets with machine-gun fire, so she went back home and set up the post in her tobacco shop instead.

Waclaw Zagorski had just finished printing leaflets for the Home Army on how the Soviet Army was to be greeted when it entered Warsaw. It was half past four when he heard the first shots, while helping his friend Staszek count the leaflets. They left the entrance door of the house stealthily because the air was now alive with bullets. A carload of German officers flashed past them, chased by a car from which young Home Army men in black raincoats fired with revolvers at the enemy.

On the other side of the street was a German factory where fuses for explosives were made and behind the closed gates were about twenty well-armed enemy troops. Zagorski and his friends went back into the workshop, armed themselves with hand-grenades and revolvers from their secret store, then with their weapons concealed beneath their clothes went out into the now silent and empty street.

A squad of about a dozen Home Army men walked quickly towards them, most of them wearing the distinctive armband but only about half of them armed. Zagorski pointed to the gates. 'There are some Germans in there,' he warned. Those Poles with arms began shooting, then all of them combined to break down the gates, rush the yard, and the guards standing there with hands up, seize their rifles and lock them up in the guardroom. One of the Poles was hit and his wounds were dressed by Wanda, a tall dark girl who lived near by.

Soon it was dark and the street was empty. A civilian said that the police in Ciepla Street were walking out of their barracks dressed in plain clothes. Some of the Home Army men ran off to seize their arms. Machine-gun fire and heavy explosions echoed from all sides of the city.

Nobody knew what was happening, or even if the command to start the Uprising was given. But everyone was aware that after five years of enemy occupation freedom was sweeping through the city like a storm.

The rule of the Nazis was ending. A red glow shone in the dark western sky, but people looked to the east, from where hundreds of Soviet tanks were coming. Had they reached the western side of the Vistula yet? But before they came the Home Army would take control of Warsaw in the name of the Polish Republic.[22]

Stefan Korbonski, a Peasant Party leader and member of the Council of National Unity, saw his wife Zosia, his closest collaborator in the underground for five years, walking quickly along Marshall Street to meet him. Before she said a word he realised from the look on her face that she had something urgent to say.[23]

She blurted it out. A close friend of both of them had called on her at 11 o'clock to say good-bye. He had said that the Uprising would begin at 5 o'clock that afternoon, and that he was taking part in an attack on the cavalry barracks.

Korbonski could not believe it and accused his wife of talking nonsense. Did she think he wouldn't know if it were true? Yet he felt a little uncertain, so leaving Zosia waiting in the street he hurried to the secret office of the Directorate of Civil Resistance, of which he was the director.

His deputy, Mr Krajewski, was on duty there and Korbonski asked him whether he had heard anything about the Uprising starting that day. The answer was brief. 'Of course. I was waiting for you, to talk it over with you. I heard about it from friends in the "Bastion" regiment. Action will begin today.'

'Have we received official notification of the matter?'

'No. I have just looked through today's mail, but found nothing about it. But you can take it from me that the rising will begin today.'

Korbonski was furious, unable to understand why this vitally important department of the underground had not been informed. It was now 1 o'clock and he had made no preparations. Arranging with Krajewski that they should meet every day in the DCR hideout he left quickly to meet his wife in the street again. He signed to her from a distance that the report was true.

110

They separated and went to find their radio operators, who were due to call up London that afternoon. Korbonski searched until after 2 o'clock before he found Jan, his operator, and told him that the day and almost the hour had come. Jan had to get quickly to Peacock Street to pick up their secret transmitter. They arranged to meet at the corner of Basket Street and Marshall Street, after which they would go on to the special hideout ready for when the Uprising would begin.

Korbonski reached the rendezvous shortly before 5 o'clock. Walking down Basket Street he saw a youth and a girl emerge from a doorway. They embraced each other passionately. As Korbonski passed the boy gave him a nod of tacit understanding. Korbonski nodded in return, showed the boy his watch and said, 'It's time.' The boy kissed his girl once more then jumped on a passing tram and went off to join his unit.

Soon after Jan arrived, staggering under the weight of a heavy bag on his back containing both the transmitter and the transformers for the radio station. Shortly after him came Zosia. By then they could hear the bursts of firing coming from the direction of Mokotow Field so they entered the house in Marshall Street, where in a loft on the top floor their secret radio station was to be accommodated.

A bleak reception had awaited Prime Minister Mikolajczyk on his arrival in Moscow late on Monday, 31 July, with the Foreign Minister, Count Romer, and Russian-speaking Professor Grabski, Speaker of the Polish Parliament. The next evening at 9.30 his meeting with Foreign Minister Molotov to discuss the agenda for the talks with Marshal Stalin had been even bleaker. Neither Mikolajczyk nor Molotov knew then that the Uprising had already started. According to Molotov, Soviet forces were then about six miles from Warsaw. 'We'll take it soon,' he had remarked airily.[24] The surprise German counter-attack was to begin that very night.

Mikolajczyk was told of the Uprising by the British Embassy and had plenty of time to study Komorowski's almost frantic appeals for help, which were passed on to him by the Embassy. 'I spent a distressing forty-eight hours scanning reports from the Warsaw Underground,' he wrote.[25] These were, of course, calls for arms, and appeals that their fateful expectation of an immediate Soviet attack on the city should at once be made solid fact.

For Mikolajczyk they were poignant days, kicking his heels awaiting Stalin's pleasure, tortured by the knowledge that his fellow-countrymen, citizens as well as the ill-armed Home Army troops, were facing alone the savage might of the Wehrmacht.

Komorowski, who had apparently let himself be pushed into launching the Uprising against his better judgement was now, as the battle raged, face to face with the forbidding shortage of arms and ammunition that had earlier held him back. Waiting to hear on 2 August how the troops had fared in their vital initial attacks upon which the seizure of the city depended must have been a nightmare, though neither then nor later did he admit it.

His anxiety took form in two more radio messages to London, dated 1 August, sent 2 August. The first read: 'Arrange immediately for arms and ammunition to be dropped…in the squares given on to the city: Filtrowa, Kerceli Square, Saxon Gardens, Avenue of the Polish Soldier, Pulawska, Belwederska Streets.'[26]

The second, also signed by Deputy Premier Jan Jankowski, showed how desperately he was waiting for the Soviet attack, Chrusciel's report of which had triggered off the Uprising: 'In view of the fact that fight to capture Warsaw has begun, we ask for Soviet help to be supplied in the shape of an immediate attack from outside.'[27]

Soon Komorowski and the Home Army leaders would know whether the tremendous zeal of his under-armed troops could outweight the greater fire-power and training of the Germans.

In the headquarters in Cracow of Hans Frank, German Governor-General of Poland, General Stahel's report early in the evening of 1 August of an apparent insurrection by the Polish Secret Army caused some alarm, though mainly for the security of the 9th Army's supply routes through Warsaw and across the Vistula to the battleground east of Praga.

At about 6 o'clock SS and Police Chief General Wilhelm Koppe, also Secretary of State for Security Affairs in the General Government, telephoned Colonel Geibel from Cracow for more news, but the Colonel had taken shelter in the basement and could only say that his men were then fighting off a furious attack.[28]

General Koppe said that he would order reinforcements of heavy tanks and artillery to make for Warsaw immediately. Geibel informed General Stahel, who said that in order to conserve his forces he would go on to the defensive until these units arrived. He then threatened over the city loud-hailer system to raze to the ground every house that contained a sniper. In Cracow meantime a state of alarm was called and the garrison was reinforced in expectation of a similar uprising.

Hitler's General Staff took the matter very seriously indeed. Characteristically, the Fuhrer at first decided upon a total withdrawal from Warsaw and a blanket bombing of the city to flatten it completely. But this plan was dropped because many Germans were already pinned down there. He therefore gave the order to Heinrich Himmler for a relief force to be sent instead.[29]

Himmler's first reaction in his headquarters in East Prussia was easy to guess; he wanted blood, to appease his sense of outrage. He chose the man he believed to be the main creator of the Secret Army. General Rowecki was shot at dawn at Sachsenhausen concentration camp on 3 August.

Himmler then assembled a relief force under the command of Lieutenant-General of SS and Police, SS-Gruppenführer Heinz Reinefarth, a lawyer who had made a lightning career in the Nazi Party and the Wehrmacht. He ordered SS-Oberführer Oskar Dirlewanger's anti-partisan brigade of two battalions of 865 released criminals, three battalions of former Soviet war prisoners, two companies of gendarmes and a police platoon, with eight flame-throwers and a five-gun battery of artillery, some 2,500 men, to entrain at once for Warsaw. Supporting it was SS-Brigadeführer Kaminski's Rona Brigade of Ukrainian collaborationists 1,585 men with a battery of four guns. Both left for Warsaw on 3 August.

The next day Himmler flew from East Prussia to Poznan, where he assembled directly under Reinefarth's command a combat group of some 8,000 men equipped with thirty-seven assault guns, four heavy mortars, 150 flame-throwers and including a motorised battalion of incendiary police and a company of heavy tanks. In support was Colonel Wilhelm Schmidt's group, 2,000 strong, consisting of three battalions of Schmidt's 603 Regiment, a battalion of grenadiers, a police battalion, two platoons of No. 500 SS Assault Battalion, a detachment of artillery, eight flame-throwers, armoured train No. 75 and fifteen heavy mortars. Total strength of Reinefarth's group was about twelve thousand men.[30]

On 3 August General von Vormann sent another 1,000 East Prussian Grenadiers to Praga to help hold the Poniatowski bridge and another three battalions of this regiment to reinforce the SS Hermann Goering Regiment, which was assigned the task of clearing the route through Warsaw to the Kierbedz bridge. Meantime Colonel Geibel obtained a company of tanks from the 'Viking' Division, consisting of four 'Tiger' one 'Panther', four medium tanks and an assault gun to reinforce his militarised police units.

Command over all of these and the other German troops in Warsaw was apparently on 3 August given to General of SS and Police Erich von dem Bach-Zelewski, a Prussian Nazi and an ardent supporter of Hitler, whom Himmler had in January 1943 appointed Chief of Anti-Partisan Combat Units. Von dem Bach, chosen for the task because of his experience and his ruthlessness, was on 1 August 1944 near Gdansk, supervising the building of fortifications on the Vistula. Immediately after Himmler telephoned and gave him the appointment he set out for Cracow to organise more reinforcements with the aid of General Koppe. He was therefore not to arrive in Warsaw until 5 August.[31]

Himmler meantime, in a special decree of unparalleled barbarity ordered that not only every insurgent but also every inhabitant of Warsaw was to be killed. No taking of prisoners was to be allowed. Rape, torture, looting, murder — nothing was forbidden. Warsaw was going to be razed to the ground to set a terrifying example to the rest of Europe.[32]

10/   First days

From the outset the Polish Home Army was faced with the problem of street fighting between units without radio links cut off from each other by intervening buildings. Each battalion, company or platoon fought independently, Polish and German positions formed a chessboard of hundreds of separate battle actions. These actions the Home Army launched with all the fervour of a revolutionary uprising in the fifteen kilometres of the city and its suburbs stretching from Bielany in the north to Mokotow in the south, and the ten kilometres from Praga in the east to Wola in the west.

Never before in history had insurgents tried to take over so big a town or city; nor had the difference in military power between the two sides ever been so marked.

Weapons apart, success in these conditions depended greatly on the capabilities, courage and leadership of junior commanders. On these levels the Poles proved themselves superior. In the first days of the Uprising, before the arrival of German reinforcements, their aggression, resilience and speedy action enabled them to outweigh the heavy armament as well as the rigidity of the German military hierarchy. Unfortunately, Polish junior commanders too often lost their lives owing to courage or impetuosity amounting to foolhardiness; but when one fell another spontaneously replaced him.

The Germans managed to maintain constant radio links between their commanders and units out in the city, whereas at some time or other during their assignments the Polish messenger women — the sole means of communication — were pinned down by heavy fire from enemy tanks or machine-gun posts, or killed.

But a way was at once improvised to allow freedom of movement from one district to another. Aided by the citizens, Home Army sappers blasted entrances in the cellar walls from house to house and created sign-posted subterranean routes. Through them voluntary traffic wardens directed the flow of wounded, arms, ammunition and messenger women. This underground system lasted until heavy bombing blasted the houses into rubble down to the very cellars.

Late in the afternoon of 2 August reports of the ebb and flow of the fighting began to reach Komorowski in his GHQ in Wola, the north-western bastion of the insurrection, where he was to spend the first six days. Wola, a working-class district, was captured early on 2 August, thus closing one of the east–west routes to the Germans for the time being. The important main Post Office building had been captured and later the water filter station and the gas works.

The fight for the vital electric power station, facing Good Street on the Vistula embankment, which guaranteed the electric power needed among other things for manufacturing weapons in the underground workshops went on for nineteen hours. Some weeks before the Uprising the Germans had strengthened the defences of this extensive plant along the river with barbed-wire, trenches and pillboxes and brought up to 150 the strength of the troops holding it inside and outside.

Just before 5 o'clock its telephone links with Stahel's and Geibel's headquarters were cut and a few minutes later a mine laid beneath one of the German pillboxes had signalled the Uprising by blowing it to pieces. Among the white-hot furnaces, the throbbing steam turbines and the whirring dynamos kept running by a skeleton staff, a battle began between Polish technicians and workers against the police, or *Werk-schutz*, as the Germans called them.

At the same time Home Army detachments launched an attack outside from Leszzynski Street, which joined Good Street at right angles opposite the main plant entrance. Fighting was fierce and casualties were heavy on both sides before the Germans gave up when the Polish director called on them to surrender after 17 hours' fighting. Although the cranes which carried the coal to the furnaces were shattered by German 88-mm artillery fire after the capture, so that wheelbarrows had to be pressed into service, the dynamos and other equipment were intact and the production of current went on without interruption.

The night sky on 2 August was lit by the angry red glow of many huge fires which raged despite the rain. Two-thirds of this inferno were occupied by the Home Army, including the Stare Miasto (Old Town) of narrow streets and tall medieval houses and churches, the districts of Powiśle and Czerniakow along the bank of the Vistula, and most of the City Centre. The Germans still held the Brühl Palace, which was Stahel's GHQ, the Szuch Avenue Gestapo HQ, the importantly situated Bank of National Economy, the Parliament buildings and other strongpoints.

The attack on Okecie Airport, possession of which was vital for the aid Komorowski and his Staff hoped would fly in from the west, began with confusion. Major Wisczowski, whose assault group was to make the attack, countermanded it at the last moment because he was too far below strength. His order failed to reach all the units in time; and at 1700 hours some of his units attacked the airport perimeter defences. They were mown down by machine-gun fire in open ground.[1]

A Polish officer then rushed up with the countermanding order and the units began to pull back, but an enemy armoured car sped up to this confused scene and shot down more than 120 insurgents, including practically all the officers. The remainder were scattered throughout the area, some retreating to Mokotow, others were killed in further battles.

Attacks on the Vistula bridges from the Praga embankment also failed. The Kierbez Bridge was defended by strong German forces in the city park. The insurgent attack was thrown back with heavy losses. No more successful was the attack on the Poniatowski bridge, carried out by an under-strength and under-armed unit which was destroyed by fire from the bridge turrets. Home Army troops also failed to occupy the near-by city park, from where they could have harassed the German defenders. The western entrances to the bridges changed hands in fierce fighting several times within the first thirty-six hours before they were finally held by the Germans.

In Praga itself strong German tank units met the initial fierce Home Army onslaughts launched by mostly understrength battalions. One battalion, commanded by Lieutenant-Colonel Stefan, in its attack on a German barracks where Home Army units were to assemble after destroying the enemy, was repulsed by tank units stationed there. Desperately, the Polish commander ordered another attack, but even heavier losses forced him to give up and take cover.

Major Ludwik's Praga detachments seized the railway control centre at the corner of Targowa Street and Wilenska Street, completely disorganising the Wilno station. His units also destroyed two German tanks and occupied a telephone exchange. But a squadron of Tiger and Panther tanks opened fire on the railway building and other near-by objectives taken by the insurgents. Many were killed, the rest forced to retreat. By night time on 2 August the Praga detachments were defending themselves in isolated groups and the Uprising there was over as a serious threat to the Germans.

Janusz Tomaszewski, aged 11, had graduated to the Baszta Regiment from the underground 'Grey Column' scouts. On 31 July he was ordered to join his platoon at a villa near to a German-occupied school at the corner of Narbuta and Kazimierzowska Streets in Mokotow, because fighting was expected to start; but it was a false alarm. Some of the men went home and others stayed in the villa awaiting the new zero hour, and among them Tomaszewski — now a captain in Warsaw's River Police. Mokotow, the Uprising's southern bastion, barred the Germans' southerly access to the City Centre and its bridges.

At 3 p.m. on 1 August Tomaszewski was issued with a revolver and a few rounds of ammunition and told to be ready at 5 o'clock for an attack on the school, occupied by three hundred SS. Like all the initial attacks on the first day it had been planned as a surprise night attack, so that when zero hour was unfortunately changed from 3 a.m. to 5 p.m. it became doubly dangerous. The Poles could no longer count on the surprise factor and the inherent dangers of an attack on this well-fortified building were much greater in daylight.

Already, before 5 o'clock, they could hear in the distance the sounds of firing and of heavy explosions. They still waited. Finally, the orders came and the attack on the school began with an advance across an open potato field. But the enemy were on the alert and this first attack was beaten back by machine-guns on the roof and in concrete bunkers at every corner of the building. The folly of mounting in daytime attacks originally planned for the night became tragically clear.

Another attack was planned for 3 a.m. Over the centre of the city they saw a red glow and clouds of dark billowing smoke, heard the distant crash of guns and the crackle of automatic fire warning them fighting had not ceased there.

It began to rain. The SS in the school now and then fired their machine-guns or tossed grenades at random in the direction of the Polish lines, clearly with the object of showing they had no shortage of ammunition. The Home Army men on their part kept quiet and did not reply, in the knowledge that every single bullet or grenade must be used to good effect.

The attack began at 4 a.m. with a rush in the rain on the German positions. Heavy explosions thudded in the darkness as demolition squads blew down gates and doors. Petrol bombs flared, grenades crashed and the sudden rattle of automatic fire signalled that the outer strongpoints were overcome and the attack had moved on to defenders on staircases and inner rooms.

At one point Janusz found himself faced by Germans in a narrow passage. He fired his revolver while the enemy were attacked from the other direction and shot down. The impetus of the night attack began to pay off and soon those Germans still alive retreated, leaving the school in Polish hands. Losses had been heavy, but the attack was successful, the strongpoint had been taken and with it a large quantity of arms and ammunition.[2]

Elsewhere in Mokotow during the night a number of other detachments which had failed to take their objectives had retired across country to the Kabacki Forest. Only small units were left in southern Mokotow. The Germans then moved in with strong forces of tanks along Sobieski Avenue, from Wilanow, and although the insurgents had built anti-tank barricades and other obstacles they were driven back by heavy gunfire. Many were killed or wounded and the rest of these forces fled to the Kabacki Forest.

Only Lieutenant-Colonel Daniel's group still hung on. In the early hours of 2 August he concentrated his remaining troops into a district of solid concrete apartment houses between Odynca and Pulawski Streets and Niepodleglosci Avenue and there held out.

During the first night's fighting, more than 2,000 Home Army troops were killed or wounded. About 5,000 left the city to hide in the surrounding woods after they had failed to take their objectives. A considerable amount of arms and ammunition had been captured, but much was lost, especially in the suburbs, where caches fell into German hands.

Chrusciel's objectives—the seizure of the city, the closure of the bridges across the Vistula and the capture of arms—had fallen far short of attainment, but the Old Town and Wola, the north-western bastion of the Uprising, were cleared of the enemy. In Praga, Okecie, Bielany, Ochota, and parts of Mokotow the Germans still held out. About two-thirds of the western river bank were in Home Army hands, including Powisle and Czerniakow, although the Germans held strongpoints in Polish areas and also dominated wedges of territory there, thus splitting them into isolated sectors.

Huge fires raged throughout the city. Petrol storage tanks were ablaze, as well as thousands of houses, the railway centre in Praga and numerous big buildings. 'The struggle is in the nature of a general action all over the city,' Komorowski reported in a radio message to London on 3 August.[3]

Focus points of the struggle are scattered over the whole area with the exception of Zoliborz. Our own forces in Zoliborz were dispersed by enemy armour and withdrew in a westerly direction.

The beginning of the struggle was quite critical, as we were fighting to retain the initiative. At present the initiative is in our hands, as the continual extension of the areas we hold shows. The spirit and morale of the commanders and soldiers is magnificent. The people are enthusiastically co-operating in the struggle. The streets of the city are intersected by numerous barricades, the national flag is flying over captured objectives.

We are fighting effectively against heavy tanks, of which we have already destroyed or damaged over a dozen. Those damaged we are already putting to good use in the advancement of our own operations.

So far the situation is not difficult for us, though the German attack is supported by armour and anti-aircraft guns...

In the centre and western part of the city the struggle is very intense. During August 2nd enemy attempts to recapture conquered positions and streets were repulsed. The enemy is attaching special importance to recovering and clearing the main thoroughfares of the city. Heavy struggles are being waged for the General Post Office, which we captured yesterday at 16.35 hours...

Attacks four times repeated on the Telephone Exchange yielded no results. The enemy is blowing up certain bunkers, which he cannot hold, and is burning buildings, especially in the suburbs.

We have inflicted very heavy losses in men and motorized equipment on the enemy; we have taken prisoners. We are afraid of nothing except a shortage of ammunition. We have not sufficient arms for the volunteers, in sporadic cases members of the Polish Workers' Party, who are reporting to us for co-operation with the Polish Home Army. No organised detachments except those of the Home Army have yet been reported.

In another message on the same day Komorowski[4] nervously complained about lack of support. 'We are waiting for supplies to be dropped. The Soviet artillery can be heard. We do not notice any Soviet attack on the city...'

German fighting tactics also drew a strong protest from him in a third message on 3 August. He requested that the accusation should be passed on through neutral channels to the German command in Warsaw that the Germans were using civilians as human shields, binding men and women to tanks and dragging them along the street, and similar atrocities. He advised the German Command in Warsaw that he had ordered 'ruthless repressive measures to be applied to Germans in the hands of the Home Army'; but nevertheless reprisals were at no time officially carried out.

Meantime, despite the dangers and discomforts which they had to face, the people of the capital made common cause with the troops. Boys, girls and women joined in the task of building barricades with anything from furniture to motor cars, while along the streets of battle national flags fluttered, a symbol of defiance and a gesture of support for the Republic. 'The whole capital, possessed with the fervour of struggle, is fighting the Germans and obliterating the traces of bondage. Not a single political organisation is fighting independently, everything is united round the country's armed forces,' noted Mr Jan Jankowski, the Deputy Premier.[5]

But already the shortage of ammunition which had dissuaded Komorowski from starting the Uprising during the last days of July had become a tormenting anxiety after little more than three days and nights of fighting. Reserves were falling quickly from hour to hour; lack of weapons prevented the great numbers of volunteers from going into action.

Komorowski knew of the technical problems which a flight with a heavy load of ammunition from England to Warsaw and then back involved, and that little support could be expected. But now that he found himself in a bloody battle against the savage German cohorts he could do no other than plead for bullets and guns. For the intensity of the fighting never flagged. Many of the Home Army's key positions in areas they had seized had been consolidated by the eager troops, while the Germans had been partially expelled from the northern suburb of Zoliborz which had at first been lost.

Everyone during these first four days was asking the same puzzling question: 'When are the Russians coming in? When will the Red Army help us?' After all, the word had gone round in the beginning that advance Soviet units were entering Praga and would soon be crossing the Vistula. And now, despite the red glow in the sky above Warsaw, the Soviet radio was silent both of appeals to fight and reports that Warsaw was fighting. Many people, listening anxiously to Moscow Radio for its response to the Uprising it had so fervently called for, were bewildered. Something seemed out of joint. They noticed that the Red Air Force had ceased operations over the city, but consoled themselves with the fact that the Luftwaffe too had for the time being vanished from the skies.

They may have surmised that both air forces were engaged in the battle east of Praga in the Wolomin–Radzymin area during the first four days of August, for the sound of artillery rumbled on and on there, a distant accompaniment to the crash and rattle of the fighting in the near-by streets and squares.

Mikolajczyk's meeting with Stalin took place as arranged at 9.30 in the evening on 3 August in the conference room in the Kremlin, the Soviet dictator juxtaposed beneath vivid oil paintings of the two great Tsarist generals Suvorov and Kutozov. Mikolajczyk tried ineffectually to impress Stalin by introducing himself as a peasant who had risen through his own exertions. Almost at once the talks began to founder over the issue of the Polish Committee of National Liberation which Stalin had sponsored in Moscow and which he recognised as the Polish administration in liberated areas; and over Poland's future frontiers.

Stalin brought the Home Army into the argument. 'What is an army without artillery, tanks and an air force' he demanded. 'They are even short of rifles. In modern warfare such an army is of little use. They are small partisan units, not a regular army. I was told that the Polish Government has ordered these units to drive the Germans out of Warsaw. I wonder how they could possibly do this, their forces are not up to that task...'[6]

'I agree that they are short of arms,' Mikolajczyk answered. 'I have a telegram from the Lublin area, where there are three divisions of the Home Army. If they were supplied with arms, they would be able to render significant service in further battles. I have the highest admiration for these men who in such circumstances have continued to fight and have even manufactured machine guns in caves...I hope, Marshal, that you share my opinion that our men of the Home Army are admirable, for, in spite of the shortages of arms, they have been carrying out the orders of their Government and have continued to fight.'

'Perhaps,' Stalin said, 'they wish to fight, but as a matter of fact they are unable to do so. What a pity. They are good soldiers, but they need arms to fight and they have none.'[7]

The meeting ended at midnight, after Stalin had insisted that Mikolajczyk should meet members of the Committee of National

Liberation on 5 August to discuss the formation of a new united Polish Government, including members of the Committee. But the talks then inevitably foundered over the Committee's wish to allocate only four cabinet seats to the London Government and keep the remaining fourteen for themselves.

General Michal Zymierski, commander of the communist People's Army, told Mikolajczyk that he had requested Stalin to supply arms for the insurgents and to issue orders to the Red Army to treat the city of Warsaw with consideration. He said that in his presence Stalin had dictated appropriate orders to Marshal Rokossovsky. Ten divisions of Rokossovsky's army were said to be between Warsaw and Deblin, sixty miles south-east, ready to turn the flanks of the Germans from south and west. Zymierski then spoke of the problem of dropping arms from the air to an embattled city. 'This could only be done in the neighbourhood of Warsaw and also in the Praga area, from whence the arms must be transported to the city. Arms must be provided, but how? The difficulty is increased by the lack of any liaison.'[8] The meeting ended without any real results.

Mikolajczyk had so far made little progress. At the same time reports of the savage fighting in Warsaw continued to reach him. His suspicions, later to grow into accusations, that the Russians were deliberately withholding aid were born in Moscow at this time. He awaited with anxiety his final meeting with Stalin.

Komorowski awoke in the early hours of 4 August with an uneasy feeling associated with the sound of battle that he could not at first understand.[9] Not far away a tank fired its heavy gun from time to time and the windows rattled. Suddenly he knew what had disturbed him. The artillery that had rumbled on and on for days across the Vistula in the east was silent. The distant noise of battle had ended. So struck was he with this fact that he awoke Pelczynski, his Chief of Staff, and Jankowski, the Deputy Premier. The strange silence across the Vistula surprised them also. Together, trying to find a reason for it, they ascribed it to a temporary lull in the fighting, but none of them guessed that it would be five weeks before they would hear that artillery again.

It was an event that for the first time cast real uncertainty over the question of how long the fighting in the city would last. For if the end of the sound of battle meant, incredibly, that the Germans had stopped the Soviets, temporarily of course, their hope that the Uprising would end in four, or at the most eight days, had all at once become a cruel joke, with a background of the starkest tragedy.

That afternoon, in the first German air raid since the Uprising began, yellow-nosed Messerschmitt fighters swooped low over Warsaw's broad avenues and huge squares to strafe troops and civilians; shortly after, twenty-four bombers launched incendiaries and high explosive bombs on Wola.

121

These two developments – the lull in the Soviet offensive and a German air raid that presaged many more – brought into sharp and painful focus the urgent question of Home Army ammunition.

Troops were still seizing ammunition and weapons in this battle for equipment, but not nearly enough, and even with their own arsenals working round the clock reports from district commanders stressed that four days were the most they could carry on fighting at the present intensity.

Komorowski knew that miracles apart an end to the fighting in four days was impossible. They would not surrender; the Germans would go on attacking. And he now had to rethink his belief in Chrusciel's report of 31 July that the Red Army would soon enter Warsaw. 'I was fully aware that the army under my command was a revolutionary one,' he wrote later. 'Its successes were due to the drive which enabled its soldiers to charge and take a strongly fortified enemy position, often without the help of even a heavy machine-gun.'[10]

To rein them in and check their drive by controlling the use of ammunition would be like taking their best weapon away from them. The consequent risk of weakening their morale would be great. Komorowski had to weigh this against the even greater danger of allowing the fighting to peter out owing to lack of ammunition and thus exposing everyone to Nazi barbarism. The answer was clear. Trigger-happy shooting and uncontrolled bursts from automatic weapons must stop. Henceforward, bullets must be fired as carefully as if they were torpedoes and operations should be launched for sound tactical reasons only.

Nevertheless, Komorowski put his pen to this order regretfully. And on the same day he sent another top priority message to London: 'I categorically demand help in ammunition and anti-tank weapons forthwith and on the days ensuing. A struggle lasting several days at least awaits us and we must be supplied throughout that time. We have staked everything on holding the capital. Muster strength for the effort.'[11] In a succeeding message he named the Jewish Cemetery, Napoleon Square and the Little Ghetto as dropping-points. 'Our ability to hold out in the struggle depends on receiving ammunition from you,' he stressed.[12]

For three years Royal Air Force Halifax and Liberator aircraft had intermittently dropped arms and ammunition into Poland at isolated places prearranged and carefully guarded. These operations were geared to a system perfected over the years of German occupation. The BBC Polish programme signalled an intended drop on any given night by playing an agreed melody and its cancellation by another one. Still another indicated the dropping-place, for each of these known places was identified by its own melody. Signal lights pointed the precise dropping zones; and now this system had been extended to Warsaw. From the night of 1 August observers were ready in captured squares and parks on the secret list.

Since the news of the fighting was received in London on 2 August Churchill had been trying to help Warsaw. Like King George VI and President Roosevelt he had received an urgent plea for help from Poland's President Raczkiewicz. It had been supported by letters from General Sosnkowski to Field-Marshal Sir Alan Brooke, Chief of the Imperial General Staff, to Sir Archibald Sinclair, Secretary of State for Air and to General Wilson, Allied Commander in the Mediterranean Area.

Churchill took action. The highly unrealistic Polish requests for the dropping of the Polish Parachute Brigade and the landing of the four Polish bomber squadrons in Poland were rightly rejected at once. But to Air Marshal Sir John Slessor, Air C-in-C for the Mediterranean and the Middle East, Churchill sent an emergency signal early on 3 August revealing the Uprising. He ordered that ammunition and weapon drops, if technically possible, be started at once from RAF bases in southern Italy, nearly a thousand miles away from Warsaw.

RAF 148 Squadron of 334 Wing was detailed for this impossible task, a formation which specialised in sorties over enemy-occupied territory. All the seven Polish crews in 1586 Flight attached to 148 Squadron and seven British crews experienced in night flights over Poland took off.

Bad weather stopped flying on the night of 3 August, but fourteen Halifaxes and Liberators set out on the night of 4 August on this long and hazardous journey over German-occupied territory. Having survived the concentrated attacks of German night-fighters *en route* their task was to fly at roof-top height through the thick blanket of smoke and the curtain of anti-aircraft fire over the flaming city and drop their containers in places signalled by the Poles.

On the evening of 4 August however the BBC played melodies signalling a supply drop outside Warsaw. Someone, it seemed, had a bad ear for music, but observer teams were on the alert throughout the capital and in the early hours an engine note unlike any German one was heard in the starry skies. Two Halifax bombers had succeeded in getting through and had dropped 24 containers of weapons and ammunition, of which 12 only fell into insurgent hands. It was, of course, chicken feed in relation to the dire needs of the Home Army's 42,000 men, yet the gallant flight cheered the city's lonely fighters with the thought that perhaps after all they were not alone. Five aircraft were lost.[13]

To Air Marshal Slessor the risk that three or four such flights would wipe out his specialist crews and long-range aircraft in return for small returns was too great. He was also convinced that the lives of his airmen should not be exposed in pursuit of impossible objectives. He imposed a ban on further flights to Warsaw.

The order caused something of an uproar among members of the Polish Government in London. And in Warsaw, having received no more drops, Komorowski signalled London on 6 August:

I have to state that in her present struggle Warsaw is getting no aid from the Allies, just as Poland got no aid in 1939. We demand that you should clearly state this fact to the British in an official declaration and leave it on record. We are not asking for material help; we claim that it should be immediately forthcoming. Failure to drop ammunition may soon put us in a difficult situation, especially if the enemy, applying the barbarous method of burning down houses, uses heavy arms in larger quantities in support.[14]

Strong pressure forced Slessor to countermand his order in favour of the Polish crews of 1586 Flight, who had volunteered to fly in the teeth of the high odds against survival. Three aircraft carrying arms and ammunition flew off on 8 August, reached Warsaw and dropped their containers. Some of these fell into the hands of the Home Army and some of them became German booty. On the night of 9 August another four Polish-crewed aircraft took off, but could not reach the city and dropped their loads in the near-by Kampinos Forest, which they knew to be the hideout of many hundred insurgents. There were no losses on these two flights, though the aircraft were badly damaged.

The nature of the struggle for Warsaw now began to change. Komorowski's order to conserve ammunition had precisely limited operations to attacks on objectives needed for consolidating present positions and attacks necessary for preparing future offensives. So inevitably Home Army impetus was checked.

The Germans however were now attacking more and more with heavy tanks. Polish arsenals undertook mass-manufacture of incendiary bottles with which to counter them, but the increase of German armour presented a difficult challenge. These Panzers, the spearhead of the counter-attack which Himmler had organised, were now about to assault the working-class suburb of Wola, western bastion of the Uprising.

11/   The Germans counter-attack

During 4 August 1944 advance detachments of the German relief force under the overall command of Lieutenant-General Heinz Reinefarth detrained near Wola, on the western outskirts of Warsaw. Reinefarth reported to General Niklaus von Vormann's headquarters at Skierniewicz, forty-five miles south-west of the city, where the 9th Army Commander informed him that the Uprising was more dangerous than had at first been believed; and that he doubted whether the relief force would be strong enough to crush it completely.[1]

At this time the Home Army still blocked the German lines of communication across the city to the Vistula bridges and so effectively that the Germans had been forced to erect two pontoon replacements, one north at Bielany and the other south, at Siekierki. All German military traffic was forced to take these roundabout routes.

The Old Town, entirely in Polish hands, and Mokotow partly so, cut the German routes to the north, west and south. Home Army troops had also seized the Post Office Station, built astride the main Warsaw railway from east to west, which they thus controlled. In the tunnel beneath they had derailed a train and near by had blown up lengths of rail. Before the Uprising an average of fifty military supply trains went through the station every twenty-four hours, but owing to this accurate demolition not one got through to the east during the entire battle.

The German 9th Army War Diary[2] reported on 4 August that while all the efforts of the 9th Army were directed at blocking the Soviet forces in the Magnuszew area (some forty-five miles south east of Warsaw) operations against the Soviet 8th Tank Corps in the Praga sector had had to be abandoned to a large extent. Referring to the Uprising it said: 'The situation in Warsaw is basically the same. The centre of the city is completely in the hands of the insurgents. The attack from the east to re-open communications could not proceed because a regiment of the Kaminski brigade, only partly in uniform, was to attack from the west towards Ochota, and it was considered desirable to avoid any mistaken fighting between the two groups.'

Reinefarth's formations, according to von Vormann's orders, were to strike east from Wola along the line of Chłodna Street–the Saxon Gardens–the Brühl Palace, in order to drive off the Polish force pinning down General Stahel there, and relieve him. The relief force was promised Luftwaffe fighter and bomber support, a company of heavy tanks from the SS Hermann Goering Regiment and artillery bombardment from the heavy guns of No. 75 armoured train.

General Rohr's group was also to fight east and parallel along Jerusalem Avenue towards the river. Altogether about 7,300 men, it consisted of Kaminski's Ukrainians, a Panzer assault company, a company from the SS Viking Division, a battalion of pioneers, about 3,000 men from Geibel's militarised police and 500 from Okecie airport garrison supported by nine tanks and a field gun.

Meanwhile on the evening of 4 August the 9th Army issued a report that the insurgents still fought fiercely, even though they had suffered heavy losses. Despite air attacks they were holding on to all the main crossroads, so that any German sortie or movement caused them heavy losses. German positions in the Ghetto ruins were under attack by insurgents with a field-gun mounted on a lorry.

Less organised insurgent groups were more or less quiet, while Praga was subdued. In the southern part of the city a large force of insurgents had been annihilated by the Luftwaffe, while in the southwest there was silence. 'It is becoming more and more apparent,' the report mistakenly observed, 'that the majority of the people are taking no part in the Uprising.'[3]

The night passed quietly in Wola. The Home Army and the population spent it digging anti-tank ditches and strengthening barricades. Fortunately some of the containers dropped by the RAF—with valuable Piat anti-tank weapons and light machine-guns—fell in Wola. Home Army Intelligence reported the arrival of German reinforcements and of the armoured train in the sector. The defenders were about four thousand strong. They were expecting a heavy attack by some twelve thousand seasoned troops supported by tanks and artillery.

What sort of troops were these with which the Germans were to counter-attack? Von dem Bach, the anti-partisan expert, on his way to command in Warsaw, testified later[4] of Dirlewanger's criminal brigade:

Although their moral qualities left much to be desired, their fighting ability was extremely high. This brigade was composed exclusively of released criminals who were offered a pardon if they showed valour in battle. They had nothing to lose and everything to win. They exposed their lives without hesitation for this reason. They knew that they were respected neither by their own officers nor the enemy. They gave no mercy in battle and did not expect any. As a result they suffered losses three times as great as those of any other German unit…They had enormous experience of anti-partisan fighting, which they had been carrying out for years. All in all, Dirlewanger's brigade possessed the highest fighting qualities. To remove it from the battle would have been nothing less than to give up any idea of an offensive.

In contrast, the Poznan police group were, in von dem Bach's view, useless for attack, because they lacked the necessary impetus. They were used for attack only when the enemy position was destroyed by flame-throwers or artillery. Yet they excelled at defending a position once this had been taken. Discipline was very much better than in Dirlewanger's brigade.

Von dem Bach said that Colonel Schmidt's reserve regiment were well-trained troops dependable for any infantry job, but matter-of-fact, lacking any sort of joy in their trade ('Freude am Handwerk'!) or any real enthusiasm for fighting like the Dirlewanger criminals he praised so much. This was counterbalanced by their experience in frontal attack, their good equipment and the fact that they were led by thoroughly experienced officers and non-commissioned officers.

The commanding officer, Colonel Schmidt, was the real source of the worth of this regiment. His experience of warfare, his tactical talent and his readiness to engage himself personally in the battle were outstanding among the officers in Warsaw. 'He was both the soul and the father of his regiment.'

The Ukrainian collaborationists, or Cossacks, led by SS-Brigadeführer Kaminski, a deserter from the Red Army, were in von dem Bach's view the lowest of the low. 'The fighting value of these Cossacks was, as usual in such a collection of people without fatherland, very poor. They had a great liking for alcohol and other excesses and had no understanding of military discipline.'

Shortly after dawn on 5 August Luftwaffe bombers flying without fighter cover zoomed low over the roofs of Wola to drop high explosive and incendiary bombs. The whole of this working-class district of mostly wooden houses was soon a mass of flames. Civilians—women, children and old people—poured out of their homes with what belongings they could carry and trudged towards the City Centre, where all looked quiet.

The German counter-attack had begun.

At 6 o'clock units of Dirlewanger's and Schmidt's infantry in tight columns behind tanks attacked along Wolska and Gorczewska Streets towards Kercely Square and down Chlodna and Ogrodowa Streets. After the tanks had shot up the Polish barricades the infantry, some using flame-throwers, rushed up to them and attacked at close quarters with hand-grenades, retiring only after many had fallen. A heavy German tank was blown up by a mine at half past eight at the corner of Mlynarska and Gorczewska Streets.

Kaminski's Cossacks had attacked along Grojecka Street towards

Narutowicz Square to try to seize the districts south of Wola on the insurgents' left flank. At the same time the Germans launched an attack on the cemeteries in this district which, held by the Home Army troops, were stopping access through Wola towards the City Centre.

Bombs and mortar shells burst among the tombstones, bullets from machine-gun crossfire whined and ricocheted among the marble statuary. Strafed from the air and heavily attacked on the ground the Poles, suffering heavy casualties, fell back from the Calvinist cemetery to Okopowa Street.

Profiting by this advance, the German troops attacked Polish positions in the near-by Evangelist cemetery and by about 4 o'clock took it by storm, going on to sweep Okopowa Street with machine-gun fire. Colonel Radóslaw, in charge of the Polish group defending Wola, reinforced the Jewish cemetery and Okopowa Street along the western boundaries of the Ghetto ruins with two battalions of shock troops. Two German tanks captured by Home Army troops opened fire on the advancing German troops and checked their advance, but the near-by hospital of Saint Mary and Saint Charles was overrun by Dirlewanger's criminal regiment and everyone there shot.

The captured tanks then attacked German positions in the Ghetto, which included a concentration camp of Jews from all over Europe. Nazi camp guards cheered wildly at the tanks' approach. In retribution for their inhuman treatment of the Jewish prisoners they were shot out of hand and some three hundred and fifty Jews set free.

A little later in the summer evening, darkened by smoke and reddened by flames leaping from whole streets of burning buildings, the two captured tanks again strafed the German infantry in the cemeteries, after which they were driven out by a Polish counter-attack, leaving behind a large number of dead and many weapons.

During the night the weary troops on both sides rested, but the Luftwaffe again heralded the next morning, 6 August, with low-level fighter and bomber attacks, sometimes no more than a hundred feet high, on barricades in Kercely Square and the Chlodna–Towarowa crossroads. The 10th and the 11th Home Army assault groups manning the barricades were decimated. Units of Dirlewanger's brigade then advanced along Chlodna and Electoralna Streets towards the Brühl Palace in Theatre Square without meeting serious opposition. Thus in a daring raid the Germans had driven a thin wedge through the Polish lines in Wola to the City Centre, while a further attack by Dirlewanger's troops in the cemetery area had pinned down Colonel Radóslaw's group.

Captain Sosna held Wronia Street, leading to Radóslaw's position and Komorowski requested Chrusciel, commander of the Warsaw troops, to order a counter-attack along this street, or along the Mirowski Market, to relieve Radóslaw's men. Chrusciel replied that he had only enough arms and ammunition for defensive action, and declared that he would sit tight and wait for the arrival of the Red Army.[5] It appears that this commander, whose belief that the Soviets were about to enter Warsaw had started the insurrection, was making it the yardstick of all his subsequent action.

Headquarters of Captain Sosna's group was in the Haberbusch Brewery, Krochmalna Street, also a 'cage' for German prisoners. At 7 a.m. on 6 August, German bombs hit the brewery, killing fifty-seven prisoners and setting a hospital next door on fire. Nurses and attendants in the hospital carried patients and wounded out from the burning building under fire from tanks.

Half an hour later Dirlewanger's criminal regiment and Reinefarth's flame-thrower unit, followed by Schmidt's regiment, attacked behind tanks along Ogrodowa, Krochmalna and Chlodna Streets in an effort to extend their wedge in the Polish positions. The main weight of the attack hit the barricade at the Chlodna–Wronia crossroads. Both Polish commanders were badly wounded here.

Captain Sosna's headquarters informed him that all ammunition had been used. He ordered a retreat and gave permission to quit the fighting area to all unarmed troops – they had been awaiting the arms of the fallen, or those of German prisoners. On receiving the order to retreat Lieutenant Berbostawki led his company in a counter-attack. He was never seen again; his troops were driven off with heavy losses.

The main Polish forces and the walking wounded in this vital area of the western City Centre fell back several hundred yards through Mirowski Square to the Palace of Justice in Leszno, leaving weak rearguards on what remained of the barricades. Aircraft first, then tanks and infantry attacked in strength the positions on Chlodna and Ogrodowa Streets and overwhelmed them, the severely weakened Home Army troops being forced back still further towards the City Centre.

At about midday on 6 August a formation of Dirlewanger's hard-fighting criminal regiment backed by heavy tanks finally broke through to the Mirowski Market and thence to the Saxon Gardens and Theatre Square. After the tanks in the open spaces had dispersed the Poles pinning down General Stahel in the Brühl Palace contact was made with the SS units defending it. The defenders were drinking heavily and ready to surrender.[6] An hour or two later and the Poles would have been able to seize the German general commanding the garrison and his entire staff. Such is the fortune of war.

The German commanders now held a conference in Brühl Palace and decided that General Stahel would stay there to direct operations, with a battalion of SS-Oberführer Dirlewanger's regiment at his disposition while SS-Gruppenführer Reinefarth's troops would reinforce and extend the wedge he had driven through the Polish positions in Wola and the City Centre. Utterly ruthless destruction of entire streets by burning and by artillery fire had made this advance possible, including bombardment by shells of the heaviest calibre from the armoured train on the railway which ran from north to south across Wola.

Neither the Poles nor the Germans kept their troops that night in fiercely burning Chlodna Street between the Zelazna crossroads and Saxon Gardens. Next morning, 7 August, the Luftwaffe were again out early, smashing the Polish barricades in the district with low-level bombing attacks. Then through the swirling smoke came two heavy Tiger tanks leading Dirlewanger's 2nd Battalion, who drove in front of them a screen of Polish women and children. They were followed by a Poznan Police battalion. No aid could arrive from Colonel Radóslaw's group in the cemetery area to the immediate north because it was held down by enemy tanks, armoured cars, mortar and machine-gun fire.

Inevitably, fire from Captain Sosna's company was stayed, but any kind of stand against the massive German force was impossible. The Poles retreated east along the broad thoroughfare of the Electoralna, leading to the Town Hall and Theatre Square. Another German wedge advanced along Leszno Street, parallel to the north. SS-Brigadeführer Kaminski's brigade of Cossack former prisoners-of-war made only slight advances from Ochota north-east towards the adjacent City Centre. To fighting, they preferred the indiscriminate slaughter and pillage of thousands of the civilian population there, including women and children.

Kaminski and his troops had become interested in a vodka factory. From the afternoon of 5 August Kaminski urgently requested air support to enable him to enter.[7] Because the 9th Army distrusted him his radio conversations were tapped and filed:

Kaminski to Reinefarth: Bandits taking up a fixed position in the grounds of the Machorka factory. Further attack only after cleansing of these grounds. Frolow.

Kaminski to Reinefarth, later: Reached the Machorka factory. Heavily occupied and defended by bandits. Factory grounds enclosed by high wall. Request urgently means for blowing up and burning.

Reinefarth to Kaminski, 6th August, 14.00 hours: Make detailed sketch map of Machorka factory immediately. Also height of the object. Because of the use of Stukas. Sketch map will be collected.

Kaminski to Reinefarth: Platoon of tanks firing at my regiment.

Reinefarth: Does armoured train or tank gun protect factory? Hurry, urgent. Reinefarth.

Kaminski: North side of factory is protected by guns. Assumption: perhaps a platoon of tanks. Frolow.

Kaminski: Bandits have finished building heavy fortifications and barricades. For the second time I ask you for heavy artillery, pioneers and flame-throwers. Three times during the assault I tried to seize the barricades. However, proved unsuccessful. I am expecting tanks and flame-throwers. Frolow.

130

Kaminski's urgent requests for aid were of course simply camouflage. Vodka had detained him. He was later court-martialled and shot.

The situation now looked bleak for the Home Army. Then during the afternoon a Polish counter-attack from Mirowski Square succeeded in driving one of the German wedges back in the direction of Wola, but a Panther tank and several armoured cars swiftly checked it. By the evening, the insurgents had retreated to their starting-point.

By about 8 o'clock in the evening of 7 August the Germans were in complete control of the Wolska–Chlodna–Elektoralna–Saxon Gardens artery, with the Kierbedz Bridge only one or two hundred yards away on the far side of the Royal Castle which the Poles still held. That evening a large crowd of Polish civilians were forced at gunpoint to clear all barricades and ruins from the streets along this line of communication to the bridge. They were afterwards shot in the Mirowski Market.

A terrible massacre of the civilian population by Reinefarth's and Dirlewanger's troops had begun in Electoralna Street, the surrounding area and in the parts of Wola in which Home Army units had been overwhelmed. Although the actual deeds were done by Kaminski's renegade Cossacks and Dirlewanger's criminal troops, German officers permitted these murders of tens of thousands of unarmed men, women and children.

On 5 August, the hospital of the Marie Curie Radium Institute had been invaded by drunken Cossacks who assembled the staff and patients, about one hundred and seventy in all, robbed them, drove some of them into the hospital garden and thence to a camp near Mokotow Field, where the women were raped. Those patients still in their beds were shot dead, the building was pillaged, saturated with petrol and set on fire. Later the staff and patients who had been taken to the camp were shot through the head by a German officer.[8] Similar barbarities were carried out at the Wola Hospital and the St. Lazarus Hospital.

After having taken Wolska Street the Germans set fire to the houses there with petrol bottles and drove the inhabitants to the yard of the Ursus factory near by. Here the Germans shot them in the back of the head and stacked their bodies in heaps ready for burning. One woman who escaped after her three children had been murdered there later estimated that there were five to seven thousand dead in the yard.[9]

One man among a throng of civilians who were driven similarly out of Elektoralna Street on 7 August later testified how they had stumbled in the darkness along Chlodna Street, where the houses were burning like torches. 'It sometimes seemed as though it was one great wall of fire. Our personal experiences, driven as we were like cattle, haunted by fear, facing endless danger from the continuous shooting among the ruins and the huge fires – took on terrible unearthly dimensions,' he wrote.[10]

The procession, marching slowly from St. Charles Borromeo's Church to Zelazna Street, suffered terrible maltreatment and even torture...For a time I carried a little girl, Basia, two years old, in my arms. The child had lost both father and mother. The attitude of the women was deeply touching. Grave and obstinate, only paying attention to their children and bundles, they marched on like soldiers, taking care not to expose the little ones to danger. During the whole time, that is, until we reached Zelazna Street, where the women were separated from us, I heard not a single complaint, no bitter weeping, no begging for help...There were moments when the heat from the burning houses made our progress quite impossible. The wind blew up clouds of biting smoke which hid everything...I saw in several places in Zelazna Street corpses of murdered people lying in the streets. They could not have been victims of bombing or of stray shots for they lay in groups.

A young women named Wanda was seized while taking shelter among hundreds of other people in the Ministry of Commerce building in Elektoralna Street. A German dragged her aside and tried to rape her, but when she resisted fiercely he chose another woman and fired at Wanda with his pistol, but missed. She ran out through the burning street into another house. The next day Wanda was driven with a procession of mostly young women with children towards Wola.[11]

They stopped at a street crossing because the insurgents were firing from Kercely Square towards them. German troops there stopped the procession and ordered the women to lie down from one side of the street to the other as a living barricade. 'We were all prepared to die, and said the Rosary aloud. Bullets whistled over our heads or past our ears... As if by some miracle they only hit the Germans...They were bewildered by the fact that only they were falling...We thought they would take their revenge on us. Stupefied and astonished they looked towards the insurgent posts and then at our quiet, resigned attitude, and the children clinging to their mothers.

'At last they let us go.'

A man called Marian among the refugees in the Commerce Ministry building in Elektoralna Street was ordered out by the Germans late in the evening of 7 August with about one hundred and fifty other men and marched to Mirowski Square where they were ordered to remove the corpses, mainly civilians, scores of which lay on the ground where they had fallen after being shot. After an hour and a half's work stacking the bodies they were marched to the Market Hall in Chlodna Street. Inside it was full of black smoke from a fire burning in a vast hole in the floor. The prisoners were ordered to stand with their faces to the wall and their hands up.[12]

There was a burst of automatic fire. Although not hit Marian fell with those beside him and heard their groans and moans. A little later he cautiously lifted his head and saw Poles forced at gunpoint to carry the bodies and throw them into the flames issuing from the hole. In the

132

smoke and the gloom he escaped into the lavatory and hid behind a partition. A little later another man, Dr Jerzy Lakota, of the Child Jesus Hospital, joined him there. Together they sat there for several hours, listening to the intermittent firing in the hall and the noise of the bodies burning in the fire hole. Just before daylight they crept out of this frightful charnel house and escaped through the flaming streets to Krochmalna Street.

The 5 to 7 of August saw days and nights of appalling horror in Wola, the western part of the City Centre and Ochota, where Kaminski's Soviet renegade troops were let loose. As part of a deliberate plan based on Himmler's order nearly 40,000 civilians were executed and burnt in this inferno.

While the tide of fighting in Wola moved nearer and nearer to his GHQ Komorowski's fears about the chances of Soviet aid were temporarily dispelled. Polish troops in the City Centre took to Colonel Chrusciel a short thick-set man of athletic build who had asked in Russian and German to be taken to the Polish Commander. He told Chrusciel: 'My name is Konstantin Kalugin. I am a Russian officer under the orders of Marshal Rokossovsky.'[13] He produced a miniature inch-square identity card out of a knot in a red handkerchief which under a magnifying glass showed this name and that he was an intelligence officer in contact with the Czarny Group, a Red Army guerrilla unit operating behind the German lines.

Kalugin said that he and a companion were dropped by parachute on 15 July near Lublin, one hundred and fifty miles south-east of Warsaw. Their assignment was to make contact with the Polish underground in the capital, but reaching it on 1 August they had lost contact with each other. Unfortunately the other man carried the radio transmitter and codes, so he now had no way of getting in touch with his commanding officers. He therefore sought permission to send a report to Stalin on the Warsaw situation with a request for aid.

Kalugin said with much confidence that the Red Army possessed overwhelming numerical superiority over the Germans and without any doubt it should enter Warsaw within the next two or three days.

Informed about Kalugin and his request, Komorowski decided that while Prime Minister Mikolajczyk in Moscow would have kept Marshal Stalin fully informed about the course of the fighting against the Germans, this confirmation from a Soviet officer could be of much value, especially as the means of establishing liaison with Rokossovsky.

He therefore authorised Chrusciel to transmit Kalugin's message to London for onward transmission to Stalin. The message asked that German concentrations in certain areas of Warsaw should be attacked from the air, that the airfields at Okecie and Bielany should be bombed and most important that arms and ammunition should be dropped in specified streets and squares. Kalugin added: 'The brave people in

Warsaw believe that you will give them the most positive help in the next few hours. Please facilitate my liaison with Marshal Rokossovsky.' He signed the message: Captain Konstantin Kalugin of Czarny Group, Warsaw. Chrusciel also transmitted a message from Kalugin to Rokossovsky via London and Moscow.

The Chief of the Polish General Staff in London acknowledged both messages: 'Proposals of both Kalugin and the O.C. Warsaw Sector, Home Army, immediately transmitted to Moscow through British channels, as were your previous requests for Soviet attacks from outside. No Soviet answer yet received.' There is no record of any Soviet reply to these messages.

Kalugin remained at Chrusciel's headquarters until some weeks later in September the Russians occupied the suburb of Praga, when he crossed the Vistula and rejoined them. During this period he was given complete freedom of movement so that he could observe the fighting in the various sectors.

The German advance through Wola brought Komorowski's GHQ into the centre of the battle. By the evening of 6 August the Kamler factory was the target of more or less continuous machine-gun fire. The humbly-named 'messenger-girls' – 'staff-assistants' would have been more appropriate – bravely risked their lives time and again in their work of liaison, but keeping links intact with the various Home Army groups had become almost impossible. Radio sets in the Kamler building, the sole means of communication with the world outside Warsaw, were also all too vulnerable.

Komorowski therefore ordered the removal of the GHQ to the Old Town, or Stare Miasto. The route lay across the ruins of the Ghetto, dominated by machine-guns on the tower of the Pawiak prison church. One of the captured tanks first shelled the tower and knocked them out. Led by a well-armed Polish infantry platoon Komorowski and his staff in single file doubled forward through paths of rubble and past the shells of buildings, bending low to avoid shots from the Germans in their Pawiak stronghold. Their journey across this lifeless wasteland lasted two hours.

In the Old Town everything was still untouched by bombing or shellfire. The tall, narrow old houses with their embellished façades and elaborate doorways, the churches, the little shops were still more or less as they were when built within the city walls by prosperous merchants in the Middle Ages. Komorowski's new headquarters were in a school in Barakowa Street which the Germans had pressed into use as a hospital. A tall building, its roof offered a panorama of Warsaw's chequerboard of battle actions.

Home Army strongpoints for the defence of the district included the Treasury Printing Building and the Royal Castle, the Town Hall slightly south of it on the northern verge of the City Centre and the

Bank of Poland on the flanks. The Old Town was immensely over-crowded. Refugees from elsewhere in the city had flooded in until there were an estimated 170,000 people there, about double the normal.

While the defeat and the massacre went on in Wola, Mikolajczyk had more fruitless meetings in Moscow with the Polish Communist National Committee of Liberation. In view of their failure his last hopes rested on Stalin. But on 6 August, before this meeting, he received a startling telegram from Jankowski. 'Since the battle for Warsaw began the Red Army on the Warsaw front has stopped all military operations,' Jankowski accused.

> A complete cessation continues even now, while for the second day running the Germans heavily bombard the town from the air. In other words, there is no Soviet intervention.
>
> This incomprehensible, passive and ostentatious behaviour of the Soviet troops at a distance of a dozen kilometres from Warsaw has its political significance, a matter which the Government must raise with Allied quarters, jointly with the Premier, who is now in Moscow. The question is urgent and its immediate solution is necessary in view of the further development of our action.[14]

Jankowski had given a dangerous political slant to the question of the Red Army's activities. It was dangerous because untrue, because in the inflammable state of Russo-Polish relations it spread like wildfire and because its slanderous content would antagonise the Soviet leaders just when the Home Army was begging for their help.

Mikolajczyk did not yet know that Rokossovsky's forces on the 1st Belorussian Front, ordered to take the Warsaw suburb of Praga by 5 to 8 August[15] and to establish bridgeheads on the Vistula's western bank south of Warsaw had by then withdrawn from their battle with the Germans a dozen kilometres east of the city with the loss of some five hundred tanks and an estimated six thousand men. Nor that the Red Air Force had temporarily lost superiority over the battle area.[16]

The Germans were by the evening of 7 August in partial control of the Wolska–Chłodna–Saxon Gardens route. Colonel Radóslaw's group was isolated in the cemetery area to the north of Wola and west of the Ghetto. As well as numerous fortified strongpoints within Polish-held districts the Germans also now held wedges of territory thrusting deep into the city. Thus they had won their secondary objective of splitting up the districts in Polish hands so that these had become three different sectors with very little liaison.

In the south of the city the Home Army held Mokotow and Czerniakow, then the City Centre – with a German wedge thrusting deep into it – abutting on to Powisle along the river bank; and in the north the cemetery sector, the Old Town and Zoliborz, separate from it but in contact with troops in the near-by Kampinos Forest area.

The immediate effects of this became quickly clear. Colonel Chrusciel found that effective command of his troops was no longer possible. He had to turn to reliable officers who could take command in their areas and fight on independently. Fortunately the Home Army did not lack them. He appointed Colonel Karol Ziemski to command the Old Town, with Zoliborz and Kampinos also subordinated to him, about 9,000 men, designated Group North; Colonel Radwan, the City Centre and Powisle, and Colonel Kaminiski (code-named 'Daniel') to command Mokotow and Czerniakow. Their tasks: to hold their perimeters and to destroy German strongpoints inside them.[17]

Colonel Ziemski also wanted to resume contact with his forces in Zoliborz and Kampinos. He knew that to defend the Old Town it was essential to prevent the Germans from occupying the Ghetto ruins and the Krasinski Gardens, for this would pin his forces down against the river. He divided his troops into three, placing the eastern section under Major Rog, the southern under Major Sienkiewicz and the western section, which joined the cemetery area, he added to Colonel Radóslaw's command. He instructed Radóslaw and Sienkiewicz to maintain close contact and help each other by intermittent counter-attacks. Ziemski also organised workshops for the repair of weapons and set up a small arsenal for the manufacture of hand-grenades with explosive removed from unexploded German bombs and shells.

Meanwhile, in Wola, after Komorowski's removal to the Old Town, Polish troops fought a rearguard action and finally withdrew on 8 August, establishing a new line of defence along the western boundary of the City Centre.

The Germans now launched a massive assault on the Polish positions guarding the remaining part of the vital route to the Kierbedz Bridge. Supported by twenty tanks, by assault guns and more or less constant attacks by dive-bombers; by burning and dynamiting houses on either side of the route, including the Polish national monument of the Unknown Soldier, over which rolled tanks and armoured cars, they won their route to it on 9 August.

The loss cut off the Old Town and the Home Army GHQ from all contact with the City Centre. The Home Army was now fighting isolated battles against the Germans with almost entire lack of liaison between the separate groups. Somehow the Poles kept their morale high. Defeatism did not exist, even though they knew well enough how desperate their situation had become, in face especially of the silence across the Vistula and the freedom of the skies above Warsaw which the Red Air Force allowed the Germans.

One can see this thinning band of Home Army fighters reading the approaching tragedy in each other's haunted eyes, then arming themselves with that blend of high courage and resolute obstinacy peculiar to their nation, and fighting even harder. The German wedge, driven in the form of a raid in force from Wola through Chłodna and Electoralna Streets to the Saxon Gardens had driven off the Polish troops besieging the Brühl Palace, but failed to expel them from the district or from their positions in the ruins bordering the route. Though far superior in terms of numbers and weapons, the Germans were still not yet strong enough on the ground to dominate what they had won largely by rigorous aerial bombardment. Persistent as volcanic lava the Poles seeped back again into positions they had lost as need called the Nazis away to other points in the city.

On 9 August, at 10.20 a.m., a furious attack by Home Army troops badly wounded Dr Fischer, Nazi Governor of Warsaw after he had left the Brühl Palace with his staff for a destination of greater safety else-where, in accordance with an order given him the day before by von dem Bach. Dr Hümel, his deputy, was killed; numerous other staff members were killed or wounded. 'Resistance is snowballing,' General von Vormann, 9th Army Commander, reported to Himmler on 10 August.

The uprising, originally very improvised and spontaneous, is now being fought on hard military lines. The rapid reduction of the uprising with our existing force is impossible. The danger is that the movement is widening its theatre of activity and may well spread throughout the country.

The actions we have undertaken are of a street fighting nature. Fighting house by house our losses are high. For our soldiers fighting on the east bank of the Vistula the situation may well become unbear-able. The supply lines, which form a great loop through Modlin, may well be cut off, as they lack men to defend them.

There is also the threat of an attack in the rear of the forces fighting in the suburbs.

What the situation demands is a division up to full strength with great quantities of armament.

General von dem Bach, the Prussian Nazi specialist in anti-partisan movements had by now taken command of the German counter-attack. Questioned at Nuremberg in 1946 about the exact date of his arrival he stoutly maintained that he took over not earlier than 13 August. He wanted to make the date as late as possible so as to clear himself of responsibility for the massacre of the civilian population carried out by Kaminski's Russian renegades and Dirlewanger's criminals. But there is evidence that he in fact arrived on 5 August and that it was he who had launched the onslaught through Wola. 'When I arrived and took stock of the position I found great confusion,' he said later.

Every unit fired in a different direction and nobody knew exactly where to aim. From the military point of view it was a very difficult situation.

At a cemetery I saw a group of civilians being captured and executed on the spot by men from Reinefarth's unit...

I went personally to Reinefarth and...informed him of the situation I had observed and of the fact that his detachments were executing innocent civilians...Reinefarth then drew my attention to the order issued by Himmler. He had received an express order not to take prisoners, but to kill every inhabitant of Warsaw. I asked him: 'Including women and children?' He replied, 'Yes, including women and children.'[18]

Von dem Bach, it must be said, thereupon risked Himmler's wrath and possible action against himself personally, and issued an order forbidding the mass extermination of the population.[19] Witnesses before Polish authorities investigating German atrocities in Warsaw after the war agreed that the mass executions were stopped in the evening hours of 5 August by order, they understood, of a German general newly arrived in Warsaw, but they recurred on a smaller scale on 6 and 7 August. Kaminski's troops in particular, the Soviet renegades, had become drunk and more or less uncontrollable.

Thus it is clear that von dem Bach was the German general behind the Wehrmacht's first effectual attempt to cope with the Uprising that split the Polish forces into separate groups. Equally that he tried, but did not succeed, in stopping the civilian massacre. On the other hand he had no scruples about destroying Warsaw through fire and bombardment with the heaviest shells, which killed civilians as effectively as the massacres.

Von dem Bach next set about his task of crushing the Uprising and securing a route for supplies to the German troops opposing the Soviet forces east of Praga by mounting an operation against the Old Town, which lay between the Citadel railway bridge and the Kierbedz Bridge. This was not practicable, however, until he secured more reinforcements. So meantime he ordered Reinefarth to seize positions from which his operations could be launched in the districts immediately to the west of it, the Ghetto and the Powazki cemetery area. German troops holding areas already cleared of insurgents were not to be used.

The final meeting between Stalin and Mikolajczyk took place in the Kremlin at 9 p.m. on 9 August. Mikolajczyk pressed Stalin again about the urgent need for arms. Declaring that the Germans were not strong enough to subdue the Poles, he said that they were trying nevertheless to open at any price two main thoroughfares leading through the town and the Vistula bridges. 'A mortal struggle is taking place at the moment and the Polish forces have to face great technical superiority on the part of the enemy,' he declared.

138

'All these struggles in Warsaw seem to me unreal,' Stalin answered bluntly. What he then went on to tell Mikolajczyk was painful indeed for the Premier to hear, knowing as he did what a bloody struggle was then being fought in the capital. 'It would be different if our armies were approaching Warsaw, but unfortunately this is not the case,' Stalin said coolly.[20]

I reckoned on our army occupying Warsaw on August 6 but we failed to do so. On August 4* the Germans brought into the Praga area four armoured divisions and the 'Hermann Goering' Division which had come from Italy. We could therefore not capture Praga and had to make an outflanking movement after the crossing of the Vistula in the area of Pilica.

At first that operation proceeded quite smoothly along a sector 25 kilometres long and 30 kilometres wide. Yesterday the Germans launched vigorous counter-attacks there with infantry and two armoured divisions. Consequently our offensive aimed at the capture of Warsaw is opposed by five new armoured divisions, three of which are still posted around Praga.

I do not doubt that we shall overcome these difficulties too, but we have to re-group our forces and bring in artillery. This demands time.

I am sorry for your men who started the battle in Warsaw prematurely and have to fight tanks, artillery and aircraft with rifles. I know Warsaw personally and I know the narrow streets of the Old Town.

What can an air-lift do?—We can supply a certain quantity of rifles and machine guns, but we cannot parachute cannons. Are you quite sure that arms parachuted from the air will reach the Poles? This might be easy in some outlying areas like Kielce or Radom, but in Warsaw, considering the concentration of German forces, it would be an extremely difficult thing to do. Perhaps it could be done. We must try. How much assistance are you asking for and where would you like us to drop the arms?

Mikolajczyk saw in Stalin's remarks a ray of hope at last, something which would transform his journey from bitter failure to triumph. 'I understand your hesitation,' he answered quickly, 'but a battle is taking place in Warsaw and nothing can stop it.' He then told Stalin that the places for parachute drops were secured by barricades so that they could not be intercepted by the enemy—an inaccurate and highly optimistic account, of course.

Mikolajczyk added that so soon as direct liaison was established between Warsaw and the Red Army it would be possible to give

* The Germans in fact began their offensive with these divisions at dawn on 1 August.

signals for air lifts. Stalin promised that 'we shall try to do everything possible to help Warsaw', and asked him to 'facilitate this and to issue all the necessary instructions'.[21] Mikolajczyk said that he would ask Warsaw to send a reply to him immediately. He gave Stalin more details of the dispositions of Polish forces in Warsaw, then took his leave, again fervently reminding Stalin of his promise that everything would be done by the Soviet authorities to bring help to Warsaw as quickly as possible. Stalin confirmed this.

In the early hours Mikolajczyk left Moscow aboard a Soviet aircraft for Tehran. In the British Embassy there he hurriedly sent a telegram to the Polish President briefly informing him of Stalin's assurance that he would send arms. He also sent a second message to his Deputy in London for onward transmission to Warsaw about the military briefing Stalin had given him.

Of great importance, militarily for the insurgents and politically for the Allies, this information could have stopped the stories about Soviet inaction that were beginning to circulate. But, consciously or unconsciously Mikolajczyk did not convey the gravity of Stalin's account, as a comparison makes clear. His message said:[22]

> Stalin was counting originally on the entrance of the Soviet armies into Warsaw on the 6th or 8th but this was prevented by the counter-attack on Praga of four fresh German tank divisions. Further, the out-flanking Soviet manoeuvre across the Vistula in the Pilica area which had begun so well was also set back by two German tank divisions.
> This makes it necessary to regroup and bring up Soviet artillery. Stalin has no doubts as to the final outcome, despite the unforeseen delay. He realises its importance for our fighting in Warsaw and promises air support to the limits of his possibilities...

Much of Stalin's emphasis, as well as his vital sentence about the Soviet forces is missing—'It would be different if our armies were approaching Warsaw, but unfortunately this is not the case.'

Whether he wished to or not, Mikolajczyk had played down the gravity of Stalin's report. Since the contents of this message would have been passed on to the British and United States Governments they too were left in doubts by it as to Soviet intentions about Warsaw.

Mikolajczyk's apparent omission to communicate the full sense of Stalin's briefing and thus stop the dangerous reports circulating about Soviet failure to aid Warsaw was to inflict far-reaching damage upon the relations between Soviet Russia on the one hand and Britain and the United States on the other.

The German picture of the fighting as seen from their 9th Army War Diary[23] confirmed Stalin's report. 'All the efforts of 9th Army Command are directed at blocking the Soviet forces in the Magnuszew area,' it reported on 4 August. And on 7 August: 'The main interest lies in today's double attack by the 19th Division and the 'Hermann Goering'

Division from the south at the Magnuszew bridgehead. Nineteenth Armoured Division began its attack around midday. Despite the heavy opposition and the over-bearing enemy odds, AOK 9 has ordered this attack to continue tomorrow. An enemy attack undertaken today from the Nasilow bridgehead, at the division of the 4th and 9th armies, is threatening the German positions. There is quiet on General Saucken's Praga front.

Continued pressure put upon Air Marshal Slessor, added to the waning of the dangerous full moon, now caused him to relax still more his ban on flights to Warsaw. Six British joined five Polish crews and the eleven aircraft took off on the night of 12 August. All of them returned to base, but only seven had dropped their containers and only five of these reached the Home Army.

Polish pleas to both Americans and British on behalf of their beleaguered fellow-countrymen continued increasingly. To President Roosevelt the Polish President Raczkiewicz telegraphed on 12 August:

> I appeal to you, Mr. President, to order the American Air Force in the European Theatre of war to give immediate support to the garrison of Warsaw by dropping arms and ammunition, bombing objectives held in the Warsaw area by the enemy, transporting Polish airborne units to take part in the fight for their capital. Any delay to afford help spells disaster to Warsaw. The Polish people could never understand why it should fall now at a moment when the common cause of the United Nations is championed by military power of unexampled strength.[24]

Ambassador Ciechanowski approached Mr Stettinius, US Secretary of State, with the message. The eventual outcome was the decision in principle to carry out a major Anglo-American air lift operation, but this was not to take place for some weeks.

In a summary of the situation on 9 August the Diary[25] reported German losses very great in the Magnuszew fighting, while Russian attacks on General Saucken's Praga front facing Warsaw made the withdrawal of some units very difficult.

The next day it revealed that German attempts at containing the Soviet crossings of the Vistula were ineffectual. Significantly, it went on to remark that the German Command believed that the Russians 'will use this area of concentration for a circular offensive against Warsaw. 9th Army Command regards these developments with great anxiety.

'It assumes that enemy concentration in the Praga area is now complete, and that soon offensive action will be launched.

'The Kaminski group is still tied down in Ochota; it would appear that for the moment it is more interested in looting than anything else.'

The Germans now stepped up their offensive in a desperate effort to overcome Polish resistance.

Reinefarth attacked in the cemetery sector on 8 August with his own, Dirlewanger's and Schmidt's forces. In this eerie district west of the Ghetto among the battered tombstones and the shattered marble slabs, about a mile long and half a mile wide, Radóslaw had placed one battalion, Zoska, in the Jewish and Evangelist cemeteries; Broda battalion with the platoon of three captured tanks in Okopowa Street, dividing the area from the Ghetto; and other units along the Calvinist cemetery and Karolkowa Street. His force was smaller, down to about 1,500 men, but captured German weapons had armed his men better.[1]

Reinefarth moved from the south—Leszno Street towards Karolkowa and Okopowa Streets—with several tanks, units of the Azerbaijan regiment and police units. Other infantry units attacked from the streets immediately to the west of the cemeteries, covered by the guns of No. 75 armoured train. Just before dawn Radóslaw had sent twenty-three picked men under Second Lieutenant Zegota in a dawn attack on this train, the sort of do-or-die action in which his men excelled. They ran into a strong German guard by the railway line, two of their machine-guns jammed, six men were killed and several wounded before they retired.

Reinefarth shelled the Okopowa Street area, about three-quarters of a mile long, with heavy artillery and mortars, and then attacked the barricades on Zytnia Street with tanks and flame-throwers. Infantry advanced on the Jewish cemetery and poured heavy fire on the insurgents holding the barricade at the junction of Ostrorog and Młynarska Streets. At 10.25 a.m. the platoon of captured tanks forced back a formation of German tanks and infantry who had advanced dangerously close to the Polish barricades at the junction of Zytnia and Karolkowa Streets.

Three hours later the Germans attacked again and managed to occupy the Calvinist cemetery. Radóslaw counter-attacked with a battalion and his tank platoon, partially drove the Germans out and captured three heavy machine-guns, but one of his tanks was put out of action.

A battle for the cemetery was now fought with hand-grenades, infantry of both sides manoeuvring among the graves and sheltering from blast and steel splinters behind ivy-clad antique marble tombstones. Polish units in Okopowa Street were at the same time pinned down by machine-gun fire from the Calvinist cemetery to the west, from Leszno Street to the south and from parts of the Ghetto to the east, especially from the tower of the church of St Charles Borromeo, until this was shattered by a shot from one of the Polish tanks.[2]

At about 1 o'clock Captain Nowak, holding part of the northern perimeter of the cemetery area, came under strong fire from Gdansk railway station, five or six hundred yards to the north-west. He withdrew his 130-strong company, but Radóslaw immediately ordered the armed platoon, about sixty men, back to its position. (A Home Unit consisted of both armed and unarmed men in these 'equipment battles', the unarmed men at hand to take over their own or the killed or wounded enemy's weapons, or those of enemy prisoners.)

Reinforced, the Germans redoubled the vigour of their offensive against the Calvinist cemetery and neighbouring streets. Polish losses were heavy, the Zytnia Street defences collapsed and the Poles fell back into Mirecki Street. After an artillery bombardment the Germans launched an onslaught against the Evangelist cemetery. Radóslaw ordered a counter-attack from the Jewish cemetery with infantry and his two remaining tanks. By about 8 o'clock the Poles had succeeded in throwing the enemy back, inflicting heavy losses and capturing six machine-guns, a mortar, about twenty rifles and a big supply of ammunition.

But Radóslaw's losses had been heavy; his group was now no more than about one thousand five hundred strong. The night passed quietly, both sides exhausted by the nervous tension and bodily fatigue caused by the battle in the cemeteries of this city roaring with flame and shuddering with explosions. The next day the Germans made no more than a few minor attacks, and on 10 August, when it rained heavily, the enemy merely probed the defences with an attack on the Jewish cemetery while bombarding Okopowa Street with mortars and artillery, causing the Poles heavy losses.

But word came on this day to raise high the Home Army's hopes of victory. Komorowski received a message from General Sosnkowski with news of the agreement reached between Mikolajczyk and Stalin on the air-drops of Soviet arms and ammunition for Warsaw. He ordered accordingly that special detachments should be assigned as outposts for receiving these supplies,[3] which was done. Eagerly the Home Army leaders now awaited the arrival of the Soviet liaison officer and of the much-needed weapons.

A final German onslaught on Radóslaw's positions started at dawn on 11 August, when an infantry attack preceded by a heavy bombardment drove the Polish forces out of their barricade at the corner of Ostrorog and Młynarska Streets. It was followed by an attack in force, 'Goliath' tanks being used for the first time in Okopowa Street. Miniature tanks loaded with explosives and controlled electrically by cable from another tank, they blew up with tremendous force when they struck an obstacle of any kind. Lieutenant Mały pioneered the technique of action by breaking the control wire with a carefully aimed hand-grenade.

The Germans, using fresh forces against the weary Polish troops, now began to make gains. After an hour's battle they finally drove the insurgents out of the Jewish cemetery. Another German battalion supported by field-guns threw back the Polish forces holding the Catholic cemetery. Radóslaw himself, with a battalion of only two hundred and fifty men and the one remaining tank in service, then led a counter-attack which hit the German flank with great impetus and for the time being stopped their advance. But the action was costly indeed.

Radóslaw was badly wounded, while sixty men, including five officers were killed and another sixty men wounded. The remaining Polish tank was damaged and immobilised, but two anti-tank guns with ammunition were captured.[4]

In the afternoon of August 11 the Germans again attacked Okopowa Street from the Catholic cemetery in the north and the Evangelist cemetery facing it further south. The Poles came under withering enemy fire. To prevent the decimation of this valuable force Colonel Ziemski ordered it to retreat through the Ghetto ruins towards Stawki Street, and at 4 p.m. under cover of the gun of the immobilised tank the battalion retired through heavy enemy fire to the line of the former Parysowska and Lubecki Streets in the Ghetto ruins. Rearguard of the retreat, Second-Lieutenant Kuba's platoon, including five girls, lost its officer and twenty men.

The headquarters of Radóslaw's group, now below half their strength, moved to Muranowska Street. The near-by Stawki Street sector now became the advance defence of the Old Town against German attacks from the hard-won Ghetto and cemetery areas westwards.

The Germans had thus won at high cost two districts vital for the city's defence by 11 August, while von dem Bach had already launched a preparatory attack on the Old Town. Large parts of Warsaw were already in ruins; tens of thousands of people were dead beneath them, or shot and then burnt by the Germans. The situation of the defenders became hourly more serious.

From day to day Komorowski and his staff still hoped for a big Soviet thrust towards Warsaw. But reports that the Soviets had arrested all commanding officers of the Home Army who had reported to them after having led diversionary actions against the Germans east of the Vistula tended to dash these hopes. Indeed, they gave rise to the suspicion that the Soviets might leave the Home Army insurgents to fight it out alone with the massive concentrations of Germans in Warsaw. Komorowski and his staff therefore awaited with growing anxiety the arrival of the promised Soviet arms.

144

The desperate Polish resistance, their apparent determination to fight to the bitter end, worried the German commanders exceedingly by mid-August. Well to the north and south of Warsaw the Soviets pressed them hard, while at the same time they needed more and more troops in the city to hold down the insurgents.

The Germans ascribed this Polish resilience to well-thought-out tactics which permitted German assault troops, flame-throwers and even tanks to advance right up to the barricades and then broke up these attacks by Piat mortars, incendiary bottles, machine-gun fire and sniping at officers. Casualties were hit mainly in the head and it was almost impossible to find out where the shots came from. They believed that the snipers were mainly on rooftops or in the higher storeys of houses, only rarely on ground floors or in cellars. The fighting hardly seemed to confirm reports of a scarcity of arms and ammunition among the insurgents.[5]

Lack of reliable information about the strength and location of the insurgent groups also confused the Germans. But it was an outcome of their own terror policy. The Poles believed they would either be tortured to obtain information, or shot out of hand, according to which unit captured them, so never surrendering, they fought to the end. The Germans were therefore attacking more or less in the dark. They knew that in Mokotow they faced a force of about four thousand fighting men, another group of unknown strength in the Old Town, a strong though much depleted force in the City Centre and other units of whose strength they were uncertain in the various suburbs, including Bielany, Zoliborz and Marymont. Partisan groups three or four thousand strong were also reported to be assembling in the forest areas around the city.

Disagreements between General von Vormann and Himmler over the quality and the quantity of forces allocated to Warsaw also caused difficulties. How little von Vormann and the Middle Army Group had to say in this matter is shown by an earlier telephone conversation between von Vormann and General Krebs, Chief of Staff of Middle Army Group, at 11.30 a.m. on 9 August:[6]

Von Vormann: I cannot manage Warsaw yet. I have not enough forces. There are one and a half million Poles. We are like a ship surrounded by water. Von dem Bach cannot do it. He reports that his task is impossible.
Krebs: Report again in writing.
Von Vormann: I have three to four thousand men against one and a half million.
Krebs: The Reichsführer SS (*Himmler*) has looked into that and will give Obergruppenführer von dem Bach the means.

Generals von Vormann and von dem Bach were convinced that upon the success or failure of Warsaw depended the spread of the Uprising throughout Poland. They also believed, incorrectly in fact, that the leaflets telling of the more brutal methods of crushing the Uprising had stayed the hands of the partisans in the forests, and that so soon as the city fell all activity in the countryside would stop. Having captured Wola and the Powazki cemetery area, they also believed at first that they had won access to the focus of the Uprising in the City Centre.

Their main task, apart from crushing the insurgents, they saw as linking up with the 9th Army by means of the routes across the city; and this necessity guided their actions. They ordered that the east–west link through the Kierbedz Bridge must be fully opened by Reinefarth's force; and that Kaminski's force would advance towards the main railway station, in order to overcome the insurgents fighting between there and Ochota suburb.

'After the achievement of these aims,' they stated, 'further action will be based on the attitude of the insurgents...who must be called on to capitulate. If they refuse they must be annihilated by encirclement and their base in the Mokotow suburb be destroyed.'[7]

After nearly two weeks' fighting, a bizarre way of life had developed around the pattern of Polish barricades and strongpoints along the German wedges through the city. Amid the crash of hand-grenades and the rattle of machine-guns attacks were repulsed and counter-attacks launched in swift succession. Air-raids followed one another so quickly that in the ceaseless alert everyone's nerves were stretched taut from dawn until the summer night brought three or four hours of quiet. Destruction by shells and bombs in daytime was the norm; the intermittent silences seemed strangely unfamiliar.

Almost every house had become a bulwark against German infantry attack. Inside, Home Army men and civilian tenants shared both their meagre rations in communal kitchens, and the ever-present danger of bombs and shells. Often they shared death. In the courtyards around which many Polish houses and apartment blocks were centred, home-built altars made from old bricks became the rule, with a cloth, garlands of leaves and flowers and a cross. Among an already religious people danger intensified the need for spiritual outlets. Priests faced death going from courtyard to courtyard to say Mass at these Christian altars.

The front line zigzagged through courtyards and up and down the floors of buildings, the Germans holding the ground floor and basement, the Poles the upper area, or the other way about. Civil authorities, hospitals, first-aid points and social welfare centres functioned night and day as little as sixty or seventy feet away from the ding-dong of battle.[8] Every area of the city and the suburbs could be hit by a variety of destructive weapons in addition to aerial bombardment.

They were assisted by patrols of Polish police named the State Security Corps, who also opposed German fifth-columnists and snipers. The Poles called these patriots 'pigeons', from their habit of perching among rooftop ruins with water and rations for several days, rifles

146

with telescopic sights firing through small holes in gables from the rear to kill men at the barricades. The Home Army organised building workers acquainted with the pattern of Warsaw's ancient rooftops to uncover their vantage-points. A Polish sniper saw a 'pigeon' aiming at a soldier in the street below, took a quick bead on him and had the satisfaction of seeing him topple earthwards before he could fire. Passwords, identity cards and check-points changed daily helped to stop the infiltration of German snipers.

Such were the conditions in which the Home Army and the civilian authorities tried to prevent disorder.

Komorowski and his Staff now felt that they had no other course but to hold on until Soviet aid did come and meantime to fight back as hard as possible. Orders were given to speed up the output of grenades and other weapons in the secret workshops. Fortunately an unexpected source of explosive came to hand. The Germans were hitting the city with shells of the biggest calibre. Sometimes the old houses collapsed into heaps of rubble in the blast of these missiles. Often, however, they failed to explode. Polish sappers removed the fuses and from the biggest of these monsters took out about six hundred pounds of explosive, which was then used to fill empty food cans or biscuit tins to make hand-grenades or mines. Captured Goliath tanks also provided a useful source of explosive.

Food for the troops was just adequate around mid-August, but monotonous. All three meals consisted of captured tinned tongue and wine from the vast cellars of a famous Polish vintner. Under fire on the barricades soldiers ate slices of ox tongue with château-bottled Bordeaux or Hungarian Tokay.

For civilians, food scarcity was becoming a food shortage. There was no meat, but plenty of sugar; in the suburbs plenty of green vegetables, in the central sectors flour, barley, dried peas and beans, just enough to maintain subsistence level, provided that these foodstuffs were exchanged between the districts.

Volunteers were called for to carry sacks of food from place to place. Soon men and women bowed under the weight of these sacks filed through streets often under enemy fire, across courtyards, along the house-to-house subterranean passages and cellars to distribution points where the food was most needed. Human pack-animals, toiling underground in every direction they became a vital part of daily life. Every day some were killed or wounded, but there was never a shortage of volunteers.[9]

The civil authorities arranged with the Peasant Party for all peasants living near Warsaw to make their first task the supply of the city with food of any and every kind. Some provisions were then taken to Home Army troops in Kampinos Forest for overnight smuggling into Warsaw and in this way a little more food arrived.

Even before the end of the fighting in the cemetery sector, units of Dirlewanger's and of another group about two thousand strong commanded by Major Reck, had begun the first preparatory attacks on the key district of the Old Town, supported by tanks and field-guns. A force of 1,357 Polish troops faced them. They were equipped with four heavy machine-guns; fifty-two light machine-guns; two hundred and forty-nine sub-machine-guns; forty-five flame-throwers; six Piat anti-tank mortars; one mortar, one field-gun, a fair number of rifles and revolvers and a substantial number of incendiary bottles and hand-grenades.[10] Another 4,953 unarmed troops and about one hundred and seventy thousand civilians were packed into these tall ancient houses leading down to the river, an area barely half the size of Chelsea south of the King's Road, or about one half a square mile.

German attacks from the west along Leszno Street towards the Town Hall, in the southern part of the Old Town, were thrown back with heavy losses. The next day, 9 August, Colonel Ziemski sent in an attack on the Gdansk station and the armoured train standing there, which had begun to bombard his positions with heavy calibre shells. Polish troops reached the station and set it ablaze, but the Germans drove them back with many wounded before they could reach the train; there were, in fact, two armoured trains. However, with their quick eye for German weapons, the Poles captured some heavy machine-guns.[11]

On 11 August the Germans launched heavy attacks against the Old Town barricades in their first effort to try to penetrate the district. Bombers, guns across the river in Praga, mortars and tanks pounded the defences or bombed the tightly-packed houses. Then, through the ruins of the castle on Swietojanska and Kanonia Streets, masses of enemy infantry with two tanks attacked from Marienstat. A determined Polish counter-attack supported by heavy machine-gun fire threw them back. Two more tanks then clattered up to the barricades defending the Bank of Poland building. One of them was destroyed with incendiary bottles and the other withdrew. Despite heavy losses the barricade, which also defended an entrance into the Old Town, was held that day.

The Home Army's aggressiveness survived even exhaustion and hunger. Lieutenant Domanski and a small detachment made a sortie that day from a barricade on the verge of the Old Town several hundred yards to Theatre Square. Here they attacked a German unit, forced it to retreat, then withdrew with rifles, ammunition and an anti-tank gun.

'From 3.30 a.m. to 1400 hours today, after yesterday's harassing enemy fire, concentric attacks were directed against the Old Town and Stawki,' Komorowski reported to London.

The attacks were supported by artillery fire, armoured trains, mortars, grenade-throwers and anti-tank guns. An enormous and crushing enemy superiority. Our counter-attacks threw the enemy back and recovered Stawki. Losses in killed and wounded. Further

148

advances in Zoliborz. The enemy air-force is strafing the city with machine-guns and guns.[12]

The defeat of Colonel Radóslaw's group that morning in the Powazki cemetery area, culminating in the fall of Okopowa Street and of the Ghetto ruins, now began to tell upon the defence of the Old Town. Reinefarth's infantry made contact with the German police troop detachments hitherto besieged in Pawiak prison, linked up first with General Stahel's units in the Saxon Gardens and then with the troops holding the Gdansk station to the north of the Ghetto. Having cut the city into three, the Germans now tried to link up their wedges to encircle the defenders.

Polish outposts in the western part of Leszno Street and the Stawki area held them up, though Radóslaw's group, which had held on to its positions in the cemeteries with such tenacity, was now tired and in need of re-forming. After his severe wound, Radóslaw had been replaced by Major Bolek.

At dawn on 12 August Lieutenant Nalecz launched a spirited attack through Długa Street and the cellars of the houses on Przejazd Street towards enemy positions on Leszno. Completely surprised, the Germans fled down Leszno to Orla Street. It was a triumph. The barricades on Leszno Street were reoccupied and a new strongpoint established in the concrete telephone building at the junction of Tłomacki Street and Przejazd Street.

The Germans responded with heavy shelling and mortaring in the area of the Stawki warehouses, smashing some and setting others ablaze. At 10 o'clock Colonel Schmidt's infantry, supported by a heavy tank, several field-guns and two armoured cars, attacked this region from the west with mortars and flame-throwers. The barricades were shattered and the Poles fell back towards the northern boundaries of the Old Town.

'We hold Zoliborz, the Old Town and the City Centre with the exception of the east–west traffic arteries,' Komorowski signalled to London during the morning of 12 August.

> Enemy attacks are made after artillery preparation from armoured trains with the support of mortars and grenade-throwers, anti-tank guns and armour, all the strength of infantry being then thrown in. We allow the enemy to come within very close distance of the barricades, and then open fire. Liaison is made difficult owing to the cutting up of the city into sections. Morale is very high, and there is a stubborn will to struggle. Silence on the Soviet side.[13]

Meantime, tanks supporting Dirlewanger's brigade had blown the barricade on Swietojanska Street to pieces soon after first light, decimating the defenders. Major Rog sent in a company to reinforce the remaining barricades there and in Kanonia Street. German infantry supported by a tank at that moment thrust into the castle ruins. A Polish lieutenant and four men surprised them with automatic fire and hand-grenades, killed several and the rest withdrew under cover of the tank.

In the afternoon the remnants of the indefatigable Radóslaw group counter-attacked Stawki Street, one of the Old Town's northern defences. They drove the Germans out of the warehouses, captured quantities of ammunition and weapons, then occupied the school and the undemolished warehouses, where for most of the night they suffered withering mortar fire. 'Today the enemy again tried to destroy our forces in the area of the Old Town,' Komorowski reported during the night of 12 August.

> The situation was critical and objectives changed hands many times. There was a hail of fire. Towards the evening the situation was mastered by a series of counter-blows. If we do not get supplies dropped on Krasinski Square tonight the situation in this area may well be hopeless tomorrow. On other sectors there are no essential changes. Silence from the Soviets...Heavy losses in life and great destruction of buildings.[14]

The appeal was successful. Two RAF aircraft with Polish aircrews successfully dropped containers into the Old Town, one of them flying low over Krasinski Square, only to be shot down by anti-aircraft fire and crash near Praga.

Komorowski and the Home Army Staff began to experience a feeling of helplessness. Having been cut off from Chrusciel's HQ by the wedge the Germans had driven through the city on 7 August, they were unable to organise linked defensive operations between the Old Town's northern group and the City Centre forces. Attempts to communicate through the sewers had so far not been successful. To make matters worse the building in Barakowa Street where the GHQ was situated came under heavy fire. To ease the situation GHQ was therefore moved to the near-by Krasinski Palace on Długa Street.

August 13 started with heavy shelling of the Old Town from the armoured trains in Gdansk station, as well as from artillery in the near-by Citadel, and from Praga, across the river. Mortar bombs were showered on the Stawki and Krasinski Gardens area. In the telephone station on Tłomackie Street the actual German orders to attack were heard. At 10 o'clock the Germans mounted their onslaught on the Old Town from Gdansk station and Stawki Street in the north, from the Ghetto in the west and the area of the Town Hall in the south.

Heavy mortar fire from all directions now drove the Poles from barricades and strongpoints. The Stawki warehouses were burnt out and the German advance was only halted further south at the edge of the

150

Muranow defences. Close-quarters infantry actions were fought here from midday. Salvoes of mortar fire which hit the Town Hall knocked down the tower, but despite very heavy casualties the Poles held on grimly. Several German tanks, an armoured car and four field-guns were destroyed.

In the evening the Poles suffered their first experience of a German booby trap. A light tank began to shell the barricades on Podwale Street. When it was attacked by boys from the Gustav Battalion the crew escaped and left the vehicle. A Polish flag was tied to it, everyone crowded round and to loud cheers it was driven behind the barricades near the Krasinski Palace.

Hearing the cheering in the square down below, Komorowski looked out of the window and with much pleasure saw the tank with its Polish flag. Suddenly a sheet of flame burst from it, there was a violent explosion and the blast threw him across the room amid a shower of glass and rubble. When he recovered after nearly a minute, he got up and staggered to the hole in the wall which had been the window.

Amid a cloud of dust was the tank, torn in pieces. Bodies and human limbs were scattered on roads, pavements and rooftops. Nearly a hundred people were found to have been killed and one hundred and fifty wounded; two houses were destroyed and part of the GHQ severely damaged. The tank had been packed with high explosive and detonated by a clockwork mechanism. Komorowski was mildly concussed and afflicted with acute sinus pain for some weeks afterwards.

At the same time, the attack went on without interruption and by the evening of 13 August the Polish defence outposts of both Stawki and Leszno had been lost. The Old Town was now completely surrounded, at the mercy of ceaseless bombardment. 'The enemy continued attacking the Old Town area with the aid of powerful guns,' the Home Army communiqué for that day reported. 'Stawki, which is in enemy hands is ablaze...The enemy are using salvo repeater mortars and Goliath tanks widely. Attacks start just after a heavy rain of fire. Great losses in men. The enemy is losing many tanks and much artillery equipment...'

The Old Town was now besieged. Help was urgently needed.

13/ Stalin changes his mind

Komorowski sent desperate messages to Home Army commanders throughout Poland ordering them to increase fighting the Germans to the limit. And to commanders in sectors within marching distance of Warsaw he dispatched on 13 August the following special order:

> The battle in Warsaw is being prolonged. It is being fought against great enemy odds. The situation demands an immediate march on the capital. I order all the disposable well-armed units to be directed immediately towards the capital in order to fight the enemy on the outskirts and in the suburbs of the city and to enter the battle raging in the town.[1]

Warsaw could yet be saved if the commanders of the thousands of armed men in the regions liberated by the Soviets could reach the city. Home Army commanders were quick to obey, but the ideological split between the Soviets and the London Polish Government obstructed the plan. Major Zegota, for example, commanding the 27th Infantry Division which had fought in Volhynia, Eastern Poland, under Soviet tactical command and still operated under its orders, sought authority from the Russian command to go at once to Warsaw's relief.

It was agreed that Zegota should take his division to the front facing the city, but instead his officers and men were ambushed, surrounded and disarmed by Soviet units. They were then directed to a new point of assembly, but when marching through a forest Zegota ordered his men to disperse.

Various other Home Army formations were stopped, the officers arrested and the troops forcibly mobilised into the Communist Polish forces. Soviet determination that all Polish men of age should be enlisted into the People's Army to take part in the battles to encircle Warsaw killed the plan. Evidence for the part the Soviets played to prevent these troops infiltrating through the lines is contained in an order the 16th Soviet Infantry Regiment issued on 24 August. Quoting Komorowski's appeal for aid and terming him the 'commander of the Polish Nationalist Army' supported by the 'Polish Émigré Government',

152

it ordered that infiltration of Home Army units towards Warsaw must be stopped at all costs; and that arms, food and equipment should be seized. Home Army units were to be disarmed and marched to mobilisation centres for transfer to the People's Army.[2]

Meanwhile General von dem Bach had received more reinforcements. By 13 August what was called Korpsgruppe von dem Bach consisted of 25,700 troops, with no less than twenty-six tanks, thirty mobile guns thirty-eight field-guns, three batteries of heavy artillery, six heavy mortars, two or three hundred flame-throwers, two armoured trains with heavy guns, an unknown number of Goliaths and the co-operation of 9th Army artillery and aircraft. As a further advantage, his command[3] was later transferred from Himmler to General von Vormann's 9th Army.

Additional reinforcements continued to arrive and four thousand two hundred infantry with armoured cars were deployed to seal off Warsaw from troops in the surrounding forests.

On 13 August, having recently occupied the water supply station just north of Ochota the Germans cut off the city's main supply, but despite repeated shelling and enemy attacks the Poles still held the power station on the Vistula embankment at Powisle.

In the Old Town the situation worsened. Shelling of the outlying defences, Muranow and Tłomackie, on 14 August, started numerous new fires. The dry old carved oak beams and the ancient buildings blazed like straw now there was no water to fight the fires. At 10 o'clock German infantry, attacking from Leszno Street through Tłomackie, overcame a barricade half demolished by the shelling, and stormed the street and the telephone exchange, where fighting with grenades was raging. But later the exchange, the near-by streets and others in the north which had fallen were retaken by costly counter-attacks.[4]

The Poles also launched night assault platoons across the Vistula to try to destroy the German guns, but they were seen in the reflected light of the numerous searchlights pin-pointing RAF aircraft on an arms-dropping mission and driven back.

Early on 15 August, the seventh day of the Old Town offensives, German attacks, preceded by heavy shelling were again launched between Krasinski Gardens and the Town Hall, Polish possession of which prevented enemy use of the Theatre Place route to the Kierbedz Bridge. Fires swept unhindered through this sector. The Krasinski Palace was razed. Mostowski Palace, taken during the day by the Germans, was retaken overnight after a long grenade battle inside. Captain Lukasiewicz, mournfully inspecting the damage within this historic place in the early hours, was shot dead by a German patrol wearing red-and-white Polish armbands which had crept in behind the lines.

By about 12 August, when the Germans had cut the Warsaw defence into three different sectors and were mounting their all-out attack on the Old Town the impression that the Russians had deliberately stayed their hand within sight of Warsaw was gaining ground among the Allies, thanks largely to the efforts of the London Polish Government. But first signs of a hardening in the Soviet attitude came in a Moscow communiqué. On 12 August Tass referred to hints in the foreign press based on Polish Government information that 'those who rose up in Warsaw were allegedly in contact with the Soviet Command, that the latter did not render the necessary assistance.' It went on:

> *Tass* is authorised to declare these statements and hints in the foreign press either the result of a misunderstanding, or else the manifestation of slander against the Soviet Command.
> It is known to *Tass* that on the side of the Polish London circles who are responsible for what is happening in Warsaw, no attempt was made to inform beforehand the Soviet Military Command, or to co-ordinate with the Soviet Command any kind of action in Warsaw. In view of this, the responsibility for all that is taking place in Warsaw falls exclusively on the Polish émigré circles in London.[5]

On the same day Mr Churchill sent on to Marshal Stalin an urgent plea for aid for the Home Army, together with a report on the severity of the fighting in Warsaw that Deputy Premier Jankowski had sent to London. 'They implore machine-guns and ammunition,' Churchill wrote. 'Can you not give them some further help, as the distance from Italy is so very great?'

Back from Moscow and anxiously awaiting the help Marshal Stalin had assured him he would give, Prime Minister Mikolajzcyk on 13 August also sent a plea to Stalin.[6] He said:

Referring to our last conversation in the matter of assistance to combatants in Warsaw, I appeal once more to you, Marshal, to give air-support to Warsaw. The following points are most important:
1. the bombing of airfields, armoured trains on the Warsaw ring-railway and other targets already specified;
2. day patrols by fighters to protect Warsaw from raids by the Luftwaffe;
3. the parachuting of huge quantities of arms and ammunition over Warsaw, most of which is now held by the Poles. This would make it possible for the fighting to continue until the arrival of your relief. The most important areas for parachuting are Krasinski Square and Napoleon Square.

Warsaw has kept up the fight by superhuman efforts in spite of an ever increasing shortage of arms and ammunition. It is both in your interest and in ours that you should reach Warsaw to liberate it, not just to clear up wreckage and bury corpses. Any assistance given by

154

the USSR at this moment will be of great political importance in future Polish–Soviet relations.

Even accepting that Stalin had failed to send arms this message is remarkable for its one-sidedness and its lack of realism. Mikolajczyk blandly ignored the fact that only four days earlier he had received from Stalin an account of the Red Army's setback and the severe battles it was then fighting with the Germans. Evidently, the British Government had not received a full account of Stalin's report from Mikolajczyk, for on 14 August Churchill, in Italy inspecting General Alexander's forces, telegraphed to Eden:

> It will cause the Russians much annoyance if the suggestion that the Polish patriots in Warsaw were deserted gets afoot, but they can easily prevent it by operations well within their power. It certainly is very curious that at the moment when the Underground Army has revolted the Russian armies should have halted their offensive against Warsaw and withdrawn some distance.
>
> For them to send in all quantities of machine-guns and ammunition required by the Poles for their heroic fight would involve only a flight of 100 miles. I have been talking to (Air Marshal) Slessor, trying to send all possible assistance from here.
>
> But what have the Russians done? I think it would be better if you sent a message to Stalin through Molotov referring to the implications that are afoot in many quarters and requesting that the Russians should send all the help they can.[7]

The Russians had of course done a great deal, but they normally sent their Anglo-American allies military reports only after a battle had been won and operations successfully concluded. Therefore Churchill could not know what was happening on this sector of the Eastern Front apart from the reports of British Military Intelligence. At this time they were making the merest conjectures about a possible Soviet setback.[8]

On 16 August Stalin in a reply to Mikolajczyk[9] retracted the assurance that arms would be sent:

> I received your letter about Warsaw. I feel obliged to let you know that after our conversation I issued orders to the Soviet Command to drop arms intensively in the Warsaw area. Moreover, a parachutist was dropped but was unable to fulfil his task because he was killed by the Germans.
>
> After a closer study of the problem I became convinced that the Warsaw action, which had been started without the Soviet Command's knowledge and without any contact with it, is a reckless adventure causing useless victims among the inhabitants.

It should be added to this that a slanderous campaign with allusions that the Soviet Command had misled the population of Warsaw, was developed in the Polish Press. In view of the foregoing the Soviet Command decided openly to disclaim any responsibility for the Warsaw adventure because it must not and cannot assume responsibility for the Warsaw affair.

It was an appalling breach of faith, but there was more to come. On the same day, Andrei Vyshinsky, Soviet Deputy Minister for Foreign Affairs, informing the United States ambassador in Moscow[10] that it was desirable to avoid misunderstanding, declared that the Soviet Government could not object to English or American aircraft dropping arms in the region of Warsaw. 'But they decidedly object to American or British aircraft, after dropping arms in the region of Warsaw, landing on Soviet territory, since the Soviet Government do not wish to associate themselves either directly or indirectly with the adventure in Warsaw.'

Already the international atmosphere was overcast by British if not American suspicions that Stalin planned to sovietise Europe. Now the London Polish Government let loose all its fury for Russia's past misdeeds in a diplomatic and press campaign charging her with deliberately staying her hand and letting Warsaw, the Home Army and the citizens be destroyed. 'They are relentless felons,' one Polish politician remarked, and it was typical of their feelings.

Mikolajczyk tried to pour oil on troubled waters and allay the harm that had been done. 'I understand very well, Marshal, that the Soviet Command assumes no responsibility for the outbreak of fighting in Warsaw which, as it seems now, was premature but the timing of which could not have been agreed upon jointly,' he said in a reply to Stalin on 18 August.[11]

> In connection with this it is quite understandable that a part of the Press, also of the Polish Press should give vent to excitement because of the tragic fate of the inhabitants of Warsaw. I can, however, assure you that in accordance with the spirit of our friendly conversations in Moscow, I am counteracting this within the limits of my powers and opportunities, and I should like to reckon on co-operation on the part of Russia also in that matter...

Mikolajczyk concluded by reminding Stalin that Warsaw had fought unaided for eighteen days. He appealed fervently for aid, notably for permission for American aircraft to land on Soviet airstrips after arms-dropping over the city. But Stalin had already withdrawn his assurance that direct aid would be given to Warsaw. It marked another change in his attitude to the London Poles.

While the Soviet armies battled to relieve Warsaw, Stalin at the same time exerted physical and moral pressure on the Polish people and its Government to secure a political system in the country subservient to Soviet Russia.

Meanwhile, Slessor had authorised full-scale flights to Warsaw again. During the four nights 13 to 16 August a total of 79 aircraft were assigned, sixty-two with British and South African crews, seventeen with Polish crews. Only twenty of the total won through to the city and made their drops. Five British, seven South African and three Polish air crews—more than one hundred highly specialised airmen—as well as fifteen aircraft, were lost. One aircraft unloaded above Krasinski Square then crashed near by. Another three crashed on landing. Many of the airmen who returned were badly wounded.

By now the experienced crews used to visual navigation by night over German-occupied Europe had either been killed or were too exhausted after the demands these flights had made upon them to carry on. Replacement pilots and navigators lacking experience of visual flying went to their deaths all too quickly in the inferno of enemy aerial attack leading to Warsaw.

From the roof of his GHQ in the Old Town late one August night Komorowski watched fifteen women of the Polish Socialist Party militia each with a hurricane lamp lie down in the darkness and form the shape of a cross in the shadow of the tall old houses in the market square. About midnight German searchlights began to pencil the starry sky until they converged on one point. German anti-aircraft fire now began to pin-point the sky with flashes. Soon, like a great moth in the light the aircraft could be seen; and at the same time the women lit their hurricane lamps to guide it.

With a roar from its four engines, the first aircraft zoomed low over the rooftops, and six parachutes bobbed quickly down to the ground. More planes entered the silver halo of searchlights, flew on through the inferno of bursting shellfire and parachuted their containers. Then from one of them flame and smoke spurted. It lost height quickly as the flames grew, but somehow the crew parachuted the containers out near Napoleon Square before it flew lower and lower across the Vistula. A sheet of flame and an explosion told its end.

Attrition of crews had all but exhausted the air supply effort from southern Italy. Five British-crewed aircraft took off on 18 August, but none reached Warsaw, while out of forty missions Polish crews flew during the next twelve days three only reached it and all their containers fell into German hands. From 15 August onwards the insurgents received not a single container, though fourteen aircraft were lost.[12]

SS-Gruppenführer Reinefarth was meanwhile energetically carrying out General von dem Bach's orders to deploy his troops for an all-out attack from all sides of the Old Town. Polish resistance was strong, yet on 16 August the Germans made small but significant gains. After tunnelling through rows of cellars they blew up a strongpoint in a block of flats on Pzrejazd Street, killing some fifty troops and widening their range of attack on Mostowski Square and the telephone exchange. The Monastery on Senators' Street, north of the Saxon Gardens, fell to them and quickly fortified, it made another strongpoint along the route to the Kierbedz Bridge.

Ignoring military etiquette, General von Vormann had impatiently been calling direct to Reinefarth instead of to General von dem Bach for a decisive attack on the Old Town.[13] But von dem Bach had insisted on the destruction first of the Home Army outposts there. Soon he would be ready for the final onslaught.

August 17 was a turning-point for everyone alive in smoke-blanketed Warsaw, then crumbling to rubble and cinders under the impact of bombardment and flame. For the first time the Germans shelled it with their heaviest rail guns throwing seven-feet-long missiles weighing one-and-a-half tons. These monsters roared over the city, smashing in one hit targets like Home Army district commands or their own captured supply depots. Happily they sometimes did not explode.

This bombardment continued for five hours, demonstrating that further resistance would be useless. Then new tactics were employed. German officers carrying a white flag marched towards the Home Army barricade near Saxon Gardens in the City Centre. To the Polish officer who met them they handed a letter from General von dem Bach to Colonel Chrusciel. It called for immediate surrender, with combatant rights for the Home Army, which involved their treatment as prisoners of war according to the Geneva Convention. If the terms were rejected, von dem Bach would order the annihilation of the city, and of everyone in it.

For Komorowski it could hardly be termed a dilemma. The gamble of starting the Uprising on 1 August just before the guns signalled the supposed entry of Soviet forces into the city had failed, bringing in its train a huge legacy of death, suffering and destruction. Moreover, the future of the Home Army, short of ammunition and split into separate groups without unified control, was hopeless. Destruction, postponed merely by desperate counter-attacks against the overwhelmingly stronger Germans, must be its fate.

Komorowski now had the chance of releasing both suffering civilians and heroic troops from this agony, even though their future lay in the grim conditions of German refugee and prisoner-of-war camps.

He knew well enough of course, that by all the rules of warfare 'a military force in our position should surrender'.[14] But, as he put it, 'all my hopes and expectations were still based on the certainty of an early renewal of the Russian offensive, which would result in the occupation of the capital. It was the only solution to our present difficulties that any of us could foresee.'[15]

The Soviets and the Germans were still engaged in hard fighting with armoured units over the approaches to Warsaw from the north and south. Cut off as he was, Komorowski had no way of knowing this; for even if the news reached London, which until the battle ended, was unlikely, Mikolajczyk would not necessarily tell him.

So after the failure of his first gamble, he now embarked upon another, in which he knew for certain how costly were the stakes in terms of human life. Perhaps his concussion had temporarily taken away his reason; for there is a kind of madness in Komorowski's rigid determination to go on swimming in this niagara of blood until the flag of Old Poland was raised for the London Government amid the hell of a Russo-German battle in the ruined city.

He makes no mention of discussion with Jankowski, the Deputy Premier. The politicians had no voice in this decision, although it was rightly a political one. 'I ordered Monter (Chrusciel) to leave General von dem Bach's letter unanswered,' he says bluntly.[16] The grounds were that the Germans could not be trusted and would kill the troops. But von dem Bach, as subsequent events made clear, was offering an agreement embodied in a document signed by both parties, similar to that which Komorowski was eventually to sign.

So the German proposal was ignored. And while the Old Town battle went on, to emphasise their disregard of the German offer Chrusciel launched a series of minor counter-attacks on isolated enemy points in the City Centre, starting with the telephone company's building. A massive concrete block, one of the tallest in the sector, it was held by a German garrison which, with well-directed fire from high windows, had stopped nearly all movement in the surrounding roads and streets, making attacks almost impossible.

Behind the Polish attack on this fortress lay that blend of the improvised, the haphazard and the heroic that ran through the whole Uprising. A man aged sixty, working as a technician in the building for many years, was refused enlistment in the Home Army on the grounds of age. In his heart he refused to accept this refusal. When the enemy turned his workplace into a fortress he put his knowledge of it to good use by starting to dig a tunnel to the basement, alone at night, from the cellars of some ruined houses nearly fifty yards away. After two weeks of solitary, unremitting toil he reached the basement wall.

He then reported his achievement and Chrusciel planned to send troops along the tunnel and storm the building as a gesture of defiance in answer to von dem Bach's letter. At 2 a.m. on 16 August the wall was blown and an assault company stormed upstairs. Surprise was complete. The attackers gained a foothold on the lower floors before the Germans knew what was happening. The enemy then barricaded every floor and corridor. A Polish women's demolition squad blew holes through the walls and a fierce battle with hand-grenades was waged from room to room. Amid the acrid cordite smoke the Germans fought right up to the

159

tenth floor. The exhausted Poles were then surprised to find the enemy had vanished. They had slid back down a steel tube to the basement.

The Home Army had gained possession of the building, but were now faced with its possible demolition by Germans in the basement. Eventually one hundred and sixteen of them surrendered, the rest were killed by flame-throwers. Having seen what the Germans had done to their women and children the Poles were little inclined to mercy. The battle for this strategically placed building had ended after ten hours. The so-called elderly man who had made it possible was rewarded by enlistment, a revolver and ammunition.

On one of the prisoners of this action a Polish soldier found a diary which reveals something of the feelings of the ordinary German soldier fighting in Warsaw. It began with an entry by the diarist, Kurt Heller, marking the start of the Uprising on 1 August. It went on:

'2.8. We are still surrounded. 3.8. Ulrich killed. S.S. Sturmfuehrer killed and many others. 4.8. Still cut off. No help from outside. We expect relief today or tomorrow. No food. Water very short. 5.8. Rudolf killed. Others killed with him. Can't keep going much longer. Luttewitz killed. Hollweg badly wounded. 6.8. At noon shelled by own artillery. Attempt at sortie failed, one killed, four badly wounded, of which one died. Fourteen of us now killed. Buried at eight this morning in the courtyard. Bad air from the dead. 8.8. Our men 100 yards away, but opposition from bandits too strong. 9.8. Food very scarce. 12.8. Hunger acute. Every day only a drop of soup and six cigarettes…When will these sufferings stop? 16.8. Terrible hunger. At night we are terrified. When first stars appear, think of home, wife, and my boy, who is buried somewhere near Stettin. 17.8. Poles tried to smoke us out by fire and bottles of petrol. More men lost their nerve and committed suicide. 19.8. No hope of relief. Surrounded by Poles. Who will be the next for the mass grave down in the courtyard?'[17]

The capture of this building gave impetus to further small attacks in the City Centre. A battle for the German police headquarters was fought with hand-grenades across the nave of the adjoining Church of the Holy Cross. In peacetime men raised their hats and women curtsied when passing it because in one of the pillars Frederick Chopin's heart was immured. Expelled from the carnage within, the Germans set the church ablaze, but happily the fire which brought down the roof timbers left the relic untouched. The hated Police HQ fell shortly afterwards, giving the Home Army a big haul of ammunition and machine-guns. Other strongpoints fell in the City Centre too. But this was not enough to rescue the Home Army from the danger of piecemeal destruction it faced.

The belief in mid-August that von dem Bach's big attack was due had caused a sense of desperation among Komorowski and his fellow staff officers in the Home Army GHQ in the Old Town. Shut up in their headquarters, with huge fires blazing in nearly every street, the aggressiveness of their troops limited by lack of ammunition, the Home Army

Staff decided that a link with Zoliborz, as the channel for arms and men from the Forest of Kampinos, was their only possible salvation.

The first move, for which the order was sent to Captain Szymon, in charge of the fifteen hundred well-armed men in Kampinos, was to be an attack on the near-by airfield at Bielany, just north of Zoliborz. Across this ran the main road from Warsaw to Modlin, which the Uprising had forced the Germans to use as one of their two communications links with the Warsaw sector of the Eastern Front.

It was an operation far beyond the strength of Szymon's forces. Seven hundred men with field artillery and armoured cars held the airport, while at near-by Boernerowo was a formation of forty tanks. Szymon attacked with three columns while the remainder of his troops went to cut the main road to Modlin. In the early morning mist it was hard to see the perimeter defences and some of his troops were pinned down by machine-gun fire. But he at first succeeded for a short time in taking the airfield and cutting the road.

Panzer reinforcements arrived from the direction of Modlin. Several tanks were knocked out by the troops holding the road, but eventually the enemy drove off the Poles and recaptured the airfield. Szymon was wounded and more than a hundred men also killed or wounded. The rest dispersed as they could, some back to Kampinos, others to Zoliborz. The assault on Bielany airfield came to an end, a total failure. A less ambitious plan of marching the remaining Kampinos forces to Zoliborz as a first step in the relief of the Old Town was then ordered.

Under Major Okon the troops began a night march. Half-way there they ran into a battalion of the 9th Army's Hungarian Division, who let them through to Zoliborz. The Polish sympathies of the Hungarians had already made the Germans suspicious. (Later it was discovered that they were negotiating to sell their artillery to the Poles for dollars and they were withdrawn from this sector.)

A flat area of allotments about half a mile long, where among the neat rows of onions, carrots and lettuce the Germans had established machine-gun nests, barbed wire and trenches, separated Zoliborz from the Old Town. The Citadel loomed on the horizon to the east. Anti-tank and anti-aircraft batteries on a neighbouring sports ground fired with monotonous regularity at chosen Old Town targets.

Lack of spare parts for the Zoliborz transmitter prevented radio contact with the Old Town at this time, and communication by land had not been attempted, yet links were essential if an attack was to be launched. A ten-year-old Polish goatherd now explained how the German let him pasture his goat in no-man's-land. He agreed to take a message, trotted off past the enemy weapon pits with one hidden in the goat's halter and came back safely in the evening with a reply, but not, unfortunately, from his journey next day. The boy was never seen again, nor was the goat.

Colonel Ziemski called for volunteers to reach Zoliborz. Three patrols who were chosen and briefed on the positions of enemy weapon sites along the route set out after midnight on 15 August. For about twenty minutes all was quiet, then suddenly machine-gun fire broke out and tracer bullets streamed through the night towards a spot about half-way over the allotments. Soon after, one patrol of three men returned carrying their wounded leader. There was no news of the other two. It seemed as though the attempt had failed.

The next evening, 16 August, two officers in stinking, filthy uniforms arrived at the GHQ. They were the two patrol leaders. Having safely reached Zoliborz the night before and delivered orders for the preparation of an attack, as well as for radio spares, they had returned through the main sewer linking the two districts. A radio link and a way through the sewers were now established. Their journey back was the first successful attempt at communication through this sewer.

In view of the Old Town's desperate situation, ringed by troops ready for a major offensive, its buildings in flames and ruins and its streets now so blocked with fallen masonry that movement was hard and dangerous, General Pelczynski proposed that he should go to Zoliborz this way and personally take charge of an attack to try to expel the German forces and link up with Zoliborz.

It was a forlorn hope. A mere few hundred infantry could do little against four or five thousand enemy troops backed by tanks, artillery and aircraft. The other members of Komorowski's staff actually opposed it, but Pelczynski evidently believed it better to die on a forlorn attack than be killed passively defending the Old Town against hopeless odds.

Just after midnight on 17 August he descended the narrow steel ladder and took his place in the pitch-black tunnel with the guide and the rest of his party to stumble through the foetid, airless atmosphere to Zoliborz. He arrived there nearly exhausted early next morning and soon after requested by radio that in view of the weakness of Major Okon's force another four companies of one hundred each should be sent through the sewer forthwith to reinforce them. Some of the Staff at GHQ opposed this, but the men were sent.

Main objective of the attack, which was to take place at 1 a.m. on 19 August, was the Gdansk railway station. Colonel Ziemski was to support it by an attack on German positions in this area from the Old Town.

From 6 a.m. on 18 August until late evening the Germans rained bombs and shells on the already blasted Old Town. Under cover of this, Reinefarth was moving his assault groups as near as possible to the Home Army barricades and strongpoints. Later, that ominous quiet which precedes a battle reigned in the half-mile space leading to the Zoliborz sector, lit intermittently by brilliant white flares in which the Germans could easily see anything that moved.

Church clocks still working in the Old Town chimed 1 o'clock in notes thin and high or low and sonorous; machine-guns rattled suddenly, grenades banged from the direction of Gdansk railway station. The attack had begun. German flares lit the sky, not only white but red now for artillery support. Within seconds the quick-firing guns on the enemy armoured train began their rhythmical chorus. Flames arose from warehouses near the station which the assault force under Major Okon had set ablaze.

The Polish attack had actually reached the open allotment sector, but then enemy shells from the Citadel guns began bursting among them. The leaders of the attack were falling, the rest wavered. Soon the survivors were retreating and making for cover. The guns thumped away for two or three more minutes, then died down, and though the night was still white with flares only the occasional fusillade broke the silence.

Beside the barbed-wire and in the carefully tended allotments lay the dead and wounded. The break-through had failed again. Reinefarth's troops tightly ringed the Old Town and from 8 a.m. next day, 19 August, the Polish troops there began their battle for survival.

General von dem Bach, loud of speech, close-cropped, tall, heavily built, methodical and severe in the Prussian manner, was desperately anxious to be able to report quickly to the Führer that he had put down the Uprising.

He personally inspected at the time of the attempted Home Army breakthrough all his troops except those few surrounded by the enemy. He observed that the northern wing of General Rohr's group, attacking the City Centre, was protected from Polish forces in Zoliborz by 9th Army Cossacks. Its southern wing was in liaison with, but did not quite join an outpost of the SS Kaminski Brigade. 'I had the distinct impression that their occupation of a vodka factory was the cause,' von dem Bach said later.[1]

He evaluated the entire situation in the city in relation to his up-to-date information in mid-August about the Russo-German battle front and then evolved a new plan. This laid down that the various districts of Warsaw were to be captured in succession by concentrating on each all the available force. He planned to make the Old Town, which was the northern part of Warsaw, the target of his heaviest attacks. 'An important factor in this decision was the ever-present threat of a Soviet attack on Praga,' he wrote:[2]

I was counting on the likelihood of the eastern bank of the Vistula falling into Soviet hands even before the end of the Uprising. Necessarily therefore the most important aim of my attack was to seize the entire western bank of the Vistula. My plan of action foresaw a pincer movement from the south along the Vistula so as to be able to create a front against the Russians at any moment.

The City Centre I had from the start seen as the last objective of my plan. The attack on the Old Town was to open the way to the Vistula for my northern group. The attacks on Mokotow and Czerniakow were to reach the same aim from the south. These forces were to join up on the river bank. I decided that Zoliborz would be the last to be attacked before the final storming of the City Centre since its commander was not in a position to attack my north wing.

Aerial photographs had shown von dem Bach that the City Centre was the most strongly fortified by barricades, and less liable to surprise attack. He was taking into account the possibility of influencing the outcome by means of negotiations, and leaflets persuading the Poles that further fighting was hopeless, and believed that a direct attack on the City Centre would only increase the will to resist.

He flooded the city with leaflets promising good treatment to those who left it, and offering to negotiate a capitulation. Simultaneously, he increased military pressure by stepping up terror bombing on residential districts and hospitals, while heavy guns shelled the whole area; street after street was on fire.

On 19 August, there was not a cloud in the sky. The sun blazed on the walls and buildings and on burned-out heaps of ruins. The soldiers' heavy boots left heelprints in the melting asphalt on the pavements. Everywhere there were swarms of flies. The unburied dead and those in shallow graves in the streets were decomposing and in places the air was heavy with the odour of corpses.[3]

Von dem Bach had strengthened Reinefarth's assault group to twenty battalions of infantry, so that he had altogether about 8,000 troops, supported by another 5,000 in the Citadel and in the garrison command.

A gunboat on the Vistula, artillery in Praga, heavy multiple mortars in Gdansk station and artillery in the Citadel began shelling early in the morning, while Stukas dive-bombed Polish strongpoints in the northern streets.

Ten infantry battalions of Reinefarth's troops launched the main attack from a semi-circle including the Citadel in the north to the Royal Castle in the south. They were backed by two battalions of sappers, a company of nine Tiger tanks with 88-mm guns, fifty Goliath tanks, twenty 75-mm assault guns, six 150-mm guns, two 280-mm howitzers, two 380-mm howitzers, one 600-mm mortar, a platoon of aerial mine-throwers, several platoons of flame-throwers and the guns of the armoured train.

The overall effect was appalling. The thunder of hundreds of tons of masonry crashing down, the shriek and roar of bombs, the drone of engines, the heavy crash of the howitzer shells and the whine of bullets sounded like a nightmare hurricane.

Under the impact of this avalanche of fire the precious old medieval houses disintegrated into heaps of timber and rubble, burying hundreds of refugees alive. Then the blaze began and the ruins burnt like tinder.

Dirlewanger's and Schmidt's infantry advanced behind Tiger tanks firing at the barricades fronting the main Home Army strongpoints in the more solid Town Hall, the Treasury Printing Building, the John of God Hospital, the Royal Palace and the Cathedral of St John. The Royal Palace, symbol of Polish nationhood, became for this reason, and because it dominated the route to the Kierbedz Bridge, a special target of German attacks. In 1939 the Nazis had stripped it of its collection of paintings, its sculpture, its furniture and carpets, and then practically gutted it.

Tiger tanks burst through the barricades around it, and Goliaths detonated their way in. German infantry stormed into the main entrance hall, hurling grenades at the defenders holding the top of a broad staircase. The Poles, fighting with a cold intensity, answered with showers of their own grenades and a fusillade of automatic fire. The battle in the throne room, the ballroom and the rooms where formerly heads of state were entertained in glittering receptions was to continue furiously for days while the German ring of steel gradually closed tighter and tighter around the Old Town.

Towards darkness the enemy bombing and shelling in the district stopped. Poles and Germans were too near each other for night bombardment. By now some Home Army units were almost paralysed by their ammunition shortage. 'We are sitting in the ruins under the heavy fire of the enemy,' Major Witold, of the Radóslaw group, reported.

> Their attacks from the Ghetto have been repelled with heavy losses. Our ammunition is very low and we do not possess a single grenade. The men are worn out. We cannot make a sortie tonight without grenades. If there is to be a sortie I beg for some ammunition; if not, then I beg to be relieved and given a day's rest...[4]

A never-ending anxiety was this shortage of ammunition. Having to conserve every round, soldiers could only fire at short range when the free-firing enemy had advanced dangerously close. It also necessitated costly sorties under fire to seize ammunition and grenades from killed or wounded enemy troops. Hand-to-hand fighting often followed these sorties. In the Gothic Cathedral of St John this close-quarters fighting began shortly after the assault on the Royal Palace and continued for nine days.

Lieutenant Korwin's platoon was holding a position in the apse and sacristy behind a barricade across the nave. Fragments of shattered marble sculpture of the saints lay here and there on the stone floor beside the bodies of the fallen. Now and then a grenade would be hurled towards the barricade from behind one of the stone columns. Through the vast hallowed space where organ music and plainsong had been heard for so long, the explosion echoed and re-echoed.

'In the Old Town from morning till 19.00 hours this was our worst day of air bombing, artillery and mortar bombardment,' Komorowski reported to London on 19 August.[5]

> Only an insignificant number of houses have remained undamaged. There is an enormous number of wounded. Enemy infantry attacks following a fierce barrage have everywhere been repulsed, but owing to systematic and mass bombing, shelling and the use of Goliath

tanks, the enemy is infiltrating into our resistance points. In the centre of the city there are desperate struggles at the barricades with intense fire from heavy mortars. Our previous hold has been maintained. In the Zoliborz area the enemy has brought up detachments of the 608th infantry regiment. The failure to carry out the bombings we asked for is making it possible for the Germans to exploit their technical superiority with complete impunity.

The bombardment continued on 20 August and all day the Old Town suffered destruction by bombs, shell and fire, interspersed by infantry attacks which followed each other with great rapidity. The Mostowski Palace came under attack from two sides at 11 o'clock by infantry supported by tanks. The Poles destroyed one tank by Piat fire and repelled the infantry, but in the afternoon shell-fire caused one of the palace walls to cave in. The Germans stormed it and fighting inside went on until 7 o'clock. The Poles then withdrew with their wounded, surrendering the ruined building to the enemy.

In the south the Germans captured Tłomackie Street and entrenched themselves between the Bank of Poland and the Radziwill Palace. Defending the Bank building, the Poles by the evening had five grenades and five rounds of ammunition to each rifle. In the northern sector they were house by house forced back from their defences. Their situation was becoming hourly more desperate.

The next day a battle began for Długa Street, which ran from near Stawki in the north along the western verges of the Old Town towards the Ghetto. After the day's first attacks by Stukas and heavy artillery Reinefarth's troops attacked from the north with flame-throwers, burst over the shattered barricades and with great energy fought their way towards Krasinski Square.

Dirlewanger's depleted band of criminals tried to force their way up from the southern end, but were unable to break the Polish resistance in the area of the Town Hall and inside the Cathedral, both of which commanded the southern entrances. Schmidt was tied down along the northern Old Town by attacks on his rear by the Zoliborz forces.

Main bastion of Polish defence in Długa Street was the old Arsenal building, already badly wrecked. Unable to take it from their positions around the Radziwill Palace, the Germans first rained incendiary bombs on it, then bombarded its walls with 75-mm assault guns. The fire got out of control. The Poles withdrew eastwards into the centre area of the district, leaving one company to hold on as long as possible.

The Germans had so far not been able to mount concurrent attacks from all sides. Consequently their attacks on individual points allowed the Poles, manning an interior defence, to strengthen them in turn as the attacks developed. So great was their fanatic courage that despite Reinefarth's huge resources in men and fire-power, his efforts at the end of two days to storm this district where the heart of Warsaw beat strongest, had met with only moderate success. 'The Polish bandits are fighting fanatically and desperately,' reported the German Middle Army Group war diarist.[6] 'The advantages gained by our detachments during these three weeks of fighting are miserable, despite our use of the most modern war equipment.'

Nevertheless, although morale was still high the military situation for the Home Army in the Old Town was catastrophic. The soldiers were worn out, so tired from lack of sleep and of nourishing food on top of the unremitting physical and nervous strain that they literally could hardly keep awake. An almost superhuman determination drove them on. Abnormally bright and glittering eyes stared out of haggard, smoke-blackened faces marked by blank and stony looks which told that they were nearly at breaking-point. Meantime Mr Churchill, who had not ceased his efforts to help Warsaw, proposed to President Roosevelt on 18 August that they should together send a personal message to Stalin. He wrote:[7]

An episode of profound and far-reaching gravity is created by the Russian refusal to permit American aircraft to bring succour to the heroic insurgents in Warsaw, aggravated by their own complete neglect to provide supplies by air when only a few score miles away. If, as is almost certain, a wholesale massacre follows the German triumph in that capital no measure can be put upon the full consequences that will arise.

On 20 August President Roosevelt and the Prime Minister sent their joint appeal to Marshal Stalin. 'We are thinking of world opinion if the anti-Nazis in Warsaw are in effect abandoned,' the message said:

We believe that all three of us should do the utmost to save as many of the patriots there as possible. We hope that you will drop immediate supplies and munitions to the patriot Poles in Warsaw, or will you agree to help our planes in doing it very quickly? We hope you will approve. The time element is of extreme importance.[8]

Stalin answered on 22 August:[9]

Sooner or later the truth about the group of criminals who have embarked on the Warsaw adventure in order to seize power will become known to everybody. These people have exploited the good faith of the inhabitants of Warsaw, throwing many almost unarmed people against the German guns, tanks and aircraft. A situation has arisen in which each new day serves, not the Poles for the liberation of Warsaw, but the Hitlerites who are inhumanly shooting down the inhabitants of Warsaw.

From the military point of view, the situation which has arisen, by

168

increasingly directing the attention of the Germans to Warsaw, is just as unprofitable for the Red Army as for the Poles.

Meanwhile the Soviet troops, which have recently encountered new and notable efforts by the Germans to go over to the counter-attack, are doing everything possible to smash these counter-attacks of the Hitlerites and to go over to the new wide-scale attack in the region of Warsaw.

There can be no doubt that the Red Army is not sparing its efforts to break the Germans round Warsaw and to free Warsaw for the Poles. That will be the best and most effective help for the Poles who are anti-Nazis.

Mr Churchill then proposed to President Roosevelt[10] on 25 August that together they should inform Stalin that they intended to order their aircraft to land on Soviet airfields unless Stalin directly forbade it, but Roosevelt declined. He said that he had 'taken into consideration Uncle J's present attitude towards the relief of the Underground forces in Warsaw, as indicated in his message to you and to me, his definite refusal to allow the use by us of Russian airfields for that purpose, and the current American conversations on the subject of the subsequent use of other Russian bases.'[11] These were those needed, of course, for the war against Japan.

Roosevelt's attitude now was that he did not see what further steps which promised results could be taken.

The agony of Warsaw's Old Town approached its zenith. Medical supplies had run out, including anaesthetics for operations for the removal of bullets. There was no bread, very little food of any kind, water only from wells or springs beneath the city and dysentery was rife. Ironically, while its defenders had by now seized from the Germans almost as many weapons as they needed they had nearly run out of ammunition. The German onslaught continued, the area held by the Home Army growing ever smaller under the impact of salvoes of fire from incendiary mortars and artillery. By 21 August, the third day of the attack, some 700 of the 1,100 houses in Polish hands had been destroyed.

In a desperate attempt to save the situation, General Pelczynski in Zoliborz and Colonel Ziemski in the Old Town planned another do-or-die attack to link the two districts so as to create the through route from Kampinos for reinforcements. Ziemski chose the most experienced and reliable officers and men from his reserve detachments to strengthen the less experienced Kampinos detachments. About nine-hundred-and-fifty men were to take part in this attempt, which included a diversionary attack on the Citadel garrison, covering fire towards the Gdansk station and destruction of the rail track to stop movement of the armoured train.

But somehow German Intelligence must have heard of the plan, for at about 10 o'clock flares shot up in front of the area where the Poles were massing. When they were deployed and ready a murderous fire was put down on them. Some battalions withdrew, others went forward. One got as far as Muranow on the northern outskirts of the Old Town, but was then caught in machine-gun fire and had to withdraw. Major Witold's men moved forward and destroyed a German bunker, but he was killed, their position was exposed and they too withdrew. Nor was the attack from the Old Town any more successful. Coming under heavy fire from all sides the troops there retreated with heavy losses.

Not only had the attempt failed, but about five hundred men were lost. Home Army morale, already tested by the setbacks of the past three days, was seriously lowered. Knowing the bleak future that awaited them, General Pelczynski nevertheless returned to the Old Town through the sewer with a party of volunteers and all the ammunition they could carry.

Home Army GHQ tried to cheer itself with the thought that while bombs and guns were the Germans' chief source of strength men and women were the Poles'. Colonel Chrushiel observed: 'All reports are showing that the enemy's attacks are weak, and where they are successful it is entirely due to the shelling and the fires. The enemy's morale is falling rapidly...They cannot stand up to our counter-attacks. Thus, attack is our only possible form of fighting.'

But the melancholy truth was that about half of these soldiers in the Old Town were out of action, wounded, or dead and buried in the graves that filled squares and courtyards to capacity. The fanatical courage of the Polish troops, the total disregard for personal safety that ammunition shortage forced on them, as well as the German blanket bombardment, had taken a heavy toll.

So after three weeks' fighting in the Old Town too few men opposed the Germans. The loads of arms dragged through the sewers from Zoliborz now only served to delay its fall. Meanwhile, Komorowski's radio links with the outside world became more and more uncertain. Three out of the four sets had been damaged or buried by falling rubble, leaving only one working, and on 23 August his Signals Officer reported that the last was on the verge of breakdown.

Komorowski took the view that a stoppage in radio communication with the outside world would be disastrous. And since the defence of the Old Town would clearly end soon he decided to move GHQ to the City Centre, where radio sets were still operating. He, his Staff and Deputy Premier Jankowski arranged to leave by the sewers two nights later.

The next day, 24 August, the Germans staged their strongest attack yet. Squadrons of Stuka dive-bombers screamed down over the defences every fifteen minutes. A barrage from mortars, mine-throwers, heavy and field artillery lasted one and a half hours. Infantry then attacked in great numbers, taking the Hospital of John the Pious after a battle which raged inside for three hours. More than a hundred insurgents were killed or wounded. At one stage the Germans captured the Radziwill Palace, but a determined Polish counter-attack drove them out. Yet the enemy had seized and held on to three footholds in the north and the west. These they held despite numerous counter-attacks, marking further erosion of the weakening Polish defences.

Komorowski ascended to the observation post to look for the last time at what had been the fabulous Old Town, unique relic of medieval Europe. All he saw now was a vista of rubble, undulating like the desert, with here and there shells of buildings not fully demolished, or a solitary chimney reaching to the sky like a forlorn cry for help. Ten days' fighting with modern weapons had smashed to pieces a treasury of domestic architecture which previous generations had conserved through six centuries. 'The ancient houses of Stare Miasto had collapsed across streets, forming gigantic barriers of hundreds of thousands of bricks,' he wrote later.

I saw our stronghold which for ten days had resisted repeated German onslaughts – the ruins of the John of God Hospital and the smashed concrete colossus of the Treasury Printing Building. Nothing but ruins now remained of Warsaw's oldest buildings: the Church of our Lady, the charred cupola of the Blessed Sacrament Convent, the shell-furrowed roof of St James's Church in Freta Street and the remnants of the Cathedral Tower. The destruction of the Old Town was the heavy price which Warsaw had paid to be able to hold on.[12]

Before Komorowski left the Old Town for the City Centre he gave Colonel Ziemski orders to hold on to the last so as to enable other districts to continue fighting until Soviet help arrived. At about 11 p.m. on 27 August he descended into the sewers with his Staff officers.

These dark and noisome passages had become a lifeline for the beleaguered Old Town troops though still a fearsome death-trap. A platoon of sixty men set out from Zoliborz with three hundred grenades, two machine-guns and several sub-machine-guns, the first such trip. Six hours later they arrived at the manhole in the Krasinski Square, so weakened by the poisonous air and their exertions that they had to be lifted out. But there were only thirty-six of them. Twenty-four had fallen and died on the way.

Except in the largest four-feet high collector-sewer travellers progressed by bending forward until almost doubled up, holding two short sticks as supports and making short kangaroo-jumps forward. It was slow, painful and exhausting. To fall meant a likely cut from the broken glass with which the pipes were strewn, and possibly septicaemia. Lack of oxygen made the soldiers' hearts pound, while the fumes in the atmosphere dried their mouths and nasal passages, causing

171

their eyes to burn and water as if from tear gas. Even the bravest men were often terror-stricken when they found it almost impossible to breathe in this pitch-black evil-smelling darkness.

Panic sometimes occurred for the most unlikely reasons. Once a nurse broke a bottle of ether she was carrying in a box of medical supplies. The smell at once caused shouts of 'Gas!' and a rush backwards in which the less fortunate were knocked down and trampled on in the thick rush of sewage.[13] One soldier, who had lost his wife during the fighting in Czerniakow, went mad and ran back. His howls were magnified a thousandfold in eerie echoes from one sewer's end to the other.

For to add to the nightmare, the sewers were like vast speaking tubes which distorted and amplified every sound. In some of the smaller tunnels a gasp or a groan grew to the proportions of a lion's roar. Bombs falling above, or the explosions of grenades tossed through manholes by the Germans boomed and crashed in a resonant pandemonium, setting the tunnel trembling in a way that stretched the overtaut nerves of the columns of wayfarers to the very limit.

Men and women stumbled forward under the weight of loads of ammunition or equipment, trying to keep their balance in the strong current, sometimes up to their waists in excrement, slithering about, falling face forward or tripping over a corpse or a bundle of abandoned equipment. People who fell behind lost their way and were never seen again. Occasionally someone's will to live would vanish completely in this hell. They slumped down in the filthy sewage, refused to move and never got up again.

Communication through the sewers was hell, but compared to life in what was left of the Old Town only relatively so. Since people in fact had to try to learn to live with sewer communication human intelligence was brought to bear upon it.

An attempt at safety and system had been made. Sappers fixed safety ropes, marked the walls with phosphorescent paint, warned of danger points in the collector tunnels where sudden rushes of sewage occurred, or built dams to control them. To prevent over-crowding sewer travellers were allowed past the sentries guarding the manholes only on production of a pass signed by a district commander.

A one-way street system with a timetable had been introduced to prevent the near-disaster which happened once or twice in the early days, when a column going north stumbled into one going south in this blackness where it was impossible for two people to pass. Thereafter, a party going from Zoliborz to the Old Town would leave at midnight and expect to arrive at about 10 o'clock, so that men and women leaving the Old Town for Zoliborz would be safe to depart an hour later at 11 a.m. Women volunteers organised in units known as *kanalarki* (Polish for sewer is *kanal*) helped to keep the sewer traffic moving, carried orders and even helped to explore safe new tunnels. The German discovery of the insurgents' use of the sewers was to lead to hand-to-hand fighting with pistols and knives in pitch darkness and waist-deep filth.

Komorowski, his staff officers, Basia, his messenger girl, the Deputy Premier Jankowski and his fellow political leaders were all roped together for this ordeal where a false step could mean a grim death. The sewer pipe to the City Centre was just under a mile long, but gasping and stumbling it took them several hours to struggle through and they were sick and exhausted on coming out into the clean air.

At this time, the end of August, the women of Warsaw sent an appeal to the Pope by radio: 'Holy Father, we Polish women are fighting in Warsaw, moved by patriotism and attachment to the land of our fathers,' they declared.

> We are short of food, arms and medical supplies. We have been defending our fortress now for three weeks. Warsaw is in ruins. The Germans are murdering the wounded in the hospitals. They are driving women and children in front of their tanks. The news that children are fighting in the streets of Warsaw destroying enemy tanks with bottles of petrol is no exaggeration.

> We mothers are seeing our sons perish for freedom and the Fatherland. Our husbands, our sons, and our brothers are not considered by the enemy to be combatants. Holy Father, no one is helping us. The Russian armies which have been for three weeks at the gates of Warsaw have not advanced a step. The aid coming to us from Great Britain is insufficient. The world is ignorant of our fight. Only God is with us. Holy Father, Vicar of Christ, if you can hear us, bless us Polish women who are fighting for the Church and for freedom.

Four days later on 4 September, Churchill and the British War Cabinet drafted a strong protest to the Soviet Government, which however, made no reference to Stalin's assertion that Soviet armies were fighting hard against the Germans in the region of Warsaw. 'The War Cabinet wish the Soviet Government to know that public opinion in this country is deeply moved by the suffering of the Poles...' it began.[14]

> Whatever the rights and wrongs about the beginnings of the Warsaw rising, the people of Warsaw themselves cannot be held responsible for the decision taken. Our people cannot understand why no material help has been sent from outside...The fact that such help could not be sent on account of your Government's refusal to allow United States aircraft to land on aerodromes in Russian hands is now becoming publicly known. If on top of all this the Poles in Warsaw should now be overwhelmed by the Germans, as we are told they must be within two or three days, the shock to public opinion

173

here will be incalculable. The War Cabinet find it hard to understand your Government's refusal to take account of the obligations of the British and American Governments to help the Poles in Warsaw. Your Government's action in preventing this help being sent seems to us at variance with the spirit of Allied cooperation to which you and we attach so much both for the present and for the future.

Out of regard for Marshal Stalin and the Soviet peoples with whom it is our earnest desire to work in future years, the War Cabinet have asked me to make this further appeal to the Soviet Government to give whatever help may be in their power, and above all to provide facilities for United States aircraft to land on your airfields for this purpose.

On the same day Winston Churchill made one more plea to Roosevelt to authorise the United States Air Force to drop arms 'landing, if necessary, on Russian airfields without their formal consent', but Roosevelt was not prepared to risk shattering the alliance by a unilateral act of this kind, especially in view of the need for Soviet aid against the Japanese.

His refusal next day took the form of a somewhat clumsy diplomatic avoiding action – or was he unknowingly harbouring Stalin's friends in his entourage? 'I am informed by my Office of Military Intelligence that the fighting Poles have departed from Warsaw and that the Germans are now in full control,' he said.[15] 'The problem of relief for the Poles has therefore unfortunately been solved by the delay and by German action, and there now appears to be nothing we can do to assist them.'

The depth of cynicism and falsity in this message must have been shattering even to worldly-wise Winston Churchill.

A last-ditch assignment was Colonel Ziemski's in the ruins of the Old Town. The Germans had barricaded below a manhole the northern sewer link with Zoliborz to stop the flow of supplies. There was little ammunition. The garrison counted between two and three thousand exhausted men. What little water still ran was mostly poisoned by the bodies which had fallen into the wells. Potato soup was almost the only food.

'I should like to mention the fact that four hand-grenades are not enough to hold this redoubt for twenty-four hours,' reported Lieutenant Kalinowski, defending the Town Hall.[16] 'It will undoubtedly lead to disaster. A relief garrison must be found, as the present one is demoralised by the numbers of dead and wounded, and exhausted as well. Blank's Palace is without defence. The civilians have all been buried in the cellars. I request a garrison for the ruins of this palace.'

But relief was impossible. Kalinowski's situation was typical of the entire Old Town defence. In the Cathedral Lieutenant Korwin's platoon had been fighting for ninety-six hours without relief, and for the past two days had neither food nor water. When they were finally relieved by another platoon with four grenades and a machine-gun they could hardly walk. On 20 August Stuka dive-bombers demolished the twenty or so remaining Old Town houses.

Further losses had reduced the number of defenders to barely two thousand men with a small number of grenades and a few rounds each for automatic weapons. They had now reached the point of complete physical inability to endure the hail of fire any more. Colonel Ziemski decided that despite the order to hold on to the last no further resistance could effectively be made.

But the issue was not surrender; it was how to get his remaining force out of the Old Town and south to the City Centre. Ziemski decided to go about it by driving a corridor south through the enemy positions in Bank Square and Mirowski Square, through which the wounded and the civilians as well could be taken out. At the same time it was agreed that Chrusciel was to mount a similar attack from corresponding City Centre positions. Major Perdzynski went there through the sewer to agree on the details. Both sides were to open fire at 11 o'clock on the night of 30 August. About six hundred yards separated the two Polish forces, held by strong German units supported by tanks and artillery. Surprise was the essence of the operation, which required exact co-ordination. Under Ziemski's command, the Old Town units were to advance in two wings, while at the same time a diversionary attack was to be made on the enemy positions in Bank Square by means of a sudden arrival from the sewer manhole there.

It was a daring and well-planned operation. The left wing under Colonel Radóslaw's command was divided into two columns. One, under Major Jan, was to advance from the ruins of the Bank of Poland, into Bank Square to link up with the group emerging from the sewer manhole there and then to fight their way down Electoralna Street to Zelazna Brama Square. The second, led by Captain Trzaska, would advance parallel from Danilowiczowska Street through Senators' Street and thence through Zabia Street, giving protection through Saxon Gardens.

The right wing under Captain Sosna, about two hundred men, was to advance from the Radziwill Palace through Tłomackie towards Rymarska Street. About six hundred and fifty men were to take part in the operation. Major Rog, with about a thousand men, was to hold all the defensive positions of the Old Town in a rearguard action while the operation was in progress, fighting his way out when a flare signalled the moment.[17]

In view of the large numbers of German troops holding the district and the extreme exhaustion of Ziemski's men the chances of success were not great; and Ziemski himself was sceptical about it. The sewer was an alternative outlet, but seemingly impossible for so many men at once. Colonel Chrusciel said that withdrawal from the Old Town would release all the German forces there for heavy attacks on the City Centre.

He therefore requested Ziemski to hold off for two or three more days after 30 August, so that the defences there could be strengthened, but Ziemski knew that his own defence was nearing the point of total collapse. Urgent action was vital.

His view was given added point on 29 August, when enemy bombing raids increased in both frequency and weight. In last desperate struggles the Poles three times gained and lost St John's Cathedral, while elsewhere among the ruins and rubble the fighting gained rather than lost in intensity.

During 30 August the walking wounded were evacuated through the sewer. At the same time Ziemski began the difficult task of withdrawing his men from their strongpoints and deploying them into their jump-off positions for the breakthrough. Then the unexpected happened. The unfortunate civilians heard of it and fearing the worst, began to panic. Desperate not to be left behind they rushed up from their cellars and thronged in a shouting crowd around the units.[18] Hearing the noise the Germans began firing at the abandoned barricades and strongpoints.

It was a dangerous moment. Ziemski managed to pull his forces back to the barricades just in time to repel enemy attacks. As a result the attempt at breakthrough had to be delayed for a time.

But the units were scattered over the whole extent of the Old Town defences. In the dark, contact with them all was almost impossible. About seventy men of Radóslaw's Zoska Battalion failed to hear the new zero hour in time and attacked alone and unsupported. German machine-gun nests and pillboxes put down a curtain of fire. Captain Jerzy led his men to refuge down a manhole into the sewers, but there in the darkness they lost their way, and came out through an open manhole in Saxony Park, which the enemy held.

It was a situation calling for immediate action. Captain Jerzy told his men to take the red-and-white armbands off their captured German SS uniforms; then forming them up two-deep with four men who spoke fluent German at their head he ordered them loudly in German to march towards Polish barricades about three hundred yards away.

An enemy patrol advanced. Quietly, Jerzy now ordered the word to be passed down the line that they were not to shoot unless attacked. But the German NCO merely warned him that any noise could bring down Polish fire. Coolly, Jerzy asked where the mines were laid in the neighbourhood, and having been told marched his men briskly towards the Polish barricade. But seeing a unit in SS uniforms advancing from German lines the Poles themselves opened fire, killing one man and wounding two. When the shooting stopped Jerzy's men rushed for the barricade, shouting in Polish—'Don't shoot!' They were saved.

The main attack was a fiasco. At first the enemy were taken by surprise, and it made progress, but they soon recovered, turned a withering fire from machine-gun nests, mortars and tanks on the flank of the Polish troops and stopped them. When there was no advance from the

176

City Centre troops, Ziemski ordered his men to return with all speed to their Old Town positions. Thus at least some of the defences were reoccupied. Tanks meantime foiled the attack from the City Centre; while men making the diversionary sortie in Bank Square were shot down while emerging from the manhole.

Thus this heroic but unrealistic effort to get the Old Town defenders out on the ground had failed. But the sewers remained, and hazardous as it was in all ways, Ziemski now planned for such an escape.

Retreat through the sewers

Ziemski's decision to withdraw alone through the sewers to the City
Centre was at first opposed by Chrusciel, who wanted him to try to hold
the ruins of the Old Town for a few more days. But Ziemski knew that
the entire defence there faced collapse. He had hardly any ammunition
and like sleep-walkers with an inhuman disregard for death his men
faced the German attacks. He pressed Chrusciel to allow him to withdraw, and it was sanctioned for 1 September.[1] 'Old Town situation
critical, impossible to hold out longer owing to lack of supplies and
the enormous losses,' Komorowski signalled to London on 31 August.

Ziemski knew that great risks were involved, for no more than about
fifty troops had so far made the journey at one time. Now there were
about fifteen hundred, as well as many civilians, numbers of whom were
exhausted and liable to panic. Moreover the Old Town barricades would
progressively be stripped of their defenders. Sooner or later the Germans
would discover this, realise where the troops were and throw grenades
or turn flame-throwers through the manholes. The Poles would be
entirely at the enemy's mercy. For even the bravest, it was terrifying.

On 1 September the unexpected intervened. It was a burning hot day;
the Germans launched a heavy infantry attack on Krasinski Square, thus
endangering the manhole to the sewers, the only escape outlet. It
electrified the Polish troops in the area.

Famished and exhausted, looking like human scarecrows, supplied
with ammunition from the last of the reserves, they now attacked like
demons. Their fire was murderous, steady and concentrated. Not a single
German entered the Square and in the evening two enemy officers with
a white flag cautiously crossed the no-man's-land there to request a
truce for a few hours so that the dead and wounded on the approaches
could be removed.

It was a heaven-sent chance. Under cover of the truce Ziemski
realised he could carry out the descent into the sewer labyrinth. He
accepted the truce and issued orders to make ready.

Now began the most extraordinary episode in the whole Uprising.
It was exactly 8 o'clock in the evening when the truce began. Shooting
stopped and an eerie silence descended over the Old Town's appalling

ruins. Leaving one token guard on each barricade, units from defences north, south, east and west began moving towards Krasinski Square and the manhole. There a queue formed, to be slowly swallowed up in it.

Everything depended upon the speed with which they stumbled the four kilometres through the sewage to the City Centre, for the truce ended at dawn. Four hours was reckoned the shortest possible time, each man holding on to the one ahead. Somehow the wounded were carried along. Now and then this human chain passed in the darkness through niagaras of falling water from bomb damage to the tunnel roof. It made breathing even worse and almost drowned some of them, but there was no time to rest.

At intervals the pitch darkness was lit by the blue light of night streaming through an open manhole. Here it was easier to breathe, but more dangerous, because the Germans with their listening points on the sewers might discover what was happening and throw down grenades. Towards the end of the journey the level of the current fell from waist to knee level, but the sludge was thicker and heavier and the poisonous gases made every breath painful.

Many could not go on and fell unconscious in the stream of sewage. Those who came behind pushed forward, hardly knowing what they were doing and trampled them down in the darkness. And there they drowned.

At 5 a.m., as dawn glimmered over the Old Town ruins and Ziemski with a few barricade guards entered the manhole, the drone of German aircraft was heard. Dive-bombers hurtled down and the two hundred soldiers still waiting to enter scattered for shelter. Bombs struck the ruins of houses all around the manhole and blocked the entrance with rubble.

But the operation had succeeded. Altogether fifteen hundred fighting men, about two thousand walking wounded, a few hundred stretcher cases and five hundred civilians, including nurses, eventually reached the City Centre. Another eight hundred managed to get through to Zoliborz.[2] Those soldiers left behind went out through smaller sewer tunnels and some survived.

German artillery, Stukas and tanks went into action as day broke. Finally, bewildered infantry led by flame-throwers stormed the silent barricades. When they were found to be empty the enemy officers suspected a cunning Polish trick, perhaps mines beneath the ruins, and pulled back their men. Civilians waving white flags went fearfully over to their positions and told them that all the troops had gone. By that time Ziemski was about to emerge in the City Centre.

Cautiously, with an advance guard of flame-throwers and grenadiers, the Germans moved in. Dirlewanger's criminal troops aided by the Ukrainian Cossacks herded the civilians together and began an orgy of violence and shooting.[3] In the cellar hospitals insurgents too badly wounded to have been carried out through the sewer were shot, or their beds were sprinkled with petrol, and they were burned alive. In the Miodowa Street cellar hospital only the intervention of German wounded saved the Polish patients.

Thirty-five thousand civilians were taken prisoner, according to German official records. More than thirty thousand had been killed, either during the fighting or when the Germans occupied the ruins.[4]

For twenty-three days the Home Army's Old Town troops had held both von dem Bach's relief force and Stahel's men at bay. Five thousand Polish troops had lost their lives. Having occupied the Old Town ruins and got access to the Kierbedz Bridge the Germans now held a wide segment of Warsaw. It stretched from Wola and Powazki in the west, through the Ghetto ruins to the Old Town and part of the Vistula embankment. Von dem Bach's task was now much simplified.

The Old Town's battle had in fact been the battle for Warsaw. Apart from taking a few isolated buildings, the thirteen thousand troops in the City Centre stayed more or less passively on the defensive instead of stoutly attacking the German offensive against the Old Town from the rear. So they let von dem Bach implement his plan to crush the Uprising piecemeal, almost without interference. Nor were really effective efforts made to bring the Kampinos detachments in to the aid of the Old Town.

The fault appears to have been lack of effective overall command. 'The immeasurable sacrifices and anguish of its defenders and its people had gained thirteen days for us,' Komorowski explained eighteen months later, when he had had plenty of time to reflect. 'Each day gained brought one day nearer the inevitable Soviet advance which would save Warsaw.'[5]

But most of Warsaw was already a heap of rubble. And Home Army Intelligence must surely have known that the Soviet forces, far from holding back, were then still fighting fierce battles with the Germans. 'The situation on the 9th Army front is intensifying,' observed the German war diarist on 26 August 1944. 'Renewed strong attacks by the enemy from two southerly bridgeheads, which were crowned with no small success.'

And on 1 September: 'The enemy continues attacks on both sides of the Radzymin–Warsaw road. Forty-seven enemy tanks destroyed. The enemy does not relinquish plans to get through to Warsaw...At all costs the enemy must be prevented from getting through to Praga until the Uprising is completely suppressed. Obstinate attempts to break through the front near Radzymin are connected with the situation in Warsaw.' On 3 September: 'The enemy are stubbornly attempting to capture Wolomin and the suburb of Praga. Information indicates the presence of parts of the 47th and 70th Armies and the VIII and IX Armoured Corps...The Germans must try quickly and completely to gain possession of the [western] bank of the Vistula so as to isolate the insurgents.'[6]

Clearly the battles with the Soviets which were being fought on the

Eastern Front were a source of much worry to the Germans. Nevertheless these actions did not seem to equal in strength and importance those of the Soviet offensive up to the end of July. In northern Poland the Soviet 2nd and 3rd Belorussian Front Armies were then involved in fighting a flanking manoeuvre from the south around East Prussia, while the 1st and 2nd Ukrainian Front Armies were enflanking German forces in the Krakow–Sandomierz area. The town of Sandomierz, about a hundred miles south of Warsaw, fell towards the end of August.

Having been pushed back with losses in their first attempt to take Warsaw by a frontal attack at the end of July, the Soviets were treating the German concentrations here with more respect. Notwithstanding the Uprising the liberation of the city was seemingly to be accomplished in due course by a pincer movement from north and south.

Meanwhile, a fleet of more than a hundred heavy bombers of the USAF now stood ready for take-off for Warsaw, awaiting Stalin's permission. Unofficial surrender talks had been going on for some time between the German command and the Bishop of Warsaw, but they came to nothing. In a message to London on 2 September, Komorowski reported: 'I have decided to defend Warsaw to the limits of possibility. We possess food till September 7, bread till September 5, ammunition is near exhaustion, how long it lasts depends on the intensity of the struggle...The possibility of holding out does not depend solely on our own powers of endurance, but also on material help from you, or on speedy success in Soviet operations in our sector.'

The Home Army leadership was thus on the one hand accusing the Soviets of doing nothing to help them and on the other declaring their intention of holding out until the 'speedy success' of Soviet operations drove the Germans out of the Warsaw sector. They relied for deliverance upon the Government and people they had accused of treachery. But only the vain hope that their troops could last until the Soviets drove the Germans out and they could install the London Government's representatives made Komorowski and his Staff keep going. Offensive operations were given up in favour of defending positions that were to be held at all costs.

Meantime, two events of importance took place. Despite the Soviet refusal, the British and United States Governments granted the Home Army combatant rights under the Geneva Convention, although these rights did not extend to the Communist People's Army, upon whom the Germans were free to pass any sentence they wished. Secondly, the Soviet 47th and 70th Armies launched offensive actions to the north and east of the Praga district. Radzymin they took on the same day.

The reaction of Generals von Vormann and von dem Bach was to speed the plan to clear the Vistula embankment of insurgents. In Marymont, between Bielany and Zoliborz, some of the weak insurgent detachments were quickly overcome and lower Zoliborz was cut off from the Vistula. The Germans now held the river embankment from this area in the north as far south as Powisle. They at once set up a defence line of about a dozen machine-gun nests along it.

On 5 September von dem Bach began heavy attacks on Powisle. For two days aircraft and heavy guns launched a high explosive and incendiary bombardment, setting the entire district aflame. Heavy shells shattered the walls of one house after another. Machine-guns sprayed the streets. People lived in the cellars like rats. Children played in the filthy water that seeped into them from burst mains.

Early on 7 September the Germans drove a crowd of women prisoners in front of their advancing troops. Seeing this crowd of women the insurgents held their fire, detecting the ruse only when it was too late. The women hurled themselves at the barricades and the Germans massed behind forced their way over too.

Attacked from all sides, the Home Army troops were compelled to retreat. Panic spread among the civilians, who fled towards the City Centre. It was a precarious situation for the insurgents. Colonel Chrusciel, however, threw in his reserves and stopped the German advance along the fashionable north–south boulevard of Novy Swiat.

The Germans were now masters of the whole river embankment except Upper Czerniakow, where the insurgents still clung to a small bridgehead, surrounded on three sides, with their backs to the river.

The loss of Powisle was a disaster. Mass shootings of prisoners and the wounded followed. The electricity power station, which workers had kept running while under fire since the start of the Uprising, was destroyed by bombs and shells. Underground arsenals, most of which used electric power, went out of action. Refugees in underground rooms, hospitals in the cellars, faced darkness.

Among the people morale deteriorated. Burials took place ever more often and with less ceremony. A deepening sense of tragedy possessed the wretched survivors. Losing hope they went about with set faces in helpless rage or deep despair.[7]

Yet the troops clung on tenaciously, in firing posts located mainly in basement or attic windows, on roof-tops or behind holes made in walls by shellfire, facing bombardments with amazing resilience. Each of the large buildings in the City Centre had its own defence unit, quick to repulse enemy attacks, undaunted by the hail of fire. It seemed as if the men of this citizen army were now shorn of that basic human quality, the instinct for self-preservation.

All this Komorowski saw in a tour of inspection. He realised how precarious was their situation and how near collapse were the civilian population, whose sufferings in their damp, dark cellars approached crisis point. But looking at the gaunt faces of the soldiers he believed he also saw the capacity to go on fighting. And he therefore decided that the Home Army would not surrender, but would hold its positions despite the worst the enemy could do.

This decision was by no means unanimous, for at least one of Komorowski's senior colleagues on the staff had earlier proposed that in view of the purposeless death and destruction they should either negotiate with the Germans or make terms with General Berling's Polish Communist Divisions across the Vistula for combined action against the enemy. Komorowski called these proposals disloyal and indignantly refused them. 'One thought alone held me to my decision to continue the fight,' he wrote later. 'The hope that the following day would bring a Soviet offensive and, with it, a complete change on the Russian front facing Warsaw...'[8]

But Jan Jankowski, Deputy Premier, and the members of the Council of National Unity, were now too concerned to agree to go on fighting blindly while the population faced starvation and disease. The first case had already been reported with the death of two elderly women too weak from lack of food to leave their room in the City Centre to go out and beg for food. Horses had long since been eaten in the need for meat. Now it was the turn of the dogs.[9]

Komorowski's rigid insistence on continued fighting was opposed by the Council of National Unity, representing the four main political parties. At their insistence Jan Jankowski and the Council's Chairman, Kazimierz Puzak, requested the Home Army command to start talks about laying down arms. It was a setback for his no-surrender policy which Komorowski had to accept.

The trend grew stronger. On 7 September German officers with white flags approached a barricade to propose a short truce for the removal of the dead lying in the streets. The truce was agreed; and at the same time the Germans requested that Polish Red Cross representatives should meet them to discuss arrangements for allowing civilians who wished to leave the city to do so. Countess Tarnowska and Mr Wachowiak then met senior German officers who proposed that all civilians, as well as the sick and wounded, should leave the city at certain agreed points during a cease-fire, and go to German refugee and prisoner-of-war camps.

Komorowski was inclined to reject the proposal, but the politicians felt it their duty to agree. The hours of the cease-fire and the places of assembly were published in the Press and on 8 and 9 September several thousand people withdrew from the city. It was a small response from among more than two hundred and fifty thousand, but people could not forget the August massacres.

Now the Germans offered negotiations. General Rohr, commander of the German forces facing the City Centre, suggested that a Polish representative should meet him to discuss 'certain proposals'. Komorowski sent Lieutenant-Colonel 'Zyndram' with orders that he should merely listen to the Germans without any discussion.

Rohr, emphasising that the Soviets were unlikely to help them, declared that Warsaw would be inevitably destroyed in the same way as the Old Town. He urged in the name of humanity that surrender negotiations should start. He asked for a reply that evening. Komorowski, still trying desperately to keep the flags flying and to fight on in the hope that a Soviet offensive would reach Warsaw, began to temporise. When the German officers approached the barricade for an answer they were told to come back the next day.[10]

Meanwhile Komorowski sent the Prime Minister, Mr Mikolajczyk and General Sosnkowski, Polish C-in-C, a blunt account of the grimness of the situation and the possible alternatives. 'Our situation... compels us to warn you of the possibility of a crisis and of our expectations in that event,' he began.

It is impossible to foresee whether the City Centre and the part north of Jerozolimska Avenue, which has been violently attacked during the last few days, can hold out. In the most favourable circumstances it may hold out even for another seven days, but the breakdown of the civilian population, which is suffering fearful losses, may compel the troops to withdraw south of the Avenue, and this may happen even within two to four days.

After the fall of part of the City Centre, with the whole of the German forces now turned against it, it would be only a question of hours before the long enduring defence of the southern part of the City Centre broke down. We cannot sacrifice the fate of the enormous number of inhabitants who have taken shelter here from all the remaining parts of the city, in order to gain so short an extension in time.[11]

He went on to warn the Government that in the event of their losing the City Centre they were faced with two alternatives. The first was, after evacuating the civil population in agreement with the Germans, 'to go on fighting to the end' – that is to die in the ruins and flames of the city. The second, surrender by individual districts (southern City Centre, Mokotow in the south, Zoliborz in the north) in succession, according to the order in which the main German blow was launched against them.

He added that the second alternative would 'give a certain extension of time' (i.e. for the Soviets to chase the Germans out) 'though then inevitably the entire city would be destroyed. The choice of one of the above possibilities will depend on the powers of resistance and the conduct of troops and civilians, and on the state of ammunition and food.'

Komorowski and Jankowski, the Government's all too faithful servants, were determined to hold on to the midnight hour and beyond, whatever the cost – in the hope of installing the London Government. For this purpose the troops who had fought so well could either fight to the end and die in the bombs and the flames; or if still alive they could

184

surrender when their district had been destroyed. It was a grim and sinister message.

So after forty days' fighting the Home Army was now poised between surrender and fighting to the bitter end. All depended upon Soviet mastery of the Germans on the Eastern Front, which was entirely beyond their control.

Meantime, von dem Bach launched concentrated attacks to try to penetrate the City Centre perimeter defences. He was still carrying out his plan for overwhelming bombardment combined with requests for surrender negotiations. The whole weight of the German forces was deployed. Many avenues were under constant shellfire and set ablaze by Luftwaffe incendiary bombs. On his way to a meeting, Stefan Korbonski hurried along Pieracki Street, a sea of flames as far as the eye could reach. Bright Street and part of Hospital Street were burning. Flaming timbers hurtled through the air, while red-hot pieces of roofing rained down. Korbonski reached his destination smarting with heat and covered with soot and dust.[12]

'The situation in the City Centre is deteriorating,' Komorowski declared with marked restraint in a message to the London Government on 9 September.[13]

The soldiers' endurance is reaching the bounds of human endurance. A hopeless situation. We are losing extensive terrain, we are being compressed into smaller and smaller islands by the enemy's mastery of Sikorski Avenue and the cutting through of our areas.

If the defence of the northern part of the City Centre collapses there may be a slaughter of soldiers and civilians. Powerful and immediate help by bombing and dropping of supplies will prolong our defence. Without that we must capitulate.

Now, when even Komorowski was on the verge of giving up, suddenly it seemed that the tide was turning at last. Late on 9 September Stefan Korbonski, member of the Council of National Unity for the Peasant Party, and throughout the occupation organiser of radio reception and transmission for the civil authority, received an urgent message from London: 'Inform Government Plenipotentiary that today Marshal Stalin promised help for Warsaw.'[14]

He ran through the pitch black streets, stumbling over the rubble to Mokotow Street, where the civil authority had its headquarters. He delivered the message to Jan Jankowski, the Plenipotentiary, Kazimierz Puzak, the Council's Chairman and their staff, who were lying in the corridor covered with blankets. Were the Soviets really coming? An excited discussion followed.

The next day, 10 September, at the hour German aircraft began their raids, the sleeping Poles were awakened not by the frightening scream of the Stuka dive-bombers, but by the steady drone of Soviet fighters circling over the city in pairs, frightening away the enemy aircraft. At the same time came the sound for which Warsaw had waited for forty-two days – the rumble of heavy artillery from the east, in the direction of Praga. On people's faces despair gave way to wild looks of incredulous hope.

That same day, 10 September, Komorowski again sent Zyndram to see General Rohr to receive any concrete proposals he wished to make, but not to talk about them. Rohr handed Zyndram a letter for Komorowski which guaranteed combatant rights for the Home Army, together with safety and adequate help for civilians in exchange for laying down their arms.

But Soviet aircraft patrolling the city skies, the approach of their armies and freedom from bombing for the first day since 1 August put fresh heart into everyone. Komorowski and his Staff saw again the likelihood of a Russo-German battle in the city's ruins during which Deputy Premier Jankowski could proclaim the rule of the London Government. Thus, by a hair's breadth, they could snatch triumph from disaster amid the ruins.

The idea of surrendering faded into the background. Playing for time Komorowski sent General Rohr a message during the evening of 10 September requesting first that General von Vormann or General von dem Bach should confirm the surrender terms; and secondly, as a guarantee, that they should be world-broadcast over the Deutschland-sender radio station. Rohr refused, stating that there would be no further talks if the Poles turned down the terms he had offered.

Everyone waited in a state of extreme nervous tension next day, 11 September, in case the Soviet offensive should peter out, but the gunfire in the east grew louder and the first Soviet shells hit German strongpoints in Praga, setting ablaze the Orthodox Church and other buildings near by. Soviet fighters attacked the few enemy bombers which ventured over Warsaw.

Komorowski saw the need to hold out as absolutely vital now, almost impossible as it was. 'There continues to be a catastrophic shortage of ammunition, the food situation is difficult,' he reported to London on 11 September. 'Without the more serious help expected from outside we cannot hold out. In the northern part of the City Centre rage battles typical of the street fighting for every cellar and house.'[15]

It was important for the London Government now to frustrate all moves towards surrendering and there is evidence that this was done. The Home Army Commander in the Cracow district sent Komorowski a message on 11 September stating that the Polish Central Council for Welfare was conferring with the German Governor-General Frank on the possibility of Warsaw's capitulation on condition that the insurgents be treated as prisoners of war in special camps: and that the rebuilding of Warsaw and the return of the population evicted from Warsaw

186

should be permitted. 'For my part I am personally paralysing all agreement attempts,' he declared.[16]

The relief of Warsaw, it was believed, and the triumph of the London Government had to come within a few days. Komorowski now made an effort to establish military liaison with Marshal Rokossovsky so that the Polish administration could play the part of rulers welcoming the entry of another power. They blindly ignored the existence of the Moscow-sponsored National Committee of Liberation, which was already ruling in the liberated areas. Komorowski sent Rokossovsky a message via London and Moscow pleading for more arms; at the same time he ordered Chrusciel – who had been promoted to General – to have patrols ready to cross the Vistula as soon as Soviet troops reached the opposite bank.

A surge of hope and excitement inspired soldiers and people alike. In the safer areas of the City Centre gaunt emaciated people, their colourless skin hanging on their protruding bones, staggered cheering and singing from the cellars despite the scream and thump of German guns. Liberation was at hand. Soon the Nazi fiends would be gone.

But in the Home Army GHQ the gravest anxiety reigned. On 12 September the Germans brought the fresh 25th Panzer Division into Warsaw and threw it into an attack on Zoliborz, the only Polish bridgehead on the Vistula north of the city. Intensive artillery bombardments varied by tank and infantry attacks broke the insurgents' barricades by 16 September and forced the defenders about half a mile back from the river into new positions.

While in Czerniakow, the Home Army's bridgehead to the south of Warsaw, and in a thin strip of the embankment north of Czerniakow and south of the Poniatowski bridge, von dem Bach pressed ahead with the next phase of his plan to occupy the entire embankment before Praga fell into Soviet hands. Intensive dive-bombing and artillery fire shattered the defenders' positions and despite frequent counter-attacks the German ring closed.

Hope that the situation might yet be dramatically transformed grew as the Soviet troops pushed back the Germans in Praga, routing the 73rd Infantry Division. Ninth Army units withdrew across the river on 13 September and the Germans blew up the Poniatowski bridge. 'The IV S.S. Panzer Corps has had to move back and open a front on the western bank of the Vistula,' the 9th Army War Diary reported on 13 September.[17] 'The day's heavy fighting has weakened the enemy. Thirty-seven enemy tanks destroyed…Bridges on the Vistula being destroyed as planned.' And on 14 September: 'In the latest fighting eighty-seven enemy tanks destroyed. But their greater strength of infantry is making itself felt and they are making progress. Nineteenth Panzer Division was pushed back in the northern part of Praga…The Magnuszew bridgehead is now completely in the control of the 8th Soviet Guards Army but all is quiet.'

On 14 September a Soviet aircraft flew low over Zoliborz, dropping a small container with a letter from the Red Army Command to the insurgents naming places where signal fires were to be lit for the dropping of food and weapons. Zenon Kliszko recalls that the first night during which the drops were to be made seemed to last for ever. He and other soldiers there stared into the bonfire they had lit, feeling joy and restlessness at once, believing that now everything would change. Suddenly, almost above their heads they heard the cough of an aircraft engine, and the small Russian biplane called the *kukuruznik* flew over. Containers without parachutes hurtled to the ground. More such aircraft then dropped their containers. Some of them were broken and the contents damaged, but the operation had a tremendous effect upon insurgent morale. Every night after this Soviet aircraft dropped supplies.

By 16 September the Soviet drops in the City Centre had yielded fifty automatic pistols, fifty thousand rounds of ammunition, two heavy machine-guns, eleven grenade guns and five hundred shells, three thousand rounds for Russian rifles, four hundred hand-grenades, five boxes of other arms and ammunition, as well as food in sacks. Weapons and provisions had also been dropped in Mokotow, Czerniakow and Zoliborz. Armour-piercing weapons were dropped thereafter. 'To the dropping of these supplies we owe the stiffening of our defence and an improvement in morale,' Komorowski signalled.[18] Soldiers and civilians alike were sure that soon the Soviets would enter the city.

This feeling was intensified suddenly at 8 p.m. on 14 September. Moscow Radio broadcast an appeal of the Communist National Committee of Liberation to the people of Warsaw to stand fast. 'The hour for liberation for heroic Warsaw is near,' it proclaimed.

Your suffering and martyrdom will soon be over. The Germans will pay dearly for the ruins and blood of Warsaw. The First Polish Division named Kosciusko has entered Praga. It is fighting side by side with the heroic Red Army. Whatever may have been the motives of those who started the rising prematurely, without agreement with the High Command of the Red Army, we are with you with all our hearts. A decisive fight is now taking place on the banks of the Vistula. Help is coming. Victory is near. Keep fighting.

Would it turn out to be July all over again? Or would it be true?

16/   Defeat, surrender and destruction

When Praga was taken by the Soviets on 15 September the entire eastern bank of the Vistula was in their hands. The Poles had lost all the western bank, except for a short stretch in the southern district of Czerniakow. This was the narrowest part of the river, little more than two hundred and fifty yards wide. Most important from the standpoint of a Soviet landing was that it should be held. To cross and land elsewhere in face of the German fortifications and weaponry would be a tremendous and costly task.

Von dem Bach was well aware of this, for on this same day in moves to secure the district the Germans drove the Home Army from the suburb of Siedce, just north of Czerniakow. They had now cut off Colonel Radóslaw's group from any hope of reinforcements from the City Centre. How long in these conditions he would be able to hold the Czerniakow bridgehead was a source of worry.

Radóslaw decided that instead of trying to reopen a way through to the City Centre he would make contact with the Soviets across the river and request reinforcements. One company from Zoska Battalion was therefore at great risk withdrawn from the line to attack the Syrena Boat Club at Czerniakow, which it captured. Radoslaw's force now held a useful landing stage for reinforcements. Envoys then made a night crossing in small craft from the boathouse and made contact with General Berling, Commander of the Polish Army with the Soviet Forces.

On 16 September amid scenes of great rejoicing the first landings of Polish Army reinforcements took place at this bridgehead — especially because these were Polish troops, even though recently conscripted and unseasoned. They were composed of two well-armed battalions and the regimental H Q of the 9th Infantry Regiment. At the same time two other attempts to land were made.

The Polish 8th Infantry Regiment crossed and tried to get a foothold at the Poniatowski Bridge; the Polish 1st Cavalry Brigade at the Kierbedz Bridge. Both of these efforts to seize the western entry to the bridges before they could be destroyed were repelled with heavy losses.

189

The Soviets now knew for certain that the western embankment—steeply rising ground—was well defended and would be costly to take.

In Zoliborz, north of the Old Town not yet attacked heavily by tanks and infantry but bombed and shelled daily, the communist leader, Zenon Kliszko felt in the tense atmosphere of waiting for liberation by the Soviets that a single moment was almost as long as a whole day. Yet there were moments of hopelessness, with the growing fears of inevitable defeat.

About fifteen hundred Home Army troops and four hundred of the People's Army in Zoliborz were encircled by some eight thousand Germans with massive armour, artillery and air support. 'We looked gloomily in the direction of the Vistula whence help and liberation was to come...From the direction of the Vistula we could hear desultory fire and...it was even assumed that some small Soviet force was trying to force the Vistula to find out what the strength of the enemy's resistance was.'[1] The harassing fire of the German artillery went on almost ceaselessly in daylight hours, pulverising and setting ablaze house after house with heavy losses.

Meantime, having received no answer to the message to Marshal Rokossovsky he had sent through London on 11 September, General Komorowski instructed that three separate patrols should cross the Vistula on different days to report to the Soviet headquarters to arrange military liaison. They took with them details of the Home Army and enemy positions, including their gun batteries. German artillery in Wola and Powazki was now bombarding the river's eastern bank, presumably to disperse Soviet troop concentrations assembling in readiness for a possible assault on the Vistula's western bank, now thick with machine-gun nests and gun batteries. Heavy fighting continued in Mokotow. Buildings changed hands time after time in attacks and counter-attacks marked by savage hand-to-hand combat.

Home Army GHQ meanwhile were hourly looking up at the skies for the fleet of over one hundred Flying Fortresses of the USAF which for days past they had expected to arrive with enough arms, food and medical supplies to enable them to hold out a few days longer. At last on 17 September the BBC played the key melody, *One More Mazurka Tonight*. It was confirmed by a message from London saying that the aircraft would fly over Warsaw between 11 a.m. and 12 noon, 18 September. On the night of 17 September a rain of Soviet fire hit German positions in the city.

The next day was fine and sunny and the Germans were not especially active. Only one or two officers at GHQ knew that the Americans were coming. Then quite suddenly everyone was looking up at the sky where very high in the north a fleet of aircraft filled the cloudless sky like silver birds flying in perfect formation. German anti-aircraft opened up all around the city, but the little clouds of smoke burst well below their thirty-thousand feet altitude. People in safe places scrambled on to the rubble heaps to try to get a better view, cheering wildly. Those under fire hoped for the best as the German guns spoke in unison.

All at once hundreds of coloured parachutes burst from the fleet. 'Parachutists!' The shout ran through the crowd, but soon disappointment replaced elation, for the containers could be seen swinging wildly. Altogether eighteen hundred of them, tight with carefully packed much-needed items, even phials of blood for transfusions and the best anti-tank weapons were dropped.

But most of them fell into German hands or floated on east over the Vistula. 'Yesterday's American expedition roused enthusiasm among the population,' Komorowski radioed to London. 'The shelters and cellars were deserted, everybody rejoiced that help had come and that we had not been forgotten. Spirits rose remarkably in the northern part of the City Centre, where the supplies were dropped. The Soviet artillery and air force continue to rake the areas of enemy resistance with fire...'

Nevertheless the expedition was a failure, owing to the numbers of containers lost to the enemy now that the Home Army held only small areas of the city. It was not repeated. 'We could merely witness this massive exhibition of power and think of what might have been, had this help reached us sooner,' Komorowski reflected later.[2]

The next day, as if to demonstrate the uselessness of aid from outside, the Germans raked the City Centre with gunfire of the heaviest type and pulverised scores of houses. General Stahel and his staff withdrew from the Brühl Palace and the Gestapo from their administrative and torture centre in Szuch Avenue. Paradoxically, it was a bad omen.

Soviet aid increased. A strong screen of fighters patrolled the city air space on 19 September, while their bombers hit German targets in Okecie airport, the Citadel and the Gdansk Station repeatedly. Soviet artillery, directed now by Home Army officers in Warsaw, smashed German targets, often causing losses to insurgents in positions near by. The Germans, so long able to smash the Poles with heavy weapons now writhed under the same punishment, as Soviet artillery shelled the Praga waterfront.

Good news now came to Zoliborz. On the night of 18 September Captain 'Karol', one of the liaison officers who had crossed the Vistula to the Soviet headquarters, returned with the definite news that the Red Army and the First Polish Army were to start an offensive on Warsaw.[3] He said that the Home Army was to be in readiness and wait for the order for combined action. But Kliszko was disturbed to hear that a battalion of General Berling's Second Polish Infantry Division had either crossed or was soon to cross the Vistula at Piekielko, near Marymont, make a reconnaissance and divert the enemy's attention from the main storming place. It was nearly two miles from the nearest insurgent positions and he knew that forces landing there were doomed to a lone fight against strong enemy forces.

Kliszko found it even more difficult to understand that the First

Polish Army HQ had made no attempt to contact the Zoliborz insurgents about help for this intended crossing. That some fighting was then going on there they knew from the boom of artillery and the crackle of small arms. This effort of the Second Polish Division to cross the Vistula was to end in complete failure and big losses. It was later reported that for this attack, carried out on his own initiative, General Berling was relieved of his command. The simultaneous main attack did not take place.

Events in the German army also influenced their operations. Owing to the defeat in Praga and the failure to break the Uprising completely a search for scapegoats was afoot in the Central Army Group. The 73rd Infantry Division commander was court-martialled. Its officers and men were forbidden leave or promotion and assigned to the hardest tasks against the Uprising. The Division's disbandment had even been mooted, but Hitler himself forbade this, blaming instead General Niklaus von Vormann, the 9th Army Commander. Von Vormann had already complained on 25 August that he had insufficient strength to defend the Praga bridgehead against the Soviets. He was removed from his command and on 21 September 1944 General of Tank Troops Smilo Freiherr von Luettwitz took over leadership of the 9th Army.[4]

From mid-September onwards, before von Vormann's fall, von dem Bach-Zelewski also felt himself under threat. He did everything possible therefore, from pressure for negotiations to a ruthless use of the heaviest weapons, to achieve success for his battle plan of cutting the Poles off from the Vistula embankment road and crushing the Uprising in the south and north before the final onslaught on the City Centre.

Czerniakow came first. Radóslaw's troops, defending an area of flat riverside land and ruined buildings about five hundred yards long by five hundred wide, were hit by a hurricane of shellfire. By 19 September, after counter-attacking repeatedly in this inferno for seven days and nights those left—seventy per cent had been killed or wounded—had reached the limits of their physical capacity. They had hardly any ammunition, no fresh water, no food and no medical supplies.

Headquarters of the group were located in a large modern block at the junction of Czerniakowska and Wilanowska Streets, the central strongpoint of the defended area. Radóslaw's HQ and a hospital were in the basement together with the exhausted remnants of two battalions. The rest of the other two were on the ground floor, with some of the men from Berling's army and a few hundred civilians.

The Germans were attacking from all sides. Eventually they blew a hole in one of the walls with a Goliath exploding tank, hurled a shower of grenades then stormed inside and occupied part of the building. Captain Wacek counter-attacked, aided by Lieutenant Maly and reserve units of Zoska Battalion, but without success. Radóslaw's HQ was now endangered by fire from the Germans, who fought back furiously, refusing to give an inch.

192

The Poles then discovered that the Germans were under fire from a Polish barricade near by and therefore could not retreat. A strange solution to the problem of getting them out was now found. It was to order the machine-guns on the barricade not to fire and let them pass. If this was not done and they held their position, they would receive reinforcements when daylight came and the defenders would be decimated.

Another counter-attack against the Germans was therefore ordered and this time the barricade machine-guns did not fire. Captain Wacek found it a hard order to give, but the stratagem succeeded. The Germans retreated from their foothold once they found that the way out was clear. For the time being the HQ was secure again.

But Radóslaw knew that the German attack would now be repeated in much greater strength in daylight and that if he waited much longer both his group and the Berling troops would be annihilated. He therefore decided to withdraw part of his forces through the sewer to Mokotow that night. The other part was to cover the withdrawal of the badly wounded troops over the river to the Praga side. It caused that irrepressible fighter, Lieutenant-Colonel Radóslaw (Jan Mazurkiewicz) no little heartburning to reach this decision, for he held an admirable landing stage for reinforcements in the bridgehead.

But his situation was known; he had requested reinforcements, and none had arrived.[5] Radóslaw and the remnants of his group descended the sewer to Mokotow in the early hours of 20 September. Under constant German fire the units covering the evacuation of the wounded by boats — troops of the 9th Infantry Regiment commanded by Major Latyszonek as well as Home Army and People's Army insurgents — held out for three more days in the hope that Soviet troops would make use of the bridgehead.

Captain Jerzy, in command of a detachment of the Zoska Battalion, decided after a conference with Major Latyszonek to transfer his detachment, the wounded and the civilian population across the river to the Soviet side. Latyszonek put forward Jerzy's request by radio to his headquarters. The Soviet 5th Division Commander promised to send one hundred pontoons at 9 a.m. each able to hold twenty people to take everyone off under cover of a smoke screen. But the help did not materialise.[6]

Later, it was promised for 8 p.m. The Germans meantime heavily shelled the buildings occupied by the Poles and by the evening all of them were on fire. At 8 o'clock still no boats came from across the river. An hour later the detachments marched out to the river and waited. Just before midnight a Soviet officer in a small boat arrived to say that headquarters had changed its plan. Instead of sending the promised pontoons all at once, fifteen smaller boats would be sent each evening.[7]

It was a heartless offer to soldiers who had withstood the German

193

attack for so many days. All chance of getting over to the other side came to an end. Desperation forced the insurgents to try anything. Some tried to swim over, others began to make rafts out of odd pieces of timber from the ruins. Captain Jerzy offered to try to lead about sixty of them through the German lines to the City Centre. Twenty-four hours later, he arrived wounded with a messenger girl and two soldiers, all four of them hardly able to stand. The rest had fallen through exhaustion or had been shot on the way.[8]

The fall of this bridgehead put the entire embankment in German hands. It also ended for the beleaguered Home Army in the City Centre, Zoliborz and Mokotow much hope of an immediate Soviet crossing, for now another bridgehead would first have to be seized. Meantime the Home Army had been receiving 'fairly large supplies of ammunition and equipment dropped by the Soviets'. This continued on 22 and 23 September, together with sacks of food, but it made little difference to the impending mass starvation. 'Only food supplies dropped wholesale can save the situation,' Komorowski told London on 23 September.

Ironically, at this approaching crisis point, a Soviet officer, Alexander Chernukhyn, 2nd Artillery Regiment, reported to General Chrusciel, saying that he came from Marshal Rokossovsky's staff. He wished to know what the Home Army's requirements were; what were their views on co-operation with Soviet forces outside Warsaw and what targets were there for Soviet artillery in the city.

Chrusciel simply suggested what appeared to him the best operational plan for the City's capture and promised Home Army support by attacking towards the Vistula in support of any Soviet drive. But no hopes were raised by this request.

General von Luettwitz was now in overall command of the German operations, while von dem Bach was in charge of negotiations and mopping up operations. The troops he had earlier used to put down the Uprising—Reinefarth's Brigade, Dirlewanger's criminal troops, the Kaminski* brigade—were removed from the Vistula front and used mainly to hem in the Town Centre to prevent the arrival of reinforcements from the forests around Warsaw, and to seal off Zoliborz from the embankment.

Von Luettwitz urged at a Central Army Group conference on 21 September that the crack 19th Panzer Division should now be allocated specially for overcoming the insurgents. At first Major-General Reinhardt opposed, but agreed with the proviso that Mokotow was to be seized in four days and Zoliborz four days later. The Central Army Group was by no means sure of the soundness of the battle plan and General von Luettwitz had to defend it repeatedly to the German High Command during the actual battle.[9]

For the attack on Mokotow General Källner's 19th Panzer Division was supported by the disgraced 73rd Infantry Division and units of the

* Von dem Bach had court-martialled and executed Kaminski a few days earlier.

Hermann Goering, Viking and Frankonian Sudeten Panzer divisions. Prolonged dive-bombing, heavy artillery and multiple mortar bombardment launched the attack south along Pulawska Street, which divided the district. Colonel Karol, who commanded the Home Army's twelve hundred armed troops there was slightly wounded, his deputy seriously. The attack changed direction swiftly to the west and the east and back again to the south. Casualties among both civilians and troops were heavy.

At dawn the next day the attacks were renewed from the south with large numbers of infantry and seven tanks and three armoured fighting vehicles from the west. 'The enemy is using all his strength to achieve the liquidation of Mokotow,' Colonel Karol reported.[10] 'The situation is very serious. Lack of help from Soviet artillery. I shall defend the position on the ruins.' Von dem Bach sent an envoy to propose that civilians should be allowed to leave, as a heavy attack was proposed. 'This enemy move and his attack I consider an attempt to demoralise us and to influence us with propaganda and I did not allow negotiations,' Karol reported.[11]

He requested through his two Soviet artillery observers artillery support from the Soviets across the Vistula. No obstacles of any kind could have prevented this, yet no fire support was given. The Soviets were shelling German troop concentrations in Ochota and also Okecie airport.

By the evening of 26 September Colonel Karol estimated his losses at seventy per cent. A truce took place during which some five thousand civilians left the district for the Pruszkow German refugee camp near by. At dawn the Germans attacked again, but Karol seemed to have lost control. Mokotow surrendered at 1 o'clock in the afternoon on 27 September. Von dem Bach wrote that day in his diary: 'At 19.15 hours the Reichsführer SS (*Himmler*) telephoned me and told me that the Führer awarded me the Ritterkreuz, Reinefarth the Eichenlaub and Dirlewanger the Ritterkreuz.' The Wehrmacht High Command obviously believed that the end of the Uprising was now a matter of days if not hours.

The day before the surrender Colonel Karol and the Home Army GHQ disagreed over the proposal to withdraw through the sewer to the City Centre. Komorowski and his staff opposed this move because the sewer system was now heavily guarded and blocked by German Pioneer detachments. He feared senseless losses. But nevertheless first insurgent units led by Colonel Karol began to go down the iron ladders at about 23.00 hours on 26 September, a scarecrow procession, with gaunt faces and open wounds covered with blood-stained rags.

Soon, as they waded forward through the stinking sludge the dangers of the journey struck them. Here and there the bottom of the sewer was clogged with the dead bodies of those who had already drowned there. Then the Germans discovered the evacuation and began to fire down the manholes or to throw hand-grenades. Those near by were killed, those behind turned back and fought in the narrow tunnels to pass those pressing on from behind. Many men and women, especially the wounded or the weaker among them, were trampled down and drowned. Others tried to escape into the smaller tunnels and never surfaced again. It was a disaster.[12]

As nothing before had done, the fall of both Czerniakow and Mokotow shocked the Home Army Staff into a realisation of the gravity of their military situation. All agreed at a meeting on 27 September that the position was untenable. They concluded moreover that having allowed the Germans to overcome the Czerniakow bridgehead the Soviets had no intention of trying to cross the river to establish another and take Warsaw by frontal attack. Nevertheless a last message to Marshal Rokossovsky was sent in the evening and the radio operator at Soviet headquarters acknowledged it.

Referring to the desperate situation of both troops and civilians, the message stated that hunger and German attacks made it impossible to hold out for more than another seventy-two hours. Unless substantial help came within this time the Home Army would be forced to surrender.

Komorowski and his staff now relied upon an eleventh hour Soviet response for their deliverance from catastrophe.

Immediately after the fall of Mokotow General von Luettwitz moved the 19th Panzer Division and supporting troops north of the city to Zoliborz—more than eight thousand men with air support. Before the attack Komorowski received an offer of negotiated terms in exchange for surrender. Still hoping against all evidence that the Soviets would turn the tables for him, he turned the offer down and ordered Lieutenant-Colonel 'Zywiciel' to fight to the end. Under the command of General Källner, 19th Panzer Division commander, the attack began with a blizzard of artillery fire from three directions followed by Stuka dive-bombing.

A hail of fire and steel fell on the streets and squares of this attractive residential district. Buildings crumbled into ruins and nothing could be done for those trapped beneath them. But in answer to pleas for help by radio Soviet artillery in Praga quickly opened fire on the German positions. 'After a whole day's artillery fire and bombing raids the losses in life and the material losses were enormous,' noted Zenon Kliszko, who was fighting with the Communist battalion.[13] 'In the evening the firing stopped...Over the town the darkness of night fell, a damp night, full of fear. The silence was so absolute that if you strained your ears you could hear the waves of the Vistula lapping at the banks. Our people were so near. I thought: it is enough to reach out over the river and touch the breast of a friend and whisper: I am in mortal danger.'

At dawn another storm of fire and steel struck the houses and the insurgents' positions. Half an hour later the Germans attacked from the south and the west with tanks, mechanised infantry, Goliaths and police troops through the fine wide streets. The intensity of the offensive paralysed liaison between the insurgents' staff and the fighting units. Each detachment fought on its own in accordance with its experience and courage. The first German infantry attacks were repulsed with heavy losses on both sides, but they came in again and again, pushing the defenders back from one barricade after another. The roar and fury of the fighting was beyond endurance.

All the time radio calls to Praga pin-pointing German targets for artillery attack went out, interspersed with futile SOS signals. 'We were waiting for a miracle, we were awaiting the forcing of the Vistula, a descent from the air. Calling for help all the time, we came to realise more and more that nobody could help us any more. We knew this but our hearts and our hands went on with their work untiringly, carrying out every action accurately, and in some cases with great precision. People died unnoticed, dropping to the ground as though they wanted to rest for a while, wrote Kliszko.'

By the late afternoon the Germans had driven deeply into the southern Zoliborz areas towards Wilson Square and Krasinski Street. Then in the evening the artillery stopped firing. The People's Army command there discussed evacuating the entire insurgent force to the Soviet side of the Vistula, in the belief that further fighting was hopeless.

That evening, 29 September, Komorowski personally sent a message to General Sosnkowski, Polish C-in-C, in London, foreseeing total capitulation:

1. We have ascertained that hunger rations of food are sufficient only for a further three days. I see no chance of the Red Army occupying Warsaw in that time, or of such defence from bombardment and food support being secured as could enable us to hold out until the city is occupied.

2. I have informed Marshal Rokossovsky of the situation, and asked for help. If, however, I do not receive it in large quantities and at once I shall be compelled to capitulate on conditions of combatant treatment, which the Germans guarantee.

3. As, after the fall of Mokotow, the Germans put forward a proposal to clear the city of its civilian population and in that event to cease further struggle, which they regard as pointless, I have entered into conversations. The evacuation of the civilian population from the City Centre is expected to start on October 1st and will last, I judge, three days.

4. Since the 29th Zoliborz has been heavily bombarded. The Germans reckon that within three days it will have ceased to exist. In this connection the problem of evacuating the civilian population from this district is very difficult.

5. In the event of a Red Army attack in the next few days the evacuation will be broken off and then I shall take up the struggle again.

At a command meeting that evening Lieutenant-Colonel Zywiciel reminded his officers of General Komorowski's order not to let the Germans break through; and that they should continue to obey that order 'if only for one more day'. Every officer would have to rely on his own judgement, but the fight had to go on, even though it would only bring defeat.

A People's Army officer then proposed that in view of the heavy losses among the civilian population and the inevitable defeat that would follow more fighting, the insurgent forces should try to cross the Vistula with the aid of Berling's First Polish Army in Praga.[15] After much argument Zywiciel accepted the proposal, saying that the front should be shortened so that certain positions could be held to enable the troops to reach the Vistula embankment. It was agreed that the Home Army and People's Army troops should carry out the first move towards the embankment together within the hour.

In his Zoliborz apartment, now in the firing line, Kliszko said goodbye to his family. At the last moment his wife decided to go with him, taking their sixteen-month-old daughter. The Germans did not shoot during the move and except for the roar of burning buildings the night was absolutely silent. After passing through a messengers' trench within sight of the German positions, they reached their destination, the six-floor Phoenix building, in safety.

Just before dawn the 1st Polish People's Army in Praga radioed that they should cross in a fleet of boats they would provide under cover of a smokescreen at 10 o'clock that morning, 30 September. The Germans now began a heavy attack on the various blocks of flats held by the insurgents. Through trenches and across streets exposed to machine-gun fire the first units taking part in the evacuation moved towards lower Zoliborz and the river bank. Then owing to a contrary wind which would have dispersed the smoke-screen the preparations for the crossing were put off to 21.00 hours that day.

Meanwhile, according to some reports strong insurgent detachments attacked the Vistula embankment that morning to try to seize a bridgehead to cover the evacuation, and many were killed. (Kliszko doubts the accuracy of this report, pointing out that there was no mention of it in Home Army or in German communiqués.)

At 17.00 hours about three hundred insurgents stood by ready to give covering fire for the crossing. The People's Army troops especially were excited over the prospect of crossing to the Soviet side and continuing the fighting from there. Then came a totally unexpected development. The sound of firing began to die down in various parts of Zoliborz. Soon there was total silence. Rumours of capitulation began to circulate.

198

Kliszko and two other officers were called to headquarters. There Lieutenant-Colonel Zywiciel said that he had indeed received an order to capitulate from General Komorowski and that he had decided to carry out the order.

Angry protests were voiced by the communist officers present. Zywiciel answered that the proposed evacuation would be impossible; the Germans knew the contents of their coded talks with General Berling and the First Polish Army, while there were mines and machine-gun nests in the area between the embankment and lower Zoliborz. He requested the People's Army Command to join him in agreeing to capitulate. Kliszko replied: 'We shall fight our way through to the Vistula at the fixed time.'[14]

The meeting ended, the People's Army Command met to discuss how they would implement their plan and at the same time German officers arrived at Zywiciel's headquarters to receive the document of capitulation. It meant that all the insurgents would now become prisoners of war. Doubts now began to haunt Kliszko and his fellow communist officers. Certainly, they agreed, to fight on in Zoliborz encircled and isolated, was senseless. But if the attempt to cross to the other side was to end in a massacre it would be better to be taken prisoner. 'So the will to resist and fight melted away like snow on the mountains when the warm winds blow. Fighting fury turned into resignation.'[15]

But promptly at the appointed time the barrage of Polish and Soviet artillery began. Kliszko and fifty others made up their minds that nothing would stop them from breaking free from the shadow of German captivity that hung over them. 'An avalanche of shells tore at the earth to enable us to get through to the Vistula under its cover.' Kliszko said goodbye to his wife and his daughter, who was sucking her finger and looking at him with terrified eyes. At that moment a Home Army officer ran up with a request from Lieutenant-Colonel Zywiciel to ask the Soviet side to stop their artillery fire.

By then the fire had almost stopped and Kliszko and his friends, including one or two women, began their run to the embankment for freedom in the moonlit night, at first in a tight group and then in scattered battle order.

Suddenly German voices were calling out 'Halt! halt! halt!' Machine-guns opened fire, to be answered with hand-grenades. A boy named Edward Patera fell to the ground with a groan. Kliszko picked him up, noticed his frightened eyes and was startled to find he weighed so little. Now came the final two hundred metres approach to the embankment, the hardest part.

By now the machine-gun fire had ceased though from the other side he heard occasional bursts of artillery and shells whistle above. The boy was bleeding and groaning faintly. His blood clotted on Kliszko's hands. Someone else took turns in carrying him. As silence returned the runners' heavy breathing seemed to grow louder.

Then they reached the edge of the Vistula, for all of them a wonderful moment, feeling they had got through alive. But where were the promised boats? And there were no signs of activity on the distant bank. Consternation grew; they dispersed as they ran to try to find a way of getting across before the Germans came. Firing recommenced and bullets zipped above them. Kliszko felt the chill of the autumn night rise from the river and the wet sand. His teeth chattered uncontrollably and he felt that he had reached breaking-point. After some minutes lying there in the silence on the sand he began to feel calm and vigilant again.

Suddenly he saw something moving on the river and soon boats coming in their direction. He fired a signal shot from his pistol as arranged and then began to count the fleet of boats coming towards the shore, more than they needed. Looking back at the red glow of blazing Zoliborz in the night sky they crossed safely without saying a word to each other and were welcomed on the eastern bank. But Kliszko never ceased to regret that Home Army insurgents in Zoliborz were ordered to lay down their arms and not make the attempt. He believed that after the war it worsened the new Government's attitude to the Home Army.

Fighting in the City Centre still went on, but now with a sense of despair in the full knowledge that surrender would not be long delayed. 'Warsaw has no chance of defence any longer,' Komorowski declared in a message to the London Government on 1 October. 'I have decided to enter into negotiations for surrender with full combatant rights, which the Germans fully recognise. Negotiations tomorrow. I will arrange that the question of the safety of the civilian population be linked with the question of surrender. I expect the surrender on October 3rd, 1944.'

Meantime the Polish Red Cross had reached agreement with the Germans on the evacuation of civilians, who were to be allowed to leave at two barricades during an agreed cease-fire for the refugee camp at Pruszkow. But few took advantage of the offer. 'Unexpected turn of events in Warsaw,' remarked the 9th Army war diarist on 1 October. 'Instead of the expected waves of civilians only a small number are leaving...' The civilians had bitter memories of the massacres of 5th and 6th August and were taking no chances. With the capitulation at hand they preferred to stay safely at home. They were more worried about something to eat and during the cease-fire thousands of them walked out past the German positions to the Mokotowska Racecourse to take potatoes, onions, tomatoes and carrots from the wartime vegetable gardens there. The German commander warned them that the cease-fire covered only a general exodus, and that next day he would fire at anyone hunting for vegetables under his soldiers' noses.

Komorowski, who in the past had steadfastly refused to discuss surrender while there were still hopes of a Russian attack, now chose a delegation of four headed by Colonel Iranek-Osmecki, head of Intelligence, known as 'Heller', to negotiate with General von dem Bach. During the night of 1 October the details of a surrender agreement to be submitted to the Germans were worked out.

They met the Germans during a cease-fire at 8 o'clock on 2 October at barricades facing the Warsaw Polytechnic. An SS major drove them past the devastated parts of the city occupied by the Germans since the fighting began and out into the country towards von dem Bach's headquarters at Ozarow. None of the four Poles had eaten anything for the past several days except barley soup and a little sugar. Heller, then aged 47, and a professional soldier, had slept no more than two or three hours a night since 1 August. He was exhausted and suffering from a splitting headache, like his three military colleagues, he was wearing a rumpled civilian suit and shirt and the Home Army's red and white armband. Owing to the shortage of water all of them were unwashed and unshaven.[15]

In the drawing-room of the country house where von dem Bach had his headquarters, with eighteenth-century pictures of Polish aristocrats adorning the walls, Heller met the Prussian Nazi with the gold-rimmed spectacles who had been the Home Army's main adversary. Formally, he introduced himself to the Polish delegation with his full title: 'Obergruppenführer S.S. und General der Polizei von dem Bach.' The Poles introduced themselves and at von dem Bach's request took their seats facing him at a large polished mahogany table. Lieutenant-Colonel Goltz, von dem Bach's Chief of Staff, and SS Major Fischer sat at a desk in the background.

Colonel 'Heller' gave von dem Bach a statement in Polish and in German signed by General Komorowski authorising him to negotiate and sign a surrender agreement covering the fighting in Warsaw. Von dem Bach read the statement carefully, then got to his feet and trying hard to subdue excitement began a short speech in a courteous tone praising the valour and courage of the Poles who had fought against the German forces, as well as the decision to surrender. It would spare the civilian population from horrors which would be bound to have followed had there been further resistance.

Despite the doubts of his superiors he had believed during the past two weeks when the Polish situation had become hopeless and the Russians made no move to help, that sooner or later the Poles would come to terms. The German front, he added, was now consolidated; the Russians had reached the high-water mark of their success. He then excused himself while he telephoned the news to Himmler and his Army Commander.

Von dem Bach then said that he realised that if at the last moment the Red Army were to renew its offensive the Poles might break off the talks and take up arms again. He had therefore been ordered to see that they were disarmed as soon as possible and he wanted some concession to show their goodwill. Colonel Heller, concentrating all his reserves of mental energy to overcome his feeling of utter exhaustion, answered that they were unable to agree to anything which would disarm them, but before even discussing this they should settle the basic conditions of the agreement.

Von dem Bach agreed, and talks began on the granting of combatant rights to all Poles who had fought in Warsaw; on the immunity of anybody in Warsaw who had taken part in any activity directed against the German State from 1 September 1939 to that day; and on the humane treatment of the civilian population.

Half-way through the morning von dem Bach called for refreshments, and a military orderly brought in a tray of sausage and tomato sandwiches and a bottle of Italian cognac.

With this taste of food and drink after so long, Heller argued with renewed energy with the German general over the finer points of the armistice. At one point von dem Bach complained plaintively that he had been wronged and injured by the Poles, for his name topped the list of war criminals responsible for the burning of Warsaw, broadcast by the BBC. He had always been favourably disposed towards the Poles, he claimed; Slav blood flowed in his veins and he came from a Polish family on his mother's side.

Lieutenant-Colonel Herman, one of the Polish delegation and Lieutenant-Colonel Goltz, von dem Bach's Chief of Staff, spent the afternoon drawing up the agreement in Polish and German. It was ready for signatures at 8 p.m.

Von dem Bach clearly regarded the event as of great importance, for he gave his Chief of Staff detailed instructions as to the ceremony of signing. A long refectory table in the dining hall was to be covered with green baize, with von dem Bach in the centre, Heller on his right and the second Polish delegate on his left, with his staff grouped behind. Reporters, photographers and newsreel men were given room to manoeuvre in front of it, while outside in the courtyard there was to be a guard of honour and a military band to play appropriate German and Polish music.

They then sat down and signed the document, von dem Bach assuming a slow, rather theatrical manner out of keeping with his normal behaviour; for Heller those moments which set the seal on their five long years of struggle, on the fate of Warsaw and the deaths of so many brave people, felt like an eternity.

Von dem Bach asked for a minute's silence to honour the dead on both sides, then in front of the microphones and the newsreel cameras he turned to Heller and praised the valour of the Home Army against the battle-tried German divisions. It was, he said, an event unique in military history and ranked the Home Army among the best in the world. The hopelessness of the defenders' position had been the decisive factor but this was because the expected help never came. And so

Warsaw, one of Europe's loveliest capitals, was in ruins and its population overwhelmed with suffering.

In reply Heller said pointedly that what had just occurred was the outcome of the inexorable laws of warfare and often these gave the victor today the role of the vanquished tomorrow. He appreciated General von dem Bach's goodwill and hoped that if he were to find himself in similar circumstances to theirs, the same goodwill would not be denied him. The German officers stood at attention in their field-grey uniforms, listening carefully.

The two men then bowed to each other and walked past the audience to the drawing-room. Von dem Bach asked Lieutenant-Colonel Goltz if all was ready for the departure of the Polish delegation. But the band had to his great regret not yet arrived nor was the guard of honour in place. He therefore urged them to stay and have supper—it was late and would be later still before they got back to the city.

The band had still not arrived after supper. Colonel Heller decided that they would leave at once. Out in the courtyard the guard of honour came to attention with a crash of jackboots. The delegation passed before the ranks, exchanged salutes with von dem Bach, then drove off in the waiting cars. On their way back the German artillery, which had so far been silent, opened up with a persistent roar and they sped to the capital in the light of their flashing muzzles.

That evening Komorowski, in one of his last messages to the Polish Government, announced that the agreement to cease hostilities in Warsaw had been concluded:

German–Polish war operations in the area of the capital will cease at 20.00 hours on October 2nd, 1944. Forces will march out of Warsaw with arms and with full combatant rights, in order to lay down their weapons outside the walls of the city—one regiment on October 4th at 08.00 hours, the remainder during October 5th. The civilian population is assured full protection within the limits of possibility, but unfortunately there has to be a mass evacuation.'

Next day the evacuation of Warsaw's population began by rail and road to Pruszkow. All, including the insurgents, were to leave by 6 October, after which, the Germans announced, they would shoot on sight anyone found in the streets or the houses. A dreadful silence now reigned over the heaps of rubble that were the Old Town, the burnt-out avenues of the City Centre and the smashed suburbs of Zoliborz and Mokotow. From dawn on 3 October, now that they knew they must leave, the people, gaunt with hunger, their eyes often bright with fever, came out of their cellars. With their bandages caked with blood and pus and unchanged for days, too exhausted to drive off the big blue flies that settled on their wounds, they looked refugees from some uncarthly inferno, which indeed they were. Endless columns of them trudged down Jerusalem Avenue to the designated exit points.

Komorowski's thoughts turned to the soldiers who had supported him so bravely during the sixty-three days of fighting. In his last order to them he said that unless they had surrendered, German technical superiority would have led to the complete destruction of the population of Warsaw and the burial of thousands more soldiers and civilians in its ruins. He had therefore decided to break off the struggle. 'You soldiers, my dearest comrades in these two months of fighting, one and all of whom have been to the very last moment constant in the will to fight on, I ask now to fulfil obediently such orders as arise from the decision to cease fighting.'

Komorowski agreed to visit von dem Bach at noon on 4 October to finalise further details of the surrender. But the German general merely wanted to stigmatise Soviet Russia as the 'common foe' against whom both nations should henceforward stand shoulder to shoulder. Komorowski stiffly declined discussion on this point. Germany was Poland's foe, he affirmed, whatever her feelings were about Soviet Russia. Von dem Bach then offered Komorowski the use of a villa from which he could supervise the evacuation of the population.

Komorowski declined this offer also, as he did the proposal that the surrender signed for Warsaw should now be extended to all Home Army units in German-occupied Poland to prevent further useless bloodshed.

On 4 and 5 October the Home Army and the People's Army detachment, women as well as men, marched out of the city of ruins and fire-blackened buildings between lines of Nazi gendarmes armed to the teeth. It was a heart-rending outcome to the years of struggle and the sixty-three days of fighting. In Kerceli Square they gave up their arms to the Germans and marched on slowly through Wola, past great fields of white crosses, the burial-ground of the enemy. Of these there were no fewer than ten thousand, with another seven thousand missing and nine thousand wounded.

Most of those marching there were sick or wounded; all of them were parched with thirst and half starving, but they kept in step, their heads held high, at least for the first few miles on their way to the railway station at Ozarow, from where they would be transported to camps throughout Germany. Little need to comment on the emotions stirred among them by this last contact with the old Warsaw, now the tomb of their hopes.

Except that they knew it was the bitterest tragedy of the Second World War.

In the hope of overcoming the invaders they had stepped into battle and offered their blood without stint. For this they had paid dearly, victims of a relentless clash of ideologies. Behind them under the city's rubble lay the bodies of many members of their families, their friends and their comrades. Ahead lay a future etched with a grim question-mark. For the misguided policies of their leaders and their Government it was indeed too high a price to pay.

In accordance with Hitler's command, the work of destruction of Warsaw began immediately on 4 October. Two or three days later, Irena Orska, then on duty as a nurse at Pruszkow camp, returned to the doomed city to help bring out the last sick and wounded. She entered on a German lorry through Wola and went on into the City Centre. Warsaw had become a cemetery, inhabited by starving cats and dogs which the Germans shot on sight. Here and there neatly stacked human bodies awaited collection.

Every few minutes heavy explosions rocked the smoky air. Demolition squads proceeded with the systematic destruction of all the city's buildings still standing. SS men first looted pictures, carpets, furniture, anything valuable from the great houses, then demolition workers, Polish civilians impressed at gunpoint, moved in with explosives. The first groups drilled holes in the walls, the second packed in the long sausages of gelignite and fused them. The third groups lit the fuses. Street after street was insanely blown to heaps of dust and rubble. Thus was Warsaw destroyed as no city had been destroyed before.

Irena Orska met a group of workmen on a corner. They shouted to her to hurry and cross the street. Not bothering to ask why, she ran to the heap of ruins on the opposite side. Before she reached it came the roar of an explosion, 'frightful in the surrounding scene of death. The air shook, and the corpse of a building fell heavily where we had stood before. Warsaw had one more grave to hide the charred bodies of nameless people underneath.'[16]

She persuaded the demolition workers to let her enter one of the doomed houses, so that she could take away a memory of the last hours of the city. While they planted their explosives in the basement, she went upstairs. The first and second floors were completely burnt out. She ascended the marble staircase. The door to the third-floor apart-ment had been torn off its hinges and thrown aside. An old-fashioned photograph of a man with a big moustache hung lop-sided on the wall inside, a fancy pram for a baby doll lay upside down on the floor among pieces of smashed furniture. What tragedy had been enacted here? A heap of debris lay in the hall and the workman with her clumsily tripped over it. He jumped to his feet, backing away. He had fallen on the charred body of a woman, covered with brick dust and rubble. They went down the stairs and out into the street. A minute later the walls of the building exploded into a heap of dust and bricks.

Starting back to Pruszkow camp on the lorry, Irena Orska turned to look once again at the ruins of the city. The heavy boom of explosions shook the air. The stumps of the dead houses of dying Warsaw pointed heavenwards. Barbarians with twentieth-century equipment, the Nazis were destroying it with frightful efficiency.

In fact they demolished eighty-five per cent of the city's buildings — houses, churches, schools, museums, university buildings, theatres, hospitals — the venerated and historic, no less than the ordinary. Trees were felled, underground water mains and sewage pipes blown up, tanks tore out telegraph poles and tramway tracks. Up to the very last day the Nazi Destruction Commandoes worked hard to carry out the Führer's decree.

When the Polish and Soviet forces finally captured what remained of the city on 17 January 1945 they found a vast ruin and a charnel house. Between two hundred and two hundred and fifty thousand men, women and children had died there, plus fifteen thousand insurgents.

What else but twentieth-century ideology could bring tragedy on so vast a scale?

But the human spirit as it flourishes in Poland rebelled against the Nazi attempt to dwarf the Polish people and destroy their capital for good.

On 13 January 1945, even before the liberation of the capital, the Polish Government, then in Lublin, decided that Warsaw should be reconstructed. All land within the city boundaries was taken into municipal ownership, so that there were no legal obstacles to changing land use, laying out new streets or putting up housing estates. The surviving buildings remained in the hands of their present owners, while the belt of land surrounding the city is still privately owned today.

Architect Roman Piotrowski was appointed director and Jozef Sigalin deputy director of the Warsaw Reconstruction Department. They were assisted by a team of other architects, professors and students. But when on a spring evening in 1945 they first saw the grey desert of ruins that had been their ancient capital they had serious doubts. They stood on the river bank and looked for landmarks. Here and there were the skeletons of once glorious buildings but the avenues, squares and streets were obliterated by acres and acres of rubble. And no plans were at hand to guide them because the Nazis had taken pains to burn the city's archives.

They had seriously to ask themselves whether indeed they could turn these ruins into a city of life and light once again. The problem was worsened by Poland's lack of heavy bulldozers and such mechanical aids. However, in one way the question was already answered, for people were flocking back determined to make their homes in what had been the city astride the Vistula.

Urgent and melancholy tasks had first to be undertaken. Thousands of corpses had to be removed from the sewage tunnels, from the twenty-five thousand graves in the streets and squares and nearly two hundred thousand more from under the debris. German prisoners and thousands of volunteer workers of every kind began clearing the streets. Architects turned to pictures by Canaletto and other artists to help them get their bearings. The main avenues were cleared, the water supply was repaired and made to flow again; by summer the last mines were removed from the Vistula embankment and demolition teams had knocked down buildings in danger of collapse. All the time citizens were flocking back to try to make their homes among the ruins. By the end of June nearly four thousand people were living there again, though in the most primitive conditions.

The reconstruction of Warsaw became a national saga. Cities and towns throughout Poland vied with each other in sending financial and material help. Historic mansions, churches and houses were reconstructed completely. The entire Old Town was re-erected street by street and house by house, even to the carvings and mural designs. But Warsaw by no means became a mere echo of the past. It was rebuilt as a fine modern city, a monument to the creative spirit of past generations, a symbol of the nation's determination to exist and to grow again.

Notes

CHAPTER 1

1 Polish Socialist Party (PPS), Peasant Party (SL), National Democrats (SN)
2 *The German Invasion of Poland*, Polish Ministry of Information (Hutchinson 1940)
3 Hans Frank's *Diary*, quoted in *War Losses in Poland* (Journalists' Co-operative, Warsaw 1960)
4 *War Losses in Poland*
5 Nuremberg Document No–3075

CHAPTER 2

1 Tokarzewski's Affidavit (Polish Underground Study Trust—PUST)
2 Stefan Korbonski, *Fighting Warsaw*
3 Ibid.
4 PUST (Polish Underground Study Trust)
5 *Polskie Siły Zbrojne*—History of the Polish Armed Forces (PSZ), Vol. 3, p. 101. (General Sikorski Historical Institute, (GSHI), London 1950)
6 Tokarzewski's report to C-in-C (PUST)
7 PUST
8 Zenon Kliszko, *Warsaw Uprising*

CHAPTER 3

1 Hans Frank, *Diary*
2 Archives of Central Commission for War Crimes Investigation, Warsaw, Vol. 6, p. 57
3 *Genocide 1939–45* (Western Press Agency, Warsaw 1950)
4 PUST, C-in-C to Rowecki, 18 and 20 June 1940
5 Documents on Polish–Soviet Relations, (DOPSR), Vol. 1, p. 66. General Sikorski Historical Institute and Heinemann Ltd.

6   Operational Report No. 54, 5 Feb 1941, PUST
7   Ibid.
8   GSHI, Coll. 17/2, DOPSR Vol. 1, Document 278
9   PUST, Ldz 247/43
10 GSHI, KGA, 7-1, 1 Sept 1941
11 Report No. 154, PUST, as quoted in PSZ, p. 262
12 PSZ, Vol. 3, pp. 202-3
13 GSHI, Coll. 17/2, 28 Nov 1942
14 Ibid.
15 C-in-C to CO Home Army, 26 Mar 1943, PUST

CHAPTER 4

1   Zenon Kliszko, *Warsaw Uprising*
2   T. Komorowski, *The Secret Army*, p. 122
3   Nuremberg Document PS 1061
4   Ldz 3085, PUST
5   Kliszko, *Warsaw Uprising*
6   Ibid.
7   GSHI, PRM-K, 105. DOPSR, Vol. 1, Document 171
8   GSHI, PRM 68, DOPSR, Vol. 1, Document 176
9   Alexander Werth, *Russia at War*, p. 580
10 GSHI, PRM, 41/4, Kersten, No. 17, DOPSR, Vol. 1, Document 159
11 Komorowski, *The Secret Army*, p. 128
12 GSHI, DOPSR, Vol. 1, Document 312
13 Werth, *Russia at War*
14 Ldz 2312, PUST

CHAPTER 5

1   Ldz 5371/tjn and Ldz 6029/43, 5 Oct 1943, PUST
2   Ldz 1420/op. tjn. 22 Oct 1943, PUST
3   GSHI, PRM 46/30, DOPSR, Vol. 2, Document 44
4   Ldz 2100, 26 Nov 1943, PUST
5   Instruction No. 1200/111, PUST; *The Secret Army*, p. 178
6   Ldz 6581, PUST
7   Komorowski, *The Secret Army*, p. 184
8   Kliszko, *Warsaw Uprising*, p. 41
9   GSHI, A.10.9/3/DOPSR, Vol. 2, Document 70
10 Stalin's correspondence, I. No. 236: 11, No. 160
11 Ibid.
12 *Strategy of the PPR National Front*, Jerzy Pawlowicz (Warsaw 1965) quoted by Jan Ciechanowski in his thesis *The Political and Ideological Background of the Warsaw Uprising*

CHAPTER 6

1 Komorowski, *The Secret Army*, p. 181
2 Ibid.
3 GSHI, Tehran Conference, 594–5 (Bohlen's Record), DOPSR, Vol. 2, No. 59
4 GSHI, PRM–L, 47/21: 25.1.44. DOPSR, Vol. 2, Document 87
5 GSHI, PRM–L, 48/96 Annex 3: 15.2.44
6 PUST, Ldz 6302, Appendix to Order 243: 23.3.44
7 PSZ, p. 587
8 Ibid.
9 Memorandum from Ambassador Count Raczynski to Foreign Office, 7.4.44. GSHI, A.12.49/WB/Sow. 5, DOPSR, Document 123
10 PUST, Ldz 6302/tjn.44
11 GSHI, A.12.49/WB/Sow. 5, DOPSR, Document 123
12 GSHI, A.12.49/WB/Sow. 4, DOPSR, Vol. 2, Document 123
13 GSHI, A.X11.3/90.2
14 PUST, Ldz 3418, 19.4.44
15 PSZ, p. 599
16 Josef Garlinski, *Poland, SOE and the Allies*
17 PSZ, p. 329
18 Ibid.
19 Ibid.
20 DOPSR, Vol. 2, Document 153
21 PUST, Ldz 13340
22 PUST, Ldz 13191
23 Encl. No. 3, Report 243, Ldz 6302: GSHI, DOPSR, Document 158
24 PUST, Ldz 6302, No. 243, 14.7.44
25 PUST, Ldz 131123
26 PUST, Ldz 132212
27 PUST, Ldz 13163
28 PUST, Ldz 6420/tjn.33

CHAPTER 7

1 W. Bartoszewski, *Warsaw Death Ring*, chap. 12
2 PSZ, p. 652
3 A. Skarzinski, *The Political Background of the Warsaw Uprising*
4 Adam Borkiewicz, *Warsaw Insurrection*
5 Komorowski, broadcast over Radio Free Europe, 15.9.57
6 Ldz 5916/tj/21.7.44/PUST
7 PSZ, Vol. 3, p. 657
8 PSZ, Vol. 3, ibid.
9 Komorowski's statement of 18 April 1951, PUST
10 Ibid.

11   PSZ, Vol. 3, p. 658
12   Memorandum from Mikolajczyk to Winston Churchill, 24.7.44, DOPSR, No. 164
13   Bulletin of Information, 27 July 1944
14   Personal statement to author
15   CO Home Army to C-in-C, Ldz 6024, 25.7.44, PUST
16   Nat. Arch. AK, Warsaw, quoted J. Skarzinski, p. 221
17   Col. Jan Rzepecki, *Diary*, Polish Military History Review, 1958 No. 2(7), p. 313
18   Ibid.
19   Ibid.
20   Ldz 6114/tjn/44, GSHI, PRM L.6, 27.4.44
21   Borkiewicz, *Warsaw Insurrection*, p. 18
22   J. Kirchmayer, *The Warsaw Uprising*, p. 55
23   Borkiewicz, *Warsaw Insurrection*, p. 25; Skarzinski, p. 233
24   S. Mikolajczyk, *The Pattern of Soviet Domination*, p. 76
25   Komorowski, *The Secret Army*, p. 213
26   PSZ, Vol. 3, p. 703
27   Skarzinski, p. 236
28   Mikolajczyk, *The Pattern of Soviet Domination*, p. 75

CHAPTER 8

1   PSZ, Vol. 3, p. 702
2   Kirchmayer, p. 126
3   Capt. Muszcak's oral evidence, quoted by J. Ciechanowski, p. 522
4   DOPSR, Doc. 173, p. 303
5   Military History Review, 1958: Rzepecki's *Diary*
6   Skarzinski, p. 246, quoting Wladyslaw Jaworski, a member of the Council of National Unity.
7   Col. Iranek-Osmecki's personal statement to the author
8   Borkiewicz, *Warsaw Insurrection*, p. 27; Komorowski, *The Unconquerables*, Reader's Digest, Feb 1946
9   Ibid., p. 129
10   Komorowski, *The Secret Army*, p. 214
11   Ibid.
12   Personal statement by Col. Iranek-Osmecki to the author
13   Ibid.
14   Borkiewicz, *Warsaw Insurrection*, p. 27
15   Ibid.
16   Korbonski, *Fighting Warsaw*
17   Information Bulletin, 25.9.44
18   Personal statement to author
19   *Military History Review*, Warsaw, 1963, No. 3/4 (29), Wlodzimierz Woleszyn, p. 85. Also Alexander Werth, *Russia at War*, p. 781, quoting the official Russian *History of the Great Patriotic War of the Soviet Union*

20 Orders of Soviet Second Army Staff, OP/018, 27.7.44, quoted in Poland's *Military History Review*, from USSR Ministry of Defence Archives

21 Operations Report of 1st Belorussian Front, OP/00209, 27.4.44, ibid.

22 Soviet Second Army Commander's Report, OP/2309, file 77, pp. 192–229, ibid.

23 Soviet Second Army Commander's Report, OP/210, 28.7.44, ibid.

24 Report of German Middle Army Group la, nrl/3955/44, ibid.

25 USSR Ministry of Defence, fond. 307, OP/4148, file 247, pp. 450, 518, op. cit.

26 USSR Ministry of Defence, fond. 307/OP/4148, file 31, pp. 46–7, op. cit.

27 USSR Ministry of Defence, fond. 233, OP/2309, file 77, op. cit.

28 USSR Ministry of Defence, fond. 233, OP/2356, file 164, op. cit.

29 USSR Ministry of Defence, fond. 307, OP/4148, file 247, pp. 450, 518, op. cit.

30 USSR Ministry of Defence Archives, fond. 233, OP/2356, file 164, op. cit.

31 Komorowski, *The Unconquerables*, Reader's Digest, Feb 1946, p. 131

CHAPTER 9

1 Hans von Krannhals, *Warschauer Aufstand*, p. 119

2 Op. cit., p. 118

3 Ibid.

4 Op. cit., p. 120, quoting AOK 9, 1a No. 3702/44. Borkiewicz, *Warsaw Insurrection*, p. 41, gives 20,000 men, all units

5 Kirchmayer, p. 168

6 Op. cit., p. 169

7 Borkiewicz, p. 57

8 Ibid.

9 Ibid.

10 Kirchmayer, p. 171

11 Ibid.

12 Op. cit., p. 169

13 Komorowski, *The Secret Army*, p. 216

14 Komorowski, *The Unconquerables*

15 Andrzej Pomian, *Military Dispatches*, p. 1

16 *The Secret Army*, p. 222

17 Ibid., p. 223

18 Ibid.

19 PSZ, p. 665

20 Kliszko, *Warsaw Uprising*

21 I. Orska, *Silent is the Vistula*, p. 12

22 W. Zagorski, *Seventy Days*, p. 21
23 Korbonski, *Fighting Warsaw*, p. 350
24 *The Pattern of Soviet Domination*, p. 78
25 Op. cit., p. 79
26 *The Secret Army*, p. 222
27 Ibid.
28 Borkiewicz, *The Warsaw Uprising*, p. 58
29 Ibid.
30 Ibid.
31 W. Bartoszewski, *Erich von dem Bach-Zelewski*
32 Ibid., quoting testimony of von dem Bach at Nuremberg

CHAPTER 10

1 Borkiewicz, *Warsaw Insurrection*, p. 78
2 Personal statement to author
3 *Military Dispatches*, p. 2 (A. Pomian)
4 Op. cit., p. 4
5 Ldz 6366/tjn/44, PUST
6 Document 180, DOPSR, Vol. 2
7 Ibid.
8 Note 186, DOPSR, Vol. 2
9 *The Secret Army*, p. 237
10 Op. cit., p. 239
11 *Military Dispatches*, p. 3
12 Ldz 6342/tjn/44, PUST
13 Garlinski, *Poland, SOE and The Allies*, p. 185 et seq.
14 *Military Dispatches*, p. 5

CHAPTER 11

1 Borkiewicz, *Warsaw Insurrection*, p. 140
2 War Diary, No. 11, 9th Army Command
3 *Warsaw Insurrection*, p. 141 (Borkiewicz)
4 Account given to Institute of National Memories, Warsaw, 1947
5 *Warsaw Insurrection*, p. 142 (Borkiewicz)
6 Ibid., quoting Franz Krug's account, 19.8.44
7 Von Krannhals, *Warschauer Aufstand*, p. 138
8 Central Commission for the Investigation of German Crimes in Poland, Vol. 1, p. 188, Warsaw, 1946
9 Op. cit., p. 205
10 Op. cit., p. 207
11 Op. cit., p. 212
12 Op. cit., p. 222
13 Komorowski, *The Secret Army*, p. 244
14 Document 184, DOPSR, Vol. 2

15 Werth, *Russia at War*, p. 781
16 Op. cit., p. 783
17 *Warsaw Insurrection*, p. 162 et seq. (Borkiewicz)
18 Bartoszewski, *Erich von dem Bach-Zelewski*, p. 38
19 Op. cit., p. 40
20 Document 189, DOPSR, Vol. 2
21 Ibid.
22 Ibid.
23 9th Army War Diary No. 11, pp. 384–7
24 Document 1919, DOPSR, Vol. 2
25 9th Army War Diary No. 11, pp. 394–7

CHAPTER 12

1   Borkiewicz, *Warsaw Insurrection*, p. 169
2   Op. cit., p. 170
3   Note 188, DOPSR, Vol. 2
4   *Warsaw Insurrection*, p. 175
5   Ibid., quoting Acts of Heeresgruppe Mitte, AOK 9, lanr. 3998 1c.
6   Von Krannhals, *Warschauer Aufstand*, p. 140
7   *Warsaw Insurrection*, p. 190
8   *The Secret Army*, p. 271
9   Ibid., p. 270
10 L. Bartelski, *Warsaw Uprising*
11 *Warsaw Insurrection*, p. 180
12 Ldz/6687/tjn/44, PUST
13 *Military Dispatches*, p. 8 (A. Pomian)
14 Ldz/6753/tjn/44, PUST

CHAPTER 13

1   *Military Dispatches*, p. 9
2   *The Secret Army*, p. 294
3   *Warsaw Insurrection*, p. 194
4   Op. cit., p. 196
5   Document 192, DOPSR, Vol. 2
6   Document 194, DOPSR, Vol. 2
7   Churchill, *Second World War*, Vol. VI, p. 117
8   Ibid.
9   Document 198, DOPSR, Vol. 2
10 *Second World War*, p. 118
11 Document 201, DOPSR, Vol. 2
12 *Poland, SOE and The Allies*, p. 191
13 *Warsaw Insurrection*, p. 209
14 Komorowski, *The Unconquerables*, p. 149
15 *The Secret Army*, p. 275

16 Ibid.
17 Ibid., p. 277
18 *Warsaw Insurrection*, p. 205

CHAPTER 14

1 Account given to Institute of National Memories, Warsaw, published in the quarterly *Dzie je Najnowsze*, Vol. 1, p. 316
2 Ibid.,
3 Zagorski, *Seventy Days*, p. 98
4 *Warsaw Insurrection*, p. 215, quoting *Journal of Radóslaw's Group*
5 Ldz 7042/tjn/44, PUST
6 *Warsaw Insurrection*, p. 228, quoting Acts of Heeresgrippehutte, AOK 9 Merkblatt, 218.44
7 Churchill, *Second World War*, Vol. VI, p. 119
8 Ibid.
9 Document 205, DOPSR, Vol. 2
10 *Second World War*, Vol. VI, p. 123
11 Ibid.
12 *The Secret Army*, p. 305
13 L. Bartelski, *Mokotow*, 1944
14 *Second World War*, Vol. VI, p. 125
15 Ibid., p. 126
16 *Warsaw Insurrection*, p. 239
17 Ibid., p. 277
18 Komorowski, *The Unconquerables*, p. 156

CHAPTER 15

1 Borkiewicz, *Warsaw Insurrection*, p. 290
2 Op. cit., p. 298
3 Op. cit., p. 299
4 Ibid.
5 *The Unconquerables*, p. 157
6 Ninth Army War Diary, pp. 460–1
7 Kliszko, *Warsaw Uprising*
8 *The Secret Army*, p. 335
9 Korbonski, *Fighting Warsaw*, p. 390
10 *The Secret Army*, p. 337
11 *Military Dispatches*, p. 20
12 *Fighting Warsaw*, p. 377
13 *Military Dispatches*, p. 22
14 *Fighting Warsaw*, p. 387
15 *Military Dispatches*, p. 22
16 Ldz 8652, PUST

17   AOK 9, pp. 489–90
18   *Military Dispatches*, p. 25

CHAPTER 16

1   Kliszko, *Warsaw Uprising*
2   *The Secret Army*, p. 350
3   Kliszko, op. cit.
4   Von Krannhals, *Warschauer Aufstand*, p. 195
5   *The Secret Army*, p. 353
6   Ibid., p. 354
7   Ibid.
8   Ibid.
9   *Warschauer Aufstand*, p. 196
10   Kirchmayer, p. 407
11   PSZ, Vol. III, pp. 784–5
12   Kliszko, op. cit.
13   Ibid.
14   Ibid.
15   Personal statement to author
16   *Silent is the Vistula*, p. 270

Bibliography

UNPUBLISHED

State papers of the Second World War Polish Government-in-exile in the General Sikorski Historical Institute (GSHI), and in the Polish Underground Study Trust (PUST).

Thesis: *The Political and Ideological Background of the Warsaw Uprising*, J. Ciechanowski (London University), (to be published by Cambridge University Press).

Personal Statements: Colonel Iranek-Osmecki; Colonel Stanislaw Komornicki; Captain Janusz Tomaszewski; and Mr A. Jankowski.

PUBLISHED

The Warsaw Uprising, J. Kirchmayer (Warsaw 1960).

The Political Background of the Warsaw Uprising, J. Skarzinski (Warsaw 1959).

Warsaw Insurrection, A. Borkiewicz (Warsaw 1957).

Warsaw Uprising, Zenon Kliszko (Warsaw 1967).

German Crimes in Poland, Central Commission for the Investigation of German Crimes in Poland (Warsaw 1946).

The Warsaw Rising (Military Dispatches), compiled by Andrzej Pomian (London 1945).

Documents on Polish–Soviet Relations, Vols. 1 and 2, edited by the Sikorski Institute (Heinemann 1968).

Warsaw Insurrection, Leslaw M. Bartelski (Iskry, Warsaw 1967).

Mokotow, 1944, Leslaw M. Bartelski (Mon, Warsaw 1971).

History of Poland, Stefan Kieniewicz (PWN, Warsaw 1968).

Poland, SOE and the Allies, Josef Garlinski (Allen & Unwin 1969).

Warschauer Aufstand, 1944, Hans von Krannhals (Frankfurt 1962).

Diary, Hans Frank (Neuhaus 1955).

War Diary No. 11, German 9th Army, Bundesarchiv-Militär-archiv.

Fighting Warsaw, Stefan Korbonski (Allen & Unwin 1956).

Warsaw Death Ring, Wladyslaw Bartoszewski (Interpress, Warsaw 1968).

The Nazi New Order in Poland, Jon Evans (Gollancz 1941).

217

In Allied London, E. Raczynski (Weidenfeld 1962)

The Secret State, Jan Karski (Hodder 1945).

The Secret Army, T. Bor-Komorowski (Gollancz 1950).

The Pattern of Soviet Domination, S. Mikolajczyk (Sampson Low 1948).

Von dem Bach-Zelewski, W. Bartoszewski (Interpress, Warsaw 1961).

Panzer Leader, H. Guderian (Cassell 1966).

Seventy Days, Waclaw Zagorski (Muller 1957).

War Losses in Poland, Journalists' Co-operative (Warsaw 1960).

Silent Is The Vistula, Irena Orska (Longmans 1957).

Russia at War, Alexander Werth (Barrie & Rockliffe 1964).

The Unseen & Silent, G. Iranek-Osmecki (Sheed & Ward 1954).

The Second World War, Vol. VI, Winston Churchill (Cassell 1954).

British Foreign Policy in the Second World War (HMSO).

History of the Polish Armed Forces, Vol. 3 (Sikorski Historical Institute).

A History of Modern Poland, Hans Roos (Eyre & Spottiswoode 1966).

Social Aspects of the Warsaw Uprising, J. Hochfeld (Journal of Central European Affairs).

Operations on the Warsaw Front, Wlodzimierz Woloszyn (in the Polish Military History Review).

The Warsaw Uprising, General von dem Bach-Zelewski: account given to Institute of National Memories, Warsaw.

Index

German: *Contd.*
Town, 148–51, 153, 157–8; booby trap, 151; on *13* August, 153; offer surrender, 158–9; fighting, 159–63; soldier's diary, 160; disposition and plan, mid-August, 164–5; propaganda, 165; fighting, 165–8, 169–71, 174–7, 178–80; reprisals in Old Town, 179–80; position, *2* September, 180; negotiations, 183–4, 186, 195, 197, 201–3; fighting, 181–2, 185, 187, 189–200; disciplinary measures in, 192. GERMAN FORCES UNITS: 2nd Army, 91, 93; 3rd Army, 63; 4th Army, 63, 141; 9th Army, 63 (at Minsk), 76, 91, 125, 126, 130, 137, 140–1, 146, 153, 180, 187, 200, 164 (Cossacks of), 161 (Hungarian Division of); 10th Army, 13; 73rd Infantry Div., 78, 87, 91–2, 187, 194, 192 (disciplined); Dirle-wanger's criminal brigade, 113, 126–7 (described), 127–8, 129, 131, 137, 149, 165, 167, 179 (reprisals in Old Town), 194, 130 (2nd Battalion). PANZER DIVISIONS: 3rd, 91, 92, 93–4; 4th, 86, 91, 93, 94, 187; 5th, 91, 92; 9th, 92; 19th, 86, 91, 92, 93, 94, 140–1, 187, 194–5, 196; 25th, 187; 39th Corps, 92, 94; Death's Head Division, 86, 93; Frankonian Sudeten Division, 195; 'Hermann Goering' Division, 76, 86, 91–2, 93, 94, 139, 195; 1st Armoured Paratroop Regiment, 92; Paratroop Regiment, 76; 'Hermann Goering' Regiment, 78, 101, 113, 126, 140–1; 'Viking' Division, 76, 86, 92, 93–4, 113, 126, 195; Police, militarised, 100, 102, 103, 113, 126, 127, 149; Reinefarth, Lt.-Gen. Heinz, assault group of, 113, 125, 129, 131, 138, 142, 149, 165, 194; Schmidt's Regiment, 113, 127 (described), 165; 603 Regiment, 113, 129, 149; No. 500 SS assault Battalion, 113; armoured train No. *75*, 113, 126, 142; Ukrainian Rona Brigade, Kaminski's, 113, 125, 126, 127–8, 130, 131, 133, 137, 138, 141, 146, 164, 194; Luftwaffe, 12, 13, 15, 120, 126, 127, 128, 130, 185; German–Russian relations, 28, 29, 30, 31; Nazi–Soviet pact, 14; Operation Barbarossa, 31; Russo-German war, *see under* Red Army
Germany: *blitz-krieg* technique of, 12; and Poles in Katyn Forest, 45–6
Glebov, Col., 39–40
Goltz, Lt.-Col., 201, 202, 203
Gomulka, Wladyslaw, 43–4, 53
Gruszko, Gen., 67
Guderian, Gen., 76

Hahn, Dr Ludwig, 68, 102
Heller, Kurt, diary of, 160
Herman, Lt.-Col., 84, 202
Himmler, Heinrich, 27, 41, 100, 101, 112–13, 124, 145, 195, 201; reprisal orders *re* Warsaw, 133, 137, 138
Hitler, Adolf, 11–12, 15, 31, 33, 69, 76, 100, 112, 192, 195, 205
Home Army of Poland (Secret Army), 152, 204; and Soviets, 77, 152–3; 27th Division, at Kowel, 59, 60–1; combatant rights for, 84, 181; IN WARSAW: initiated, 19, 20–2, 23; *1942:* activities, 40–3; and Communists, 43–4; *Information* Bulletins,

40, 42; new leaders appointed, *1943*, 49; *1943:* instructions to, 50–1; activities, 52–3; *1944:* 'Tempest' Operation, 56, 58–61, 64–7; 27th Division, at, 59, 60–1; and Red Army, 58–61, 64–7, 72–3, 144; *see also* Secret Army *and* Union for Armed Struggle
Hümel, Dr, 137
Hungary, 28; Hungarian Division in 9th German Army, 161

Iranek-Osmecki, Col. ('Heller'), 74, 77, 83, 84, 85, 86, 87–8, 89; in final negotiations, 201–3
Italy, RAF bases in, 123, 155, 157

Jan, Major, 175
Jankowski, Jan; delegate from London, 44, 57–8; Deputy Prime Minister in Warsaw, 61, 69, 70, 72, 73, 75, 76, 80, 82, 84, 85, 86–7; in Uprising, 103, 105, 112, 119, 121, 135, 154, 159, 170, 173, 183, 184, 185
Japan, 31, 57, 169, 174
Jelesnia village, 15
Jerzy, Capt., 176, 193, 194
Jewish Socialist Organisation, 13
Jews, in Warsaw, 40–1, 95, 128
Jozef, Capt., 86

Kabacki Forest, 117
Kalinowsky, Lt., 174
Källner, Gen., 191, 196
Kalugin, Konstantin, 133–4
Kaminski, SS Brig., 127, 130–1; Cossack brigade of, 113, 125, 126, 127–8, 130, 131, 133, 137, 138, 141, 146, 164, 194
Kaminski, Col. ('Daniel'), 136
Kamler, Lt., 103; tobacco factory of, Secret Army GHQ, 102–6, 134
Kampino Forest, troops in, 124, 136, 147; attempts to link with Old Town, 161–3, 169–70, 180
'Karol', Capt., 191, 195
Katyn Forest, Officers' graves in, 45–6
Killinski, Jan, 16
Kliszko, Zenon, 108, 188, 190, 191, 196; escapes, 198–200; wife of, 198, 199
Komorowski, Gen.; character and early career, 26; in Cracow, 26, 27, 29–30; first visits Warsaw, 27–8; appointed C-in-C Secret Army, 49; *1943:* orders, 50–2; *1944:* 'Tempest', 56–62, 64–7; *1944:* considerations *re* Uprising, 67–82; decision taken, 83–9; 97, 98, 99; at Uprising, 101–8, 111–12, 115, 121–2, 128, 133, 134, 143, 144, 147, 149–50, 152, 157; messages to government in London, 74, 105, 112, 118–19, 122, 123–4, 133–4, 148, 149, 150, 166–7, 178, 181, 184, 185, 188, 191, 197–8, 203; failure of radios, 170; refuses surrender, 158–9; transfers HQ through sewers, 171, 173; 160, 170–1, 180, 182–8, 190, 191, 194–6, 198–201, 204
Komorowski, Irena, 29–30, 88
Koniev, Marshal, 69
Konigsberg, 54
Kopanski, Gen., 75
Koppe, Gen. Wilhelm, 112, 113

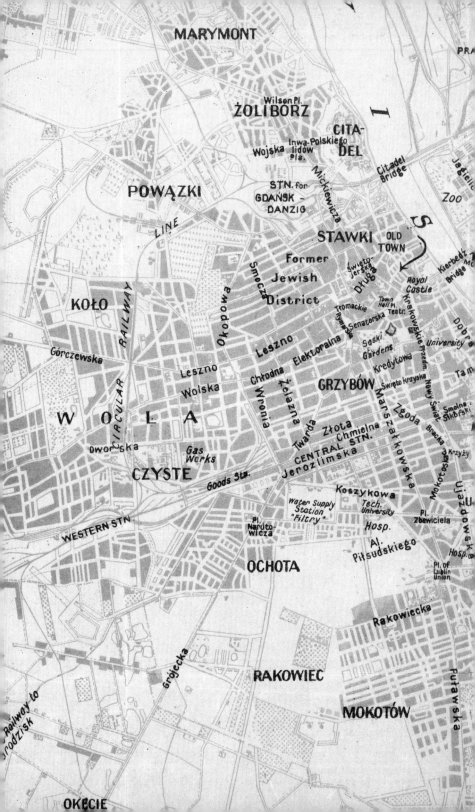